MINNESOTA GUIDE FOR ARMED CITIZENS

HOW TO SURVIVE AN ATTACK PHYSICALLY, MORALLY, LEGALLY AND FINANCIALLY

Written by
Gene German and Tim Grant

Published by
LEOSA Trainers, Inc.

Minnesota Guide for Armed Citizens

Published by the LEOSA Trainers, Inc.

Nothing contained in this book is considered as the rendering of legal advice for specific cases and readers are responsible for obtaining such advice from their own legal counsel. The reader's individual legal counsel must fully research original and current sources of authority. This book and any techniques, charts, forms or other sample documents are intended solely for educational and instructional purposes.

Second Printing, November, 2015

TJA Group LLC   TF Grant LLC
PO Box 202   4722 Forest Circle,
Excelsior MN 55331   Minnetonka, MN 55345
612-388-2403   952-935-2414

Library of Congress Cataloguing-in-Publication Data

LEOSA Trainers, Inc.

ISBN 978-1-4675-8154-7

Minnesota Guide for Armed Citizens

Printed in the United States of America by Dunn & Semington,
5250 West 73rd Street, Suite F, Edina, MN 55436 (612) 866-7225

Written by Gene German and Tim Grant
Design and Layout by Gene German and Tim Grant
Typesetting by Dunn & Semington

Photos by Oleg Volk and Gene German. Used by permission

Forward

By Suzanna Gratia Hupp

I was not raised in a house with guns, and I am not a hunter. I was, however, raised in a house in which my father was an expert on the founding of this great country and I was steeped in the meaning of our Second Amendment. I grew up understanding its importance for not only protecting "We the people" from a tyrannical government, but also for the more personal reasons of protecting family, property, or even oneself. Once I began my professional life, a patient of mine who happened to be an assistant district attorney in Houston, TX convinced me to carry a gun for personal protection.

On October 16, 1991, my parents and I were eating lunch in a crowded cafeteria. As we lingered over coffee, a truck suddenly came crashing through the floor-to-ceiling window at the front of the building. The driver stepped out of the vehicle and slowly, methodically began to shooting patrons. He had complete control over the room. I remember thinking, "I've got this guy." He was standing up, everyone else was down. I have hit much smaller targets at much greater distances. I reached for the gun in my purse on the floor next to me. Then I realized that a few months earlier, I had made the stupidest mistake of my life. My gun was a hundred feet away in my car, completely useless to me. I had begun leaving it there because at that time, in the state of Texas, it was illegal to carry it and I was afraid of losing my chiropractic permit.

In the end, I made it out, my parents and twenty one others did not. At that time, it was the largest mass shooting this country had ever seen.

We had not been in a dark alley on the seedy side of town. We had been in a crowded restaurant on a sunny day. I have had people say, "Suzanna, you could have missed!" and "What if your gun had jammed?" Both things were possible. But one thing no one can argue with: IT WOULD HAVE CHANGED THE ODDS.

I am guessing that if you are reading this book, you already believe in your right to protect yourself. However, you may have loved ones who are uncomfortable with the whole idea of guns. Have them imagine being in a restaurant when a crazed gunman enters and begins murdering innocent people. But instead of having their parents with them, let them imagine they have children or grandchildren at their sides. At the point that the gunman is leveling his weapon on their two year old's forehead, even if they have chosen not to carry a gun, don't they hope the guy behind them has one and knows how to use it?

Suzanna Gratia Hupp
Author of *From Luby's to the Legislature:*
One Woman's Fight Against Gun Control

Suzanna Hupp is my hero. She is an excellent example how a personal tragedy can give a person the strength and inner drive to change millions of lives for the better. I am honored that she agreed to write the forward to this book.

One day in 1991 as she was having lunch with her parents at Luby's Cafeteria in Killeen, TX, a lunatic drove his pickup truck through the window. He got out and methodically went from table to table shooting people. He shot 44 people in all, murdering 24 of them including both of Suzanna's parents. The police were having a meeting in a hotel just a block away from the restaurant and could not arrive in time to save these lives. Under Texas law at the time Suzanna could not have her gun with her.

This event caused Suzanna to become an advocate of an individual's right to carry a concealed weapon. She was elected to the Texas House of Representatives in 1996. She authored the Texas concealed-weapons bill which was signed by then-Governor George W. Bush. Suzanna has also testified all across the United States in support of concealed-handgun laws. I first met her at a Wisconsin Senate hearing where we both testified in 2005.

Suzanna has been recognized for her work by numerous organizations including: the American Family Association, Free Market Foundation, the Texas Association of Business, the Chamber of Commerce, Texas Alliance For Life, Texas Eagle Forum, the Young Conservatives of Texas, the Texas Right to Life Committee just to name a few.

She is a co-founder of the Civil Liberties Defense Foundation which is a non-profit legal foundation dedicated to providing educational information and legal services relating to the protection of civil liberties guaranteed by the Bill of Rights to the United States Constitution.

Suzanna has also written a book *From Luby's to the Legislature: One Woman's Fight Against Gun Control*, published by Privateer Publications, San Antonio, Texas.

Suzanna Hupp testifying before the Senate Judiciary Committee, February 12, 2013

A short lesson about human nature

Col. Dave Grossman is a former West Point psychology professor, Professor of Military Science, and an Army Ranger who has combined his experiences to become the founder of a field of scientific endeavor, which has been termed "killology." In this new field Col. Grossman has made revolutionary contributions to our understanding of killing in war, the psychological costs of war, the root causes of the current "virus" of violent crime that is raging around the world, and the process of healing the victims of violence, in war and peace. One of Col. Grossman's more famous observations of the human condition is the perfect introduction to our book. Thank you, Col. Grossman.

On sheep, wolves and sheepdogs

One Vietnam veteran, an old retired colonel, once said this to me: "Most of the people in our society are sheep. They are kind, gentle, productive creatures who can only hurt one another by accident." This is true. Remember, the murder rate is six per 100,000 per year, and the aggravated assault rate is four per 1,000 per year. What this means is that the vast majority of Americans are not inclined to hurt one another.

Some estimates say that two million Americans are victims of violent crimes every year, a tragic, staggering number, perhaps an all-time record rate of violent crime. But there are almost 300 million Americans, which means that the odds of being a victim of violent crime is considerably less than one in a hundred on any given year. Furthermore, since many violent crimes are committed by repeat offenders, the actual number of violent citizens is considerably less than two million.

Thus there is a paradox, and we must grasp both ends of the situation: We may well be in the most violent times in history, but violence is still remarkably rare. This is because most citizens are kind, decent people who are not capable of hurting each other, except by accident or under extreme provocation. They are sheep.

I mean nothing negative by calling them sheep. To me it is like the pretty, blue robin's egg. Inside it is soft and gooey but someday it will grow into something wonderful. But the egg cannot survive without its hard blue shell. Police officers, soldiers, and other warriors are like that shell, and someday the civilization they protect will grow into something wonderful. For now, though, they need warriors to protect them from the predators.

"Then there are the wolves," the old war veteran said, "and the wolves feed on the sheep without mercy." Do you believe there are wolves out there who will feed on the flock without mercy? You better believe it. There are evil men in this world and they are capable of evil deeds. The moment you forget that or pretend it is not so, you become a sheep. There is no safety in denial.

"Then there are sheepdogs," he went on, "and I'm a sheepdog. I live to protect the flock and confront the wolf."

If you have no capacity for violence then you are a healthy productive citizen, a sheep. If you have a capacity for violence and no empathy for

your fellow citizens, then you have defined an aggressive sociopath, a wolf. But what if you have a capacity for violence, and a deep love for your fellow citizens? What do you have then? A sheepdog, a warrior, someone who is walking the hero's path. Someone who can walk into the heart of darkness, into the universal human phobia, and walk out unscathed.

Let me expand on this old soldier's excellent model of the sheep, wolves, and sheepdogs. We know that the sheep live in denial, that is what makes them sheep. They do not want to believe that there is evil in the world. They can accept the fact that fires can happen, which is why they want fire extinguishers, fire sprinklers, fire alarms and fire exits throughout their kids' schools.

But many of them are outraged at the idea of putting an armed police officer in their kid's school. Our children are thousands of times more likely to be killed or seriously injured by school violence than fire, but the sheep's only response to the possibility of violence is denial. The idea of someone coming to kill or harm their child is just too hard, and so they chose the path of denial.

The sheep generally do not like the sheepdog. He looks a lot like the wolf. He has fangs and the capacity for violence. The difference, though, is that the sheepdog must not, cannot and will not ever harm the sheep. Any sheep dog who intentionally harms the lowliest little lamb will be punished and removed. The world cannot work any other way, at least not in a representative democracy or a republic such as ours.

Still, the sheepdog disturbs the sheep. He is a constant reminder that there are wolves in the land. They would prefer that he didn't tell them where to go, or give them traffic tickets, or stand at the ready in our airports in camouflage fatigues holding an M-16. The sheep would much rather have the sheepdog cash in his fangs, spray paint himself white, and go, "Baa."

Until the wolf shows up. Then the entire flock tries desperately to hide behind one lonely sheepdog.

The students, the victims, at Columbine High School were big, tough high school students, and under ordinary circumstances they would not have had the time of day for a police officer. They were not bad kids; they just had nothing to say to a cop. When the school was under attack, however, and SWAT teams were clearing the rooms and hallways, the officers had to physically peel those clinging, sobbing kids off of them. This is how the little lambs feel about their sheepdog when the wolf is at the door.

Look at what happened after September 11, 2001 when the wolf pounded hard on the door. Remember how America, more than ever before, felt differently about their law enforcement officers and military personnel? Remember how many times you heard the word 'hero'?

Understand that there is nothing morally superior about being a sheepdog; it is just what you choose to be. Also understand that a sheepdog is a funny critter: He is always sniffing around out on the perimeter, checking the breeze, barking at things that go bump in the night, and yearning for a righteous battle. That is, the young sheepdogs yearn for a righteous battle. The old sheepdogs are a little older and wiser, but they move to the sound of the guns when needed right along with the young ones.

Here is how the sheep and the sheepdog think differently. The sheep pretend the wolf will never come, but the sheepdog lives for that day. After the attacks on September 11, 2001, most of the sheep, that is, most citizens in America said, "Thank God I wasn't on one of those planes." The sheepdogs, the warriors, said, "Dear God, I wish I could have been on one of those planes. Maybe I could have made a difference." When you are truly transformed into a warrior and have truly invested yourself into warriorhood, you want to be there. You want to be able to make a difference.

There is nothing morally superior about the sheepdog--the warrior--but he does have one real advantage. Only one. And that is that he is able to survive and thrive in an environment that destroys 98 percent of the population.

There is no safety for honest men except by believing all possible evil of evil men. - Edmund Burke

When you are finished reading this book, you should have a clear idea that you are either a sheep or a sheepdog. If you determine you are a sheep, when you kiss your family good night you can sleep like a baby. If it turns out that you are a sheepdog, we hope this book will be your guide to take care of yourself and the sheep you love.

Chapter 6:

Chapter 7:

Chapter 8:

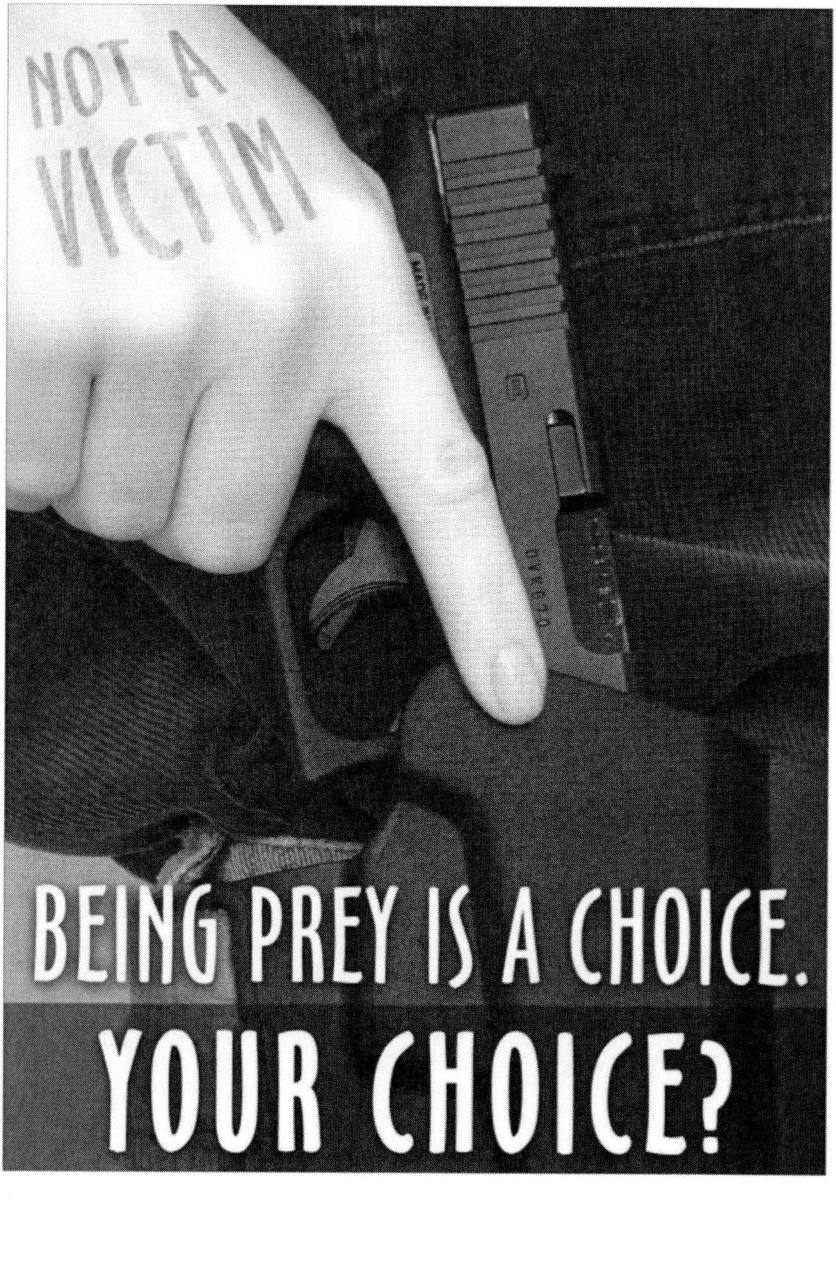
NOT A
VICTIM
BEING PREY IS A CHOICE.
YOUR CHOICE?

CHAPTER 1
What This Book Is All About

Ever stop to think how different the world would be without you? How would your family, your friends, or the world in general get along if suddenly you were gone, dead, deceased, finished, or departed?

These were the questions asked in the classic movie *It's a Wonderful Life*.

George Bailey questioned the value of his life until his Guardian Angel Clarence showed George all the lives he touched and how different his community would be without him. In the movie, George gained a keen perspective of his value to others (not to mention his value to himself) and how very important he was to those he had touched.

Just like George, your life is precious to yourself and those you touch in too many ways to list here. So close your eyes and consider for a moment how the world would change if someone wrongfully took your life. What future accomplishments will never occur? How would your spouse's life be changed? How different would your children's lives be without you? It is not a pretty picture and the ripple affect of your absence is infinite. So you have a decision to make. To what lengths are you willing to go to be prepared to protect your life for yourself, for those who love you, and those who depend upon you?

This book will help you understand the physical, moral, legal and financial issues surrounding the decision to carry a firearm for personal protection of yourself and those you love.

Carry laws

A bit of background, first.

Legislating carry law is almost exclusively a function of state government. Federal law has a lot to say about who can own a firearm and some restrictions as to where you many possess a firearm. Carry laws are enacted at the state level with federal law deferring to the states in many areas of federal gun law. Within state gun laws there are, three basic legislative schemes under which a citizen may carry a firearm in the United States: "constitutional carry," "shall issue," and "may-issue". In some states, Wisconsin for example, citizens can carry under constitutional carry and shall issue carry. In Minnesota, carry is only allowed under a shall issue permit system.

"Constitutional carry" has become the moniker for states that allow its citizens to carry a firearm, openly, and in some states concealed, without any type of permit or any type of training. One must be able to lawfully possess a firearm under federal and state laws. Every state that has Constitutional carry has one or more restrictions as to how, when and where a firearm is carried. In addition, certain federal laws will apply to constitutional carry. The Federal School Zone law is an example of federal law that applies to those that constitutionally carry.

The second category is the "shall-issue" states. Minnesota, is in this group. In "shall-issue" states, any objectively qualifying adult can get a permit to carry simply by taking and passing the appropriate training, having their background examined, filling out and filing a form with the issuing authority, and paying a fee. The majority of states have "shall issue" laws.

In "may-issue" states, permits are issued only at the discretion of the local authorities who are free to issue or deny permits for any reason, or no reason at all. This system is the most discriminating between equally qualified citizens based on which bureaucrat makes the decision. This was Minnesota's system prior to passage of the Minnesota Personal Protection Act (MPPA) in 2003 and again in 2005.

As a Minnesota permit to carry holder you decide when and how you want to carry a firearm. The permit just gives you the option of carrying a handgun and nothing more. Carrying a firearm does come with significant responsibilities. These responsibilities need to be taken seriously, very seriously. About the only thing we can promise you when carrying a handgun is: A gun never solves problems.

At best, the lawful use of a handgun can substitute one set of serious consequences for another. If you have a defensive gun use (DGU) in a public place you should expect to be arrested, possibly prosecuted for any one or more of a long list of firearm related crimes, spend a tidy sum of money on attorney fees, and have persistent emotional and possibly even permanent physical injuries. In addition, there will be the instant infamy of being judged by the court of public opinion about what you did, the way you did it without benefit of the facts. On the other hand, you could be dead. Even if you are found innocent of all criminal charges, there is a possibility of a civil lawsuits if you accidentally shoot an innocent bystander.

Why this book was written

Cars are not just for mechanics, and automotive hobbyists; medical care is not just for doctors and nurses; and your personal safety is not the job of law enforcement officers. Maintaining one's personal constant state of peace is the responsibility of each person. Minnesota's carry law added the choice of carrying a firearm to maintain your constant state of peace.

If you have decided that you are going to carry a firearm there are things you must know before you ever leave your home. Whether you carry everyday or only occasionally this book is your personal reference resource. The *Minnesota Guide for Armed Citizens* is about carrying and using a firearm for personal protection in Minnesota. As such, use it to refresh yourself if its been awhile since you last carried a firearm or a question arises amongst your friends and family. We would like you to consider sharing this book with anyone who's firearm education has come from TV or the movies. There are portions of both Minnesota carry and Minnesota self defense laws that leave a person saying, "That just does not make sense." Self defense and firearms laws have evolved over time through case law and legislative changes. Professional politicos often say that making laws is like making sausage but with many more cooks. Unintentional consequences of how laws work and work with other laws already on "the books" can be very tricky. This often leaves it to the courts figure out the application of the laws.

Additionally, laws are retroactively applied to your situation requiring you to anticipate the future outcome when relying on your "lawful use of reasonable force" (up to and including lethal force) to stop a threat. Our goal is to help you understand the laws and how they apply thereby increasing the probability you will avoid serious consequences by making better decisions.

Until the MPPA passed, Minnesota was a "may issue" state which made the concealed carrying of handguns in public by citizens difficult. Few permits were issued throughout the state. The MPPA was the result of years of lobbying and teaching legislators and cajoling the public that armed citizens are perfectly normal.

This book was written because Minnesota laws are unique to Minnesota, and state statutes are colored through court decisions interpreting how they are to be applied. The MPPA changed how a permit to carry is issued in Minnesota but did not change case law defining the use or threat of deadly force. Those who wish to carry in Minnesota need to know what the laws are in Minnesota. The opposite is also true. When traveling to other states you must be prepared to follow the applicable laws in that state.

If you are going to carry a handgun in Minnesota, you should know the difference between what is common sense and what is legal. Just because something is legal does not automatically make it sensible.

This book was written to explain how the MPPA integrates with other existing statutes not explained in the legislative text.

This book will help you understand what is involved in getting a permit and carrying a handgun in both legal and practical terms.

If you already have a personal safety concern, a stalker, an abusive ex-spouse, or you work or live in a bad neighborhood this book was written for you. You will gain legal and practical advice about surviving your current predicament.

Learning how you are perceived as an armed citizen and how it affects all other armed citizens is important and discussed.

If you are an experienced gun owner this book was definitely written for you. Many people who have owned guns for most or all of their lives have never dealt with the laws and mechanics of day-to-day handgun carry.

Regardless of how you feel about firearms or people carrying handguns in public it is our goal to help you understand the benefits and responsibilities of fully exercising your rights. It is impossible to appreciate the rights you have not used. It is life changing for many people once they fully exercise all their right of citizenship. Oddly enough the appreciation of freedom comes as a surprise to most people.

This book was also written for a relatively small number of people who may think that carrying a handgun around in public is fun and cool. We sincerely hope and expect to change the attitudes of those people.

Who we are

LEOSA Trainers, Inc. (LTI) provides Minnesota permit to carry training for citizens and LEOSA training and firearms qualification services for separated local, state and federal officers who reside in Minnesota.

LEOSA was enacted to provide qualified former officers with the means to carry a concealed firearm for their self-defense. Since no "permit" or "license" is actually issued by any state or governmental agency, this authority is most similar to constitutional carry.

LTI has expanded its permit to carry training footprint to Wisconsin, Illinois and Missouri. LTI training is also recognized by Utah and Florida.

For most of his adult life, **Gene German's** profession was a commercial insurance broker, counseling business owners about their business risks, negotiating the transfer of the risks to an insurer and suggested appropriate risk management techniques to manage risks his clients chose to keep.

As president of LEOSA Trainers Inc, Gene applies similar risk management techniques to train instructors and their students to know how to protect themselves from the unexpected threats they may encounter. He has taught citizens in Minnesota and Wisconsin how to responsibly carry lethal force in public since 2004.

Gene became a member of the leadership team and served as the Executive Director of Gun Owners Civil Rights Alliance (GOCRA) a Minnesota grassroots Second Amendment advocacy group. GOCRA was instrumental in passing the Minnesota Personal Protection Act (MPPA) in 2003 and for its re-passage in 2005. Gene and Joe Olson worked together as registered lobbyists on firearm related issues representing Minnesota's 500,000 firearms owners at the Capitol in St. Paul. Gene has testified before the Minnesota and Wisconsin legislatures on several occasions concerning carry laws.

As the NACFI (formerly AACFI) Wisconsin State Director Gene began working in 2004 with legislative leaders in Madison to successfully enact in 2011 what is now the Wisconsin Personal Protection Act. Gene and Tim Grant wrote Wisconsin's first constitutional carry course in 2009, and the current NACFI Wisconsin License to Carry course. Gene is also the co- author with Tim Grant of the Wisconsin Guide for Armed Citizens, and the Illinois Guide for Armed Citizens.

In 2012, Gene founded LEOSA Trainers, Inc. to provide the training necessary for separated law enforcement officers who reside in Minnesota and wish to carry a firearm nationwide. Gene designed LTI's training to be much more than just administering a shooting qualification. LTI offers a unique combination of Minnesota carry training and LEOSA training to clients who desire both. LTI's training also includes how a client could properly insure themselves for a defensive gun use so their life savings does not have to be at risk in retirement.

Gene formally resigned his NACFI positions and severed LTI's partnership with NACFI in August of 2014. This decision was necessary to enable him to provide continued support for LTI's instructors and to devote his time on expanding LTI's permit to carry training business in Minnesota, Wisconsin Missouri and Illinois.

Tim Fleming Grant, President of NACFI, is a political activist and marketing professional. Grant's interest in firearms and self defense began in February of 1996 when his cousin was killed in a drive-by shooting in Golden Valley, Minnesota. After four years of committed part-time work on the leadership team of Concealed Carry Reform, Now!, Grant left his position as National Sales Manager for a division of Norstan and later, Siemens to focus more time on changing Minnesota's carry laws. As CCRN's lead strategic planner and elections manager, Grant played a key role in developing and guiding the Minnesota Personal Protection Act through the Thomas, graduate credits from St. Paul Seminary and a Bachelor of Arts degree in Political Science and Economics from the University of Minnesota. Grant holds an MBA from the University of St. Thomas, graduate credits from St. Paul Seminary and a Bachelor of Arts degree in Political Science and Economics from the University of Minnesota. He also holds both Instructor and Certifier ratings from NACFI.

A handgun and a fire extinguisher

Thankfully the vast majority of people who carry a handgun will never have a defensive gun use. Coincidentally, those people who wisely own a fire extinguisher hope they never have to use it either.

When you buy fire a extinguisher you hope and expect that you will never have to use it, but you also know that, should your home catch fire, a convenient fire extinguisher may make what could have been a horrible incident a lot less horrible. A fire extinguisher is only one of the things a prudent homeowner buys in order to protect themselves and the family: smoke detectors and good locks are every bit as important.

And so it is with handguns. They are purchased and often time carried in case of a life threatening attack. Random acts of violence occur randomly so a handgun, a defensive weapon, needs to be readily available all the time. Being caught without a handgun when a random attack finds you is something no one wants to experience.

Interestingly, both a home fire and a life threatening attack are what we call, "low frequency, high consequence events". No one would call you paranoid for having a fire extinguisher at home to keep a small fire from burning the house down. Likewise, carrying a firearm for defense against a life threatening attack is just as responsible.

Humor

Carrying a handgun in public is a serious matter, and must be taken seriously. That does not mean that a little humor every now and then is a bad idea, in fact, we think it is essential. We hope that the occasional touches of humor in this book will be appreciated.

There are, however, things we do not consider funny. Joking about pointing a gun at another human being or carelessly handling your firearms are acts that diminish all armed citizens. It is your responsibility to make a positive impression.

Keeping it simple

We believe in keeping things simple whenever possible. There are sound psychological, legal, and physiological reasons for this when it comes to life-threatening encounters initiating a defensive gun use.

However, some topics cannot be oversimplified. The law and its application are complicated. We have synthesized many of the legal concepts to universally applicable formulas to assist you when making split second life and death decisions.

What a permit changes

Legally speaking, a permit to carry changes one thing and one thing only: a permit to carry allows you to carry a loaded handgun in public in some situations or places where it would otherwise be unlawful to do so.

It does not change the law of self defense in or out of the home. It does not change whether or not you are allowed to own firearms. It does not change the laws involved in storing handguns at home or at your place of business. It does not make it suddenly legal for convicted criminals to carry firearms. Most importantly is does not give anyone the right to just shoot someone!

The important thing a permit changes is the right to carry a loaded handgun in public.

It is not a "junior G-man badge

The chart that follows covers a majority of the situations involving carrying of a firearm. It does not change the legal right people have to defend themselves under Minnesota law.

Although we are offering a great deal of sound advice, we are not offering formal legal advice. For that, you should consult an attorney.

Rights	Non permit holders	Permit Holders
Owning firearms	Yes	Yes
Carrying loaded/unloaded firearms at home	Yes	Yes
Carrying loaded/unloaded firearms at place of business	Yes	Yes
Carrying firearms, unloaded, in a case, in the trunk of the car	Yes	Yes
Use of lethal force in self-defense	Yes	Yes
Carrying a firearm into school zones	No	Yes
Carrying a firearm in most public places	No	Yes
Carrying a loaded firearm in the passenger compartment of a car	No	Yes
Carrying firearms onto schools grounds (K-12)	No	Yes Storage in Parking Lots only
Acting as a police officer	No	No
Need permit to purchase	Yes	No

And remember: a gun never solves problems.

Reference # 12345678   Expires 2008-06-25

STATE OF MINNESOTA
PERMIT TO CARRY A PISTOL

FIRST   MIDDLE   LAST NAME
STREET ADDRESS
CITY   MN 55433

DRIVERS LICENSE #
Driver's License/State ID/Passport#

Bruce Andersohn   Anoka County
Issuing Sheriff   Issuing Sheriff's Office

Minnesota
State of Issue

Chapter 2
Why Would Anybody
Want a Permit to Carry?

Across the United States, millions of people have a permit to carry. The reasons vary as much as the people do.

Some have them because they need to be able to carry a firearm in order to protect other people or other people's money, bank guards for example. Some people have permits in order to protect their own assets. Many permit holders are small business owners who want to protect both their bank deposits and themselves during the sometimes-harrowing trip to the bank at the end of the day. In rural areas, in many states, some people have permits to carry because it enables them to lawfully keep their firearms in the passenger compartment of the car or truck, rather than locked in the trunk.

Most people who have permits to carry have them for personal protection. Some are worried about a specific threat, such as a stalker or an abusive ex-spouse. Others hold risky jobs, such as convenience store clerks, pizza delivery drivers, and cab drivers. What they all have in common is the desire to exercise their right to be their own first responder.

People who carry guns lawfully are far less likely to be victims of violent crime. We emphasize carry because most armed citizens do not appear as easy victims to the bad guys. Their demeanor, the way they carry themselves, and the level of situational awareness they project convinces the bad guys into looking for a softer target. Armed citizens present themselves this way because they are armed. Whether the bad guy sees the gun or not is irrelevant. If he is watching you closely, he can tell you are not a soft target. Carrying the gun is the easy part. Ever having to use it is the hard part. That is where solid training pays off.

Our experience shows us that many people who have permits to carry do not regularly carry a handgun in public. Their reasons vary widely.

One of the few universal truths about a handgun is that it never gets lighter as the day goes by. Defensive gun uses are low frequency high consequence events. Permit holders who do not regularly carry their handgun are betting on "low frequency" to mean "zero." A handgun is useful if the rare life-threatening situation confronts you, unless you decided to leave it at home. The burden of carrying a handgun is not carrying it.

It is your responsibility, both for moral and legal reasons, to maintain control of your handgun. Leaving a handgun unattended is only looking for trouble.

There are other issues. For the majority of armed citizens this means concealing the handgun. For personal, situational and communal reasons armed citizens value this form of carry. Exposing the handgun can not only startle people, but can also result in the police being summoned to a "man with a gun" call. That can be not only annoying, but potentially dangerous.

The problems do not stop there.

People carrying handguns have to *remember* they are armed. This may sound odd, but it can be like forgetting you put your glasses on your head. While it may be illegal to take a pair of nail scissors through the security checkpoint at an airport, somebody who forgets he has a pair of scissors really does not have anything to worry about beyond losing it. A permit holder who forgets that he or she has a handgun at the checkpoint will have some serious explaining to do.

In Minnesota, a permit holder going to pick up his or her children at school has to remember to stay in their vehicle when carrying a firearm on school property or be prepared to store the firearm if leaving the vehicle to enter the school. This applies to any school activity taking place on school property.

"I forgot I was armed" is not a legal defense.

Even ordinary social situations can become difficult at times.

Minnesota law allows permit holders to carry in bars. This is because guns do not drink. The law allows an armed citizen to consume only a small amount of alcohol. Should a permit holder desire a couple of cocktails, the best solution is unloading and storing the firearm in a case as a non permit holder would do when transporting a firearm or store it at home before hitting the bars.

As you have read, many reasons for not carrying exist. So why would any reasonable person ever want to? It is simple. On those rare occasions when a handgun is necessary in self defense, there is no good substitute.

Less than lethal options, like pepper spray, billy clubs, or purses require an attacker to get very close, and often do not work well against an armed attacker. Karate and other martial arts training are fine in theory but, in practice, they are useful for only the most proficient and fit practitioners. Improvised weapons like car keys or a heavy flashlight are not effective substitutes for a gun.

Statistically, the single most effective way to deter or stop a determined attacker is to produce a handgun and be prepared to use it. Fortunately, for the attacker, they can decide to flee before being shot by their intended victim. It is better for everyone if the attacker leaves the scene rather than engaging the victim in a fight the attacker is most likely to lose, and lose big. Despite surviving the attack many victims suffer some physical injury before they can stop the attacker.

Armed citizens have a positive effect on the overall crime rates. John Lott's studies have shown that when enough people take out permits it lowers violent crime rates. This phenomenon is called the "halo effect" and tends to occur when at least 1% of the state's population is perceived to be lawfully armed.

Research by criminologists confirm that criminals are responding to information about their own risk[1]. The fact that there may be armed citizens present, either as the criminal's would-be victim or as bystanders persuades some career criminals to make different choices because of their increased perception of risk to themselves. Of the thousands of law enforcement officers (LEOs) in Minnesota, at best 30% are on duty at any given time. Criminals having to also worry about tens of thousands lawfully armed citizens increases a violent criminal's chance of a bad result.

---

[1]Armed and Dangerous, by James D. Write and Peter H. Rossi (Aldine de Gruyter: New York; ISBN 0-202-30331-4), was the result of a study of over 2,000 convicted felons. Of these, two-thirds admitted having been "scared off, shot at, wounded, or captured by an armed victim," and two-fifths of them had decided not to commit a crime because they knew or believed that their intended victim was armed.

An attacker may decide to move to a different locale where the risk of being shot is less or switch to breaking into unoccupied cars. The abusive ex-spouse may worry more about the possibility of being shot while trying to beat up his or her ex than the consequences of violating an Order for Protection.

Regardless of why "shall-issue" laws lower violent crime, the important point is that they do.

We know that permit issuance is a good thing for society in general because of its effect on violent crime and for ordinary day-to-day civility. As Robert A. Heinlein wrote, "an armed society is a polite society." Heinlein was writing about fictional societies. Still, incidents of lawfully armed citizens behaving badly are nearly impossible to find. Conversely, it is possible that the presence of armed citizens have caused some loud and rude people to behave better in public.

No permit holder should ever do anything to encourage being feared by the community. The old axiom, "don't do anything to scare the women or the horses" may be a little dated, but still has a ring of truth. As you will see, when you carry a handgun, you must take more precautions to avoid confrontations that could escalate.

Getting a permit to carry because of a safety concern

In Minnesota it is possible to get a permit to carry issued within hours because of an immediate threat. A sheriff may issue and emergency permit without any training. If you have already completed training, a sheriff may be more likely to expedite you permit application.

It makes much more sense to get a permit in advance of a known threat and then make day-to-day decisions regarding carrying should a threatening situation appear.

Carrying a handgun may be an important part of personal protection it is not the only part of it. Those people who have specific personal safety concerns such as: a stalker, a physically abusive relationship, a criminal one may be testifying against in court, should consult their attorney, the local police and other safety professionals as to what else should be done. A temporary restraining order or the equivalent order is not difficult to get. While it is just a piece of paper of questionable effect, it can be very useful in dealing with the police if summoned.

Why somebody may not want to have a permit to carry

It is simply a fact that the majority of eligible citizens will not get a permit to carry. They are sheep! There are both good reasons and bad reasons why somebody would not want to obtain a permit, or even own a firearm for self defense at all. Let us look at a few.

"My gun might be taken away and used against me"

That is a very serious problem for police officers. Unfortunately, too many police officers are killed or shot annually with their own firearms. However police have very different exposure to criminal threats than citizens. Police officers carry their firearms openly, and frequently come into close contact with criminals, often needing to fight with them in order to subdue or to make an arrest which is not the job of an armed citizen

The notion of a citizen drawing a gun in self defense and having their own gun turned on them is an urban myth. Perhaps the reason for this is that it happens on TV shows every once in a while, but in real life rarely if ever. It is difficult to find an instance of a citizen being disarmed. This is understandable; when an attacker is confronted by an armed citizen most of the time the attacker flees.

"There are all those gun deaths"

Every fatality, no matter what the reason, is tragic. The facts show that firearms are among the least common causes of accidental fatalities in the United States. The National Safety Council (NSC), a nonpartisan organization, reported in 2008 the ratio of death from various causes versus a accidental firearms discharge;

1. Motor vehicle accident 67 times greater
2. Intentional self harm 60 times greater
3. Falls 40.5 times greater
4. Assault by firearm 20.6 times greater
5. Car occupant 18 times greater
6. Pedestrian 9.4 times greater
7. Motorcycle rider 8.7 times greater
8. Accidental drowning 6 times greater
9. Exposure to smoke or fire 5 times greater
10. Cyclist 1.5 times greater

When you look at the list, most are considered everyday activities that we would participate in without any undo concern. However , each activity is more dangerous than handling a firearm, some much more so.

That said, firearms safety is very important. If you make a habit of always following the basic rules of firearms safety, your chances of accidentally or negligently injuring, much less killing, yourself or somebody else is zero.

Safety is *no* accident.

"Guns are a lousy way to settle personal disputes"

This is absolutely correct.

Guns are not just a lousy way to settle a dispute, they are an illegal way to settle any kind of dispute. The only legally justifiable reason to point a gun at another human being is because of your reasonable belief of an imminent threat of death or great bodily harm. Using guns to settle heated arguments with family, neighbors, or strangers is unlawful.

Of the millions of permit holders across the nation, it is nearly impossible to find one who has used a firearm in an illegal way.

Beyond the bad reasons

The main reason most eligible people do not get a permit to carry is that they cannot or would not use a gun defensively. They are sheep. Sheep have the mistaken belief that someone else (the police) will always be there to save them. Sheep also live in a world of denial in that a random act of violence will never befall them.

We believe becoming an armed citizen is beneficial to you and your family. It is a very personal decision only you can make. Active decision making about a permit to carry is the only way to learn about its benefits, responsibilities, and your capabilities.

A few people may believe they are incapable of controlling their temper and dare not provide themselves easy access to a tool that can do a lot of damage in one uncontrolled moment. We think they are making a good decision.

It may come as a surprise that approximately 20% of students taking our permit to carry training class do not apply for a permit. Once the responsibilities and gravity of the split second decisions that are required when applying lethal force are understood carrying a gun everyday is something some students decide against.

At least make an informed decision!

Is it right for you?

No one can decide that for you. We can say that qualifying for and getting a permit to carry does give you some options.

Getting a permit to carry, carrying a firearm and using a firearm are three entirely different issues. Before ever applying for a permit to carry some soul searching must be done. Do you just want to carry a firearm, or are you capable and prepared to use it? The choice of being able to use lethal force including shooting an attacker is a individual and very personal decision. Your soul search will include your upbringing, religious training, and personal set of moral values. Along with training you will be better prepared to make an informed decision.

Our recommendation is to read about it and think about it. If you decide a permit is right for you, take a training course from LTI.

And remember: a gun never solves problems.

CHAPTER 3
Staying Out of Trouble

The most important thing for a permit holder to do is to avoid conflict.

The advantages of avoiding conflict are obvious: a violent confrontation that you avoid will mean you are not injured, killed, prosecuted, or a headline. Many people who have survived lethal confrontations, even if they manage to avoid being injured themselves suffer from a variety of psychological affects, depression, anxiety, Post-Traumatic Stress Disorder, etc. This is a very short list covering the most dramatic of reasons to avoid conflict. In reality, the list is a lot longer.

Even when lethal force is justified legally, morally, and tactically there are serious important and lasting consequences. Using lethal force even when entirely justified, has negative effects on everybody involved. Those who defend themselves against violent attacks are still victims. They are just "victims of a different type."

Being involved in a defensive gun use is an awful thing, and going to some trouble to avoid it is a good idea for everybody, particularly those who choose to carry handguns in public.

Your tactical options

In facing a threat you will have four clear tactical options. For our purposes we will define "a threat" as being a person who, even when unprovoked, has **both** the capability and intent to do you harm. Each option has its benefits and risks and the specific situation will determine which options are available. Maintaining alertness, often called "situational awareness", allows you to keep more of the options available. Your decision of which option to use and when probably will change during the course of the attack.

Each option may be both reversible and / or scalable. By reversible we mean that if you take this action, can you stop and reverse it. Scalable means you can increase or decrease the action you are taking.

Your first option is to do nothing.

You may choose to remain in a situation and go with the flow, electing not to take any action at all. Your situational awareness is heightened, and you calculate any number of options. You are collecting data. So you are very busy "doing nothing" as you are doing nothing. Doing nothing is reversible because you can decide to do something. To the extent that you are paying more or less attention to the situation "doing nothing" is scalable. What you decide to do may be scalable. You are keeping options open as the situation evolves.

Your second option is to leave if it is safe and practical.

When a situation makes you uncomfortable, the best thing to do might be to leave before any trouble starts. By practicing situational awareness you should know where the available exits are. Other considerations for this option include who is with you and can everyone safely leave. Is the level of threat to others too high for you and your party to exit? Leaving should not be reversible. If you had a belief that you were in imminent danger of death or great bodily harm and managed to escape, there is no point in going back. If you are carrying a gun, you cannot go back. It is scalable, because you can move from one point of cover to another or (either) walk or run away.

Your third option is to use less than lethal force.

Your defensive action may be anything from issuing a verbal command to be left alone, to physical actions such as striking or shoving an attacker to stop the threat. This option is reversible, if you have taken action you can stop that action. It is also scalable because you can increase or decrease the level of less than lethal force you have taken.

Your fourth option is to use lethal force.

For our purposes, this begins with the threat of lethal force (e.g., drawing your gun from its holster), and most certainly includes firing a handgun or using any other type of force that could reasonably be expected to cause death or great bodily harm. Lethal force is only partially reversible. It is reversible up until the moment you pull the trigger and shoot the attacker. After that, there is no taking the bullet back. It is scalable. You can shoot one or more times, but only as many times as it takes to stop the threat. Then you must stop shooting or you have used excessive force which is a crime.

Certainly your goal should be to escape without having to use force, lethal or otherwise. Your ability to do so will largely depend on your level of situational awareness to your environment. The earlier you recognize a threat the greater your opportunity to exercise your first option and leave.

Situational awareness

The key to avoiding problems is maintaining a reasonable level of alertness or situational awareness. This is particularly true for avoiding street crimes like mugging, assault, robbery, and rape. Being situationally aware has two advantages: it helps you avoid trouble, and appearing to be alert helps to persuade trouble to avoid you. Generally speaking, criminals are opportunists. As trainer Clint Smith puts it, "If you look like prey, you will be eaten."

When you are unaware of your surroundings and any possible threat for example, when you are asleep, it would take some serious effort to gain your attention. Being "unaware" is necessary to sleep, and should also be OK, at home with the doors locked watching TV. By being unaware of your surrounding, any unusual disturbance may cause a startle reflex.

The next level of situation awareness is when you have a deliberate awareness of your surroundings and make it a habit to pay attention to what is going on around you. You are calm, relaxed, and not concerned about an immediate threat, but looking for things out of the ordinary. When you are waiting at a bus stop, you watch the folks around you, rather than burying yourself in a newspaper or a book. When you are driving you make it a habit to look in the rear-view mirror and notice if you are being followed. It is not a matter of making major changes in how you live your life: it is a matter of being constantly aware of what is going on around you and how people are acting.

It is a good idea to make a habit of staying this alert whenever you are out in public. It is not just a matter of personal safety although awareness is the key to that. Life is just more interesting when you are paying attention to what is going on around you.

The next level is when you have identified a possible threat based upon their capability and intent to hurt you. It is time to consider your tactical options.   If others are with you, a plan to get them out of harms way is required. If you do not have a plan for this eventuality you should create one. Perhaps have a secret word or phrase ; such as; "rockcut" or "go check the dog" to alert family member what to do to temporarily create separation from you and to call the police.

The good news is the situation is either going to improve or continue to get worst. If it gets worse your mind-set needs to move to one of "I am going to survive" by fighting for my life. Because you are under attack you have to protect yourself by any reasonable means. Should an opportunity to retreat or leave presents itself, take it. When you are safe, call for help including medical assistance if needed then find your family.

We will discuss all of the physiological and psychological implications later. For now, the best time to figure out how to handle a problem is before it happens.   Think about "what if" scenarios when you are going about your day. What if I was attacked right now? What are my options? When under attack, you will go into survival mode and revert to how you have trained. Practicing "what if" is a basic form of training.

Avoiding conflict

"Alternative Means of Conflict Resolution" can be looked at as a fancy way of saying, "Do not escalate an argument into a fight." It is a good idea to cultivate a thick skin if you are carrying a handgun. It is important to avoid conflict because any conflict you are involved in automatically is escalated to the level of an armed conflict. This is true if for no other reason; you are armed even if the other person is not. How police respond to an armed conflict is considerable more dangerous for everybody than their response to an unarmed conflict.

For example, you are an armed citizen who has just been involved in a fender bender. Some idiot just backed into you, damaging your new car. You may be understandably annoyed and the other person may be equally upset. You may be tempted to leap out of your car and go shout at the other driver. Understandable, perhaps, but not a good idea. He or she may start shouting at you. You must resist the temptation to shout back You should be constantly evaluating the situation. Is the idiot just blowing off steam by shouting and swearing, or does he have the capability and intention to attack you? Can you calm him down with words or perhaps is it better to let him shout for awhile? In any case, stay alert and avoid escalation if possible. Stay calm and aware and call the police. You are armed. At this point your responsibility is to be civil and to not escalate the argument into a confrontation. This is good advice for everybody, but it is even more important for armed citizens.

The proper conclusion to this incident is for the police to show up, hand you accident report forms, see that you exchange pertinent information and you each go your separate ways.

Congratulations, you just demonstrated that an armed society is a polite society!

Being aware of what is going on around you, is situational awareness.

Avoid the conflict, and avoid the consequences

And remember: a gun never solves problems.

CHAPTER 4

Morally Surviving an Attack

"Oh my god, I just shot someone, am I going to go to hell now?"

This question may be among the first thoughts of a person who just had a defensive gun use (DGU) whether or not their attacker is dead. Those of you who were raised in a church or synagogue in any of the majority of American religious faiths have had the Judeo-Christian Ten Commandments burned into your psyche, and God's commandment, "thou shall not kill" is as clear as it can be about what is a violation of God's law.

Law enforcement officers and armed citizens all have to wrestle with whether there is ever any justifiable taking of another's life. Can one morally kill someone without also condemning themself to hell at the same time?

It may surprise some people that the Minnesota statutes regarding the use of force, up to and including lethal force, to defend yourself or others are very similar to the Jewish and Catholic moral teachings regarding the use of force for self defense and it only makes sense. Our society has determined what is righteous behavior and what is criminal behavior by relying upon the millennial wisdom of two of the world's great religious theologies to form the legal basis of how our laws treat the taking of life. Most Protestant faiths largely agree with Jewish and Catholic teaching on self defense. The bottom line is that Judeo-Christian theology and U.S. criminal statutes have more in common than not.

Some victims, who have found themselves in a position where they must use force to protect themselves or others, have suffered guilt or have questioned if they can somehow morally justify their behavior. Do not put yourself in this horrible position. Those who have survived a defensive gun use do so, in part, because they have taken the opportunity to educate themself and come to a moral decision on this issue before having to use lethal force for self preservation. Each of us must contend with that personal decision and until you do please reconsider carrying a firearm for personal protection.

Elements of an Attack

If we look at a DGU and break it down to understand what is happening, it can more easily be compared with the moral teaching of the Judeo-Christian faiths. The preconditions of a DGU are:

The Attacker

This person has elected to threaten and/or use violence sufficient to cause his victim to honestly and actually believe they will suffer imminent death or great bodily harm. The wellbeing of the victim is of no interest or concern to the attacker.

The Attacker is willing to murder or inflict great bodily harm upon his victim without regard for the consequences.

The Victim

At the time the attack began the victim posed no threat to the attacker and did nothing to cause the attack or escalate the attack. They were just in the wrong place at the wrong time. In some cases it may be that the attacker and the victim knew each other. Perhaps the victim petitioned the court for an order for protection, or filed reports with the appropriate law enforcement agency documenting an ongoing threat. Having had a relationship with an attacker in itself does not negate your right to remain safe now or in the future. Once an attack has started the opportunity to safely retreat or escape has passed. The victim's belief of the threat is real, with the attacker having the means, intent and opportunity to carry it out.

The victim's use of force is intended only to stop the threat, to cause the attacker to either break off the attack or to rendered the attacker incapable of continuing the attack. Only the amount of force that is necessary to cause the attacker to stop his attack may be used. A victim's intent should never be to murder anyone.

It is this way because our religious precepts have understood the difference between murder and killing in self defense. Murder is what the attacker intends to do to his victim, and has been against God's law since Cain murdered Abel. In fact, some Bible translations of the ten commandments read, "Thou shall not murder". The killing of one's enemies, be it done as a part of war, the proactive use of force by law enforcement, or a citizen's unintended killing of an attacker as a consequence of stopping a violent attacker has been morally justified throughout recorded history.

With the attacker and victim conditions above let us examine the moral teaching of Judaism, Catholicism, and the majority of the Protestant faiths to see how each one treats the use of force, including the use of lethal force, for self preservation.

The Judeo-Christian Teachings

Judaism

"Homicide is justifiable when it is committed in obedience to duty, as in executing a condemned criminal, or in defense of human life or chastity, or even in killing the thief who breaks in at night, whether the killing is done by the proprietor of the premises or by a stranger". (The Jewish Encyclopedia, 1909)

What can also be said, with some certainty, is that the Torah offers nothing to support an argument that defensive violence or killing is inherently wrong. To the contrary, the law which God gave to the Israelites *required* use of deadly force in self defense and defense of others. Deadly force was allowed in circumstances in which there was strong, but not incontrovertible, evidence that a criminal aggressor had murderous intent. Deadly force was not allowed in mere defense of property when there was not an implicit threat to the life on the property. Abraham and Moses, the greatest heroes of the Torah, both used force to protect innocents. Under the Torah, using force to protect innocents was not only a right, but a positive moral duty. (David Kopel, 109 Penn State Law Review 17, 2004)

Despite a trend of more liberal Jewish congregations to exhort a more pacifist belief regarding self defense, The teachings of the Torah clearly support self defense and defense of others as morally correct.

Catholicism

The legitimate defense of persons and societies is not an exception to the prohibition against the murder of the innocent that constitutes intentional killing. "The act of self defense can have a double effect: the preservation of one's own life; and the killing of the aggressor. . . . The one is intended, the other is not."

It is clear that the above text contains "theologian speak". The first sentence tells us that you may not kill innocents for any reason. Doing so would be murder. The second sentence tells us that using force for self preservation is morally acceptable providing your intent was not to kill your attacker. Using force to save yourself is righteous even if the attacker dies as long as that is an unintended consequence.

Love toward oneself remains a fundamental principle of morality. Therefore it is legitimate to insist on respect for one's own right to life. Someone who defends his life is not guilty of murder even if he is forced to deal his aggressor a lethal blow.

If a man in self defense uses more than necessary violence, it will be unlawful: whereas if he repels force with moderation, his defense will be lawful. . . . Nor is it necessary for salvation that a man omit the act of moderate self defense to avoid killing the other man, since one is bound to take more care of one's own life than of another's.

Legitimate defense can be not only a right but a grave duty for one who is responsible for the lives of others. The defense of the common good requires that an unjust aggressor be rendered unable to cause harm. For this reason, those who legitimately hold authority also have the right to use arms to repel aggressors against the civil community entrusted to their responsibility. *(The new Catechism of the Catholic Church, 1996)*

Catholic theology, appears to be the most definitive teaching on legitimate self defense with its foundation in the Jewish faith and with insight from the Second Vatican Council of the mid 20th century through the adoption of the new Catechism of the Catholic Church in 1996.

Protestantism

Mainline Protestants are the members of the National Council of Churches. Mainline denominations include the United Methodist Church, the Evangelical Lutheran Church in America, the Episcopal Church, the Presbyterian Church (U.S.A.) and the United Church of Christ. The mainline denominations have historically been dominant in American Protestantism.

The commandment is, *Thou shalt not kill.*

The sins forbidden in the commandment against killing are, all taking away the life of ourselves, or of others, except in case of public justice (capitol punishment), lawful war, or necessary defense. "Necessary defense means self defense" and as long as the intention of violence is to preserve ones life, then the killing an attacker is seen as lawful. *(Westminster Confession of Faith, 1640)*

Martin Luther's Large Catechism says that "no one should harm another for any evil deed, no matter how much he deserves it." However, in

What Lutherans Believe, W. E. Schramm says that "In a few exceptional cases the taking of human life is justifiable. If I am attacked, I may defend myself. If an invader enters my home, I may protect my family. If in the defense of my life or in the protection of my household I am compelled to maim or kill, neither the law of the state nor the law of God will hold me guilty of crime." *(Christianity, guns and Self defense, Louis Williams)*

The Presbyterian Church (U.S.A.) is also against its members arming themselves for self defense. The General Assembly of the Presbyterian Church has publicly stated it is opposed to the killing of anyone for any reason. *(Christianity, guns and Self defense, Louis Williams)*

The board of Church and Society of the United Methodist Church headed by the Rev. Allen Brockway states; For though the burglary victim or women accosted in the park by a rapist is (not) likely to consider the violator to be a neighbor whose safety is of immediate concern. Criminals are members of the larger community no less than others. As such they are our neighbors or as Jesus put it our brothers, though violent criminals act wrongfully, it is equally wrong for the victim to kill, save in those extremely rare circumstances when the unambiguous alternative is one's own death". *(Christianity, Guns and Self defense, Louis Williams)*

For Baptists, the Law of God establishes the basic right of self defense. A person has a duty to defend himself or his family whenever they are attacked or their lives are endangered. Any weapon is permissible for use in self defense. The Law of God does not say that the homeowner is guilty if he uses a sword, but innocent if he uses a club. The issue is not one of weapons, but the right and duty of self defense. *(Christianity, guns and Self defense, Louis Williams)*

As Protestantism has evolved into a number of competing religious faiths the teaching of self defense have blurred. The Baptist have remained true to the very early teaching of Protestantism, while other faiths have elected martyrdom over self preservation.

The salvation of one's soul is between every person and God. This primer is intended to assist you in reaching your decision about how you would reconcile the conflict between saving your own life or allowing someone else to wrongfully take it away from you. It may be this is just the start of your education on the morality of self defense before you arrive at a decision.

And remember: a gun never solves problems.

CHAPTER 5
Lethal Force, in Law and Practice

You are not going to be buried with a lot of legal jargon in this chapter. However, when it comes to the lawful use of force, there is just no way around getting into some of the nitty-gritty of the legalities and we have to deal with those.

This chapter is intended to be a general discussion of the judicious use of force for self defense and the affirmative self defense law in Minnesota. We also discuss the law associated with a Minnesota Permit to Carry. While this book was written with the help of some very experienced attorneys, the authors are not attorneys and cannot give you specific legal advice. Legal advice is the job for your attorney.

The law is never simple. Even when principles seem clear and well-developed the exact facts of each situation (at every moment, even as they change) can cause the legal answer to vary. This chapter discusses general principles. Only your own legal counsel, armed with the specifics of the law and the facts of your own situation can give you "legal advice" on which you can depend.

You will notice that court cases are cited. Statutory law is colored over time by judicial rulings. How a specific ruling affects the application of a specific law can be very important. In this chapter are the discussion of legal principles, and appropriate judicial rulings that may apply.

It is important for you to know that Minnesota is a "preemption state." This means that, with very few exceptions, the State Legislature has absolute control over the regulation of firearms. The laws and case law we discuss apply border-to-border. No local unit of government can enforce or enact an ordinance or resolution unless it is the same as or similar to or no more stringent than a state statute. Preemption also means that a local unit of government cannot create ordinances or resolutions to regulate that which the state does not regulate. For example, the state does not regulate how many guns you can carry. Preemption prohibits local governments from enacting ordinances to limit the number of guns permit holders may possess in public.

Justification

As we have said, the possession of a permit to carry does not change Minnesota law about the use of force, one way or another.

The legal definition of "justification" means that you (the defendant in a case) admit to the violation of a statute while simultaneously claiming that the magnitude of the harm avoided by your violation outweighs the harm (or behavior) the statute seeks to prevent. Therefore, the otherwise criminal act is justified in this particular instance, and you are not guilty of the crime.

Under Minnesota law, self defense is a "justification" defense. In effect, by claiming self defense in the use of force, you are admitting that you did something that is normally illegal, but is justified in this case because your response to the threat met each and every element required to justify your use of lethal force.

Remember, there is a proportionality aspect to any claim that the use of force is justified. This limitation rests on the common law principle that the amount of force used must bear a reasonable relation to the magnitude of the harm sought to be avoided.

Minnesota court decisions further develop this proportionality theme with *express rules* in regard to (1) defense of person, (2) defense of a dwelling or premises, or (3) defense of property. In each situation, the law identifies levels of harm which may justify the use of physical force and expressly identifies the more serious threats justifying the use of lethal force. For example, the actual *use* of lethal force (e.g., discharging a firearm at another person) is justified only where the degree of threatened injury is equally severe. *Remember this principle!* The law carefully specifies the threats which are of sufficient magnitude to justify the use of lethal force.

Self defense

Minn. Stat. § 609.06 authorizes the use of *non-lethal* reasonable force as follows:

609.06 AUTHORIZED USE OF FORCE.

Subd. 1. **When authorized.** Except as otherwise provided in *subd.* 2, reasonable force may be used upon or toward the person of another without the other's consent when the following circumstances exist or the actor reasonably believes them to exist:

(1) when used by a public officer or one assisting a public officer under the public officer's direction:

(a) in effecting a lawful arrest; or

(b) in the execution of legal process; or

(c) in enforcing an order of the court; or

(d) in executing any other duty imposed upon the public officer by law; or

(2) when used by a person not a public officer in arresting another in the cases and in the manner provided by law and delivering the other to an officer competent to receive the other into custody; or

(3) when used by any person in resisting or aiding another to resist an offense against the person; or

(4) when used by any person in lawful possession of real or personal property, or by another assisting the person in lawful possession, in resisting a trespass upon or other unlawful interference with such property; or

(5) when used by any person to prevent the escape, or to retake following the escape, of a person lawfully held on a charge or conviction of a crime; or

(6) when used by a parent, guardian, teacher, or other lawful custodian of a child or pupil, in the exercise of lawful authority, to restrain or correct such child or pupil; or

(7) when used by a school employee or school bus driver, in the exercise of lawful authority, to restrain a child or pupil, or to prevent bodily harm or death to another; or

(8) when used by a common carrier in expelling a passenger who refuses to obey a lawful requirement for the conduct of passengers and reasonable care is exercised with regard to the passenger's personal safety; or

(9) when used to restrain a person who is mentally ill or mentally defective from self-injury or injury to another or when used by one with authority to do so to compel compliance with reasonable requirements for the person's control, conduct, or treatment; or

(10) when used by a public or private institution providing custody or treatment against one lawfully committed to it to compel compliance with reasonable requirements for the control, conduct, or treatment of the committed person.

For our purposes, the key phrase is: "when used by any person in resisting or aiding another to resist an offense against the person." You can use *reasonable* force to "resist an offense"—to protect yourself against someone trying to commit a crime against your person, for example. In Minnesota, lethal force may not be used to resist an offense against only property unless the property is in your dwelling and its destruction or theft will constitute a felony. [2]

Minn. Stat. § 609.065 creates an exception that specifically authorizes the use of lethal or deadly force.

609.065 JUSTIFIABLE TAKING OF LIFE.

The intentional taking of the life of another is not authorized by section 609.06, except when necessary in resisting or preventing an offense which the actor reasonably believes exposes the actor or another to great bodily harm or death, or preventing the commission of a felony in the actor's place of abode.

The use of deadly force is further restricted by *Minn. Stat. § 609.06. Subd. 2*

---

2   A dual-effect crime, targeting both your person and your property, is treated as the more serious threat; that is, to your person.

Deadly force used against peace officers. Deadly force may not be used against peace officers who have announced their presence and are performing official duties at a location where a person is committing a crime or an act that would be a crime if committed by an adult.

Minn. Stat. § 609.065 provides language for the justified taking of life that is similar to statutes which most states apply to the actual *use* of deadly force. Minnesota law is consistent with a majority of states in defining "deadly force" as meaning:

> Deadly Force means force that the actor uses with the purpose of causing or that he knows to create a substantial risk of causing death or [great] bodily injury. Purposely firing a firearm in the direction of another person or at a vehicle in which another person is believed to be constitutes deadly force. A threat to cause death or [great] bodily injury, by the production of a weapon or otherwise, so long as the actor's purpose is limited to creating the apprehension that he will use deadly force if necessary [i.e., authorized by law], does not constitute deadly force.

Therefore, the above language can be used to argue that *only* if the firearm is discharged and a death ensues, do the "deadly force" rules of *Minn. Stat. § 609.065* apply. In other situations, the "reasonable force" rules contained in *Minn. Stat. § 609.06* provide the sole criteria governing the authorized use of force. The purpose of presenting this argument is to differentiate the <u>display</u> of the firearm from the <u>use</u> of the firearm. In doing so the display of the firearm is governed by authorized use of force standard under *Minn. Stat. § 609.06* and not justifiable taking of a life standard under *Minn. Stat. § 609.065*.

Self defense reflects a *conscious* decision on your part to *intentionally* use reasonable force to stop a threat. Remember that for the lawful use of reasonable force in self defense, the four elements must be present *all* of the time that you are using force.

Case Law - elements of self defense

Minnesota's most recent Supreme Court decision regarding self defense delineates the requirements for a successful self defense claim in State vs. Basting (C5-96-493, December 18, 1997).[3]

"The elements of self defense are (1) the absence of aggression or provocation on the part of the defendant; (2) the defendant's actual and honest belief that he or she was in imminent danger of death or great bodily harm; (3) the existence of reasonable grounds for that belief; and (4) the

---

3   The full State vs. Basting ruling can be found in Appendix B

absence of a reasonable possibility of retreat to avoid the danger. State v. McKissic, 415 N.W.2d 341, 344 (Minn.App.1987) (citing State v. Johnson, 277 Minn. 368, 373, 152 N.W.2d 529, 532 (1967)); Minn.Stat. § 609.06, *subd.* 1(3) (1996).

The degree of force used in self defense must not exceed that which appears to be necessary to a reasonable person under similar circumstances. McKissic, 415 N.W.2d at 344 (citing State v. Bland, 337 N.W.2d 378, 381 (Minn.1983)).

A defendant has the burden of going forward with evidence to support a claim of self defense. State v. Graham, 371 N.W.2d 204, 209 (Minn.1985).

Once it is raised, the state has the burden of disproving one or more of these elements beyond a reasonable doubt. State v. Spaulding, 296 N.W.2d 870, 875 (Minn.1980).

As you have read, there is a lot of statutory and case law for you to know, understand and then properly apply. We have synthesized all of this material into a formula of elements that must be present for the successful claim of self defense. These elements can be quickly recognized and assessed.

To successfully claim self defense
Claiming self defense requires you meet the following.

1. *You have the burden of "injecting" the legal issue of self defense into the case.* The defendant, usually through his or her lawyer, has the burden of going forward with evidence to support a claim that the use of protective force was justified. A trial judge's decision to deny a requested self defense instruction will not be reversed on appeal absent an abuse of discretion.[3]
2. *You must reasonably believe that every element of the justification defense existed at the time protective force was employed.* This means not only that you (1) act[4] ally believed the element of defense existed (e.g., the object in the assailant's hand was a gun) *but also that* (2) you were reasonable in so believing (e.g., the object was silver and was held and pointed in the same manner in which a gun would be handled). The standard is "reasonable belief"—a matter of perception, not fact (e.g., that the silver object turns out to be a cell phone is not relevant).
3. *The ultimate burden of proof never shifts to the defendant.* This means if there is any evidence to support self defense, the prosecution must prove beyond a reasonable doubt that the use of deadly force was *not* justified.

What does "reasonable" really mean?

The key word "reasonable," is an external, *objective* standard. It is what a hypothetical prudent person in your situation would believe. Honesty

---

4   But a defendant is entitled to a self defense instruction to the jury if there is any evidence to support each element of the defense theory. In evaluating the evidence, it must be viewed in the light most favorable to the party requesting the instruction, State v. Edwards, 717 N.W.2d 405, 410 (Minn. 2006).

and sincerity are not sufficient; you also must have reasonable ground for your belief. The totality of the situation must support your claim or you have committed a crime.

In a legal context, whether or not something is "reasonable" is determined by a "trier of fact"—usually a jury, and a jury may not only disagree with you, but can also get it wrong. If the prosecutor has any doubt that your belief was "reasonable," he can put you in front of a jury and let them decide with whom they agree.

A "reasonable belief" is an objective test. Everyone in the legal process (prosecutors, juries, and judges) gets to "second guess" whether or not you were reasonable in believing that a particular factual element existed.

Defense of others

Coming to the defense of others requires the same tactical and legal justification as to protect oneself. There is however, one big hurdle to overcome before coming to the defense of another. You must be psychic! To meet a prosecutor's challenge to the defense of a third person, the armed citizen, must have complete knowledge and understanding of the victim's condition (how they came to this place, at this time and in this situation) and state of mind. Being able to articulate how another person feels and what that person is thinking (along with what the attacker is thinking) is for practical purposes impossible. In addition, the armed citizen would need to know the relationship between who is perceived to be the victim and the attacker.

As an intervener into a situation, as the second gun in the fight you may be perceived as another threat to both the attacker and the victim. Your intent is not known, therefore, you are going to be considered a danger to all involved in the incident. This misunderstanding alone can get you killed. One of the original parties to the attack is an undercover police officer attempting to make an arrest.

Before becoming the third person involved, consider your four tactical options carefully. A situation like this can snowball very quickly into a gunfight and the line between who is the good guy and who is bad guy will get very blurry very quickly. Most likely you will decide your best option is to use your cell phone to summon the authorities and take mental notes.

You may decide to do nothing. There is no law requiring you to intervene or put yourself in harm's way. One LTI instructor comments that "if the victim is not willing to take the steps necessary to learn how to defend themselves, why would they expect me to risk my life to save them." It may sound harsh, but is true.

Assessing the situation

This is a lot to think about and may seem overwhelming. Armed citizens must learn how to take backward looking laws and apply them in a forward thinking fashion. Law is generally written to overlay upon a particular set of historical circumstances to determine if what happened was lawful. Armed citizens have split seconds to apply a set of laws to what they reasonably believe is an imminent threat. The question is, am I being reasonable if I take these actions right now?

The Minnesota Supreme Court has established the elements of self-defense are (1) the absence of aggression or provocation on the part of the defendant; (2) the defendant's actual and honest belief that he or she was in imminent danger of death or great bodily harm; (3) the existence of reasonable grounds for that belief; and (4) the absence of a reasonable possibility of retreat to avoid the danger.

This requires a systematic method for quickly assessing the situation, deciding on a course of action, and taking the action. Below is a process to help you through the assessment, decision, and action cycle while under extreme time constraints and stress. They are called *the four elements*.

For justification of self defense to apply, all four elements must be present. The moment any one of the elements is no longer present, the justification of self defense also ceases. What were justified actions just a moment before are now criminal. We cannot overstate the importance that all four elements must be present for the entire time you are acting under the justification of self defense.

The four elements

1. **Reluctant participant**

   You cannot be the aggressor in the situation. The situation must be occasioned or developed through no fault of you, the armed citizen. You cannot provoke an attack and then later claim the justification of self defense.

   If there is any question or doubt as to whether you started or contributed to the altercation you may reestablish your status as a reluctant participant. You must in good faith withdraw from the fight and give adequate notice thereof to your attacker. The louder and more public your notice the better.

   The best example of a reluctant participant is the run of the mill mugging victim. A person just walking down the street minding their own business and suddenly confronted by one or more attackers seeking either money or to cause injury.

The practice of avoiding conflict and situational awareness will go a long way in establishing your meeting the reluctant participant requirement. Being able to articulate and support the status of reluctant participant is critical to claim the justification of self defense. This is the first link of the self defense claim that must be present.

2. An actual and honest belief that you were in imminent danger of death or great bodily harm; with the existence of reasonable grounds for that belief.

"Actual and honest belief" is the language taken directly from the Minnesota Supreme Court decision *State v. Basting, 572 N.W.2d 281, 285 (Minn. 1997)*. A successful justification for self defense will require that you articulate the existence of *reasonable grounds* for your actual and honest belief.

In believing something, a person takes the information available and processes it against their life experience, knowledge and training. Believing any given set of circumstances or conditions will not be the same for each person. Because of this even when the facts are the same, believing that one is in imminent danger will be different for each person because their experience knowledge and training is different. Additionally, this process is going to take place under a great deal of stress that will affect one's ability to think rationally.

The court will allow you to use in your defense only that information that contributed to your decision to use lethal force. This information is, critical in proving the existence of reasonable grounds for your belief. Thus both the defendant and the trier of fact (the jury) may consider what the defendant knew of the aggressor's violent nature, reputation for violence, customary carry of weapons, etc. Anything learned about your attacker after the gun goes bang was not a part of your decision to pull the trigger and will not be considered.

Because this element has many subjective attributes, making a black or white case can be difficult. Gray does exist so it is very important you clearly articulate your belief of the threat. Convincing the court your decisions and actions were justified is what matters.

A determination as to the threat being "imminent" must be made. Imminent is something that is about to occur, impending or likely to occur at any moment. By contrast, this differs from immediate which is occurring without delay, having no time intervening, or the next thing about to happen. For example, A

tornado watch is an imminent warning that the conditions exist
for a tornado to form. A tornado warning is an immediate warning that a tornado exists in your vicinity. Imminent is a broader
standard, providing additional time for the armed citizen to make
good decisions and take proper actions.

Death may seem an obvious condition. However, it is not quite
that simple. All people die for the same reason: lack of oxygen to the
brain. How the brain became starved of oxygen can vary greatly. This
may not provide any insight into how one determines if death is imminent, but does provide a definition for clarification.

As with the first element, having a belief of imminent death
or great bodily harm must be present the entire time to claim the
justification of self defense. The claim is only valid until the threat
has ceased. When the threat ceases because of something you did
or for some other reason this second link in the chain claiming self
defense breaks. Once broken, your claim of justification is over.

3. No lesser force will do

The degree of force used in self defense must not exceed that
which appears to be necessary to a reasonable person under similar circumstances. The easiest way to determine if lesser force will
stop the threat is to ask yourself, "If I didn't have a gun, what
would I do?" Then, do that. You (the armed citizen) may intentionally use only such force or threat of force that you reasonably
believe is necessary to prevent or terminate the unlawful offense
against you or another person. You may not intentionally use
force which is intended or likely to cause death or great bodily
harm unless you actually and honestly believe that such force is
necessary to prevent imminent death or great bodily harm.

The level of force needed to stop the threat can change during the course of an attack. The attacker may escalate the level of
force against you by introducing a weapon or accomplices. You
may therefore need to increase the level of force needed to stop
the threat.

If less than lethal force fails to stop the threat, using lethal force
is justified, by definition. For our purposes using lethal force begins
with drawing your gun, not when you pull the trigger. Pointing a gun
at an attacker has a chilling effect on their willingness to continue the
attack (92 times out of 100 the attacker decides to flee). If the attacker
decides to continue the attack, you must be prepared and willing to
shoot.

This element is the third link of the chain and must be present to claim the justification of self defense and ceases when the threat ceases. Regardless of the level of force you used, being able to articulate your decision to use force is important.

4. **Retreat is not practical**

The Minnesota Supreme Court states the duty to retreat as "the absence of a reasonable possibility of retreat to avoid the danger". The absence of a reasonable possibility of retreat may include your lack of knowledge that an avenue of retreat existed.

Retreat is a very good option if it is practical. Being practical is nothing more than weighing the level of danger in safely retreating versus the danger of staying. If you are practicing avoiding conflict and situational awareness, your intuition and instinct should warn you in advance of danger. Leaving (or retreating if practical) to avoid conflict is preferable, making it your first best choice. The skills you learned to avoid trouble throughout your life when you were not carrying a gun become even more important to practice now that you are an armed citizen.

Retreat saves you from personal anguish, being a victim, financial distress, and allows you to maintain your constant state of peace. The wisdom of retreat is well founded.

As the fourth link in the chain, should the opportunity of retreat become available, your right to the justification of self defense ceases.

Self defense is a chain

Think of your right to use lethal force in self defense as a chain that you are desperately trying to hang on to as you are dangling over a prison cell that (obviously) you do not want to fall into. The chain has exactly four links. If any one of those links is missing or if, at any time, any one of them breaks, your justification to use or threaten lethal force ends at that very moment, and if you continue, you fall.

We have repeated "until the threat stops" a number of times because it is incredibly important. Self defense is not about killing or even wounding an attacker. We desire to change the behavior of the attacker. It is about stopping a threat to maintain your constant state of peace. To stay out of prison your justification to apply lethal force ends once you have changed the attacker's behavior and stopped the threat. Your use of force must end immediately. One more trigger pull than necessary is the difference between self defense and prison.

Understanding the four elements necessary to threaten or apply lethal force is critical to saving your life and staying out of prison. Know when the four elements are present, and just as important, know when the chain of elements breaks.

Although you use self defense as your defense, in order for the state to convict you of a crime, the state only has the burden of disproving that at least one of the self-defense elements were missing beyond a reasonable doubt. If they do, you are going to prison. *State v. Spaulding, 296 N.W.2d 870, 875 (Minn. 1980).*

Defense of dwelling

It is important to know how the crime of "burglary" applies to your dwelling. Although most people associate the term burglary with someone stealing their stuff, burglary also means the unlawful breaking and entering of another's property with the intent of committing any criminal act.

Minnesota has four levels of burglary.

First Degree Burglary: Burglary in any one or more of the following circumstances:

- Of a dwelling or home while someone is present;
- With the possession of a dangerous weapon or item made to look like a dangerous weapon; or
- If the defendant assaulted another person in the commission of the offense.

Second Degree Burglary: Burglary in any of the following circumstances:

- Of a dwelling or home even if no one is present;
- Of a bank or other financial business that receives securities or other valuable papers or of a pharmacy, and this is committed by force or threats; or
- With the possession of a tool or tools to aid in gaining access to money or property.

Third Degree Burglary: Burglary in any other circumstances when the defendant enters a building without consent and commits a felony or gross misdemeanor.

Fourth Degree Burglary: Burglary in any other circumstances when the defendant enters a building without consent and commits a misdemeanor other than theft.

So, this seems to say that you can just shoot someone who attempts to unlawfully enter your home. For the sake of discussion, let us say you called the police and they arrived in time to catch the burglar, arrested him and he was found guilty of breaking into your home. Do you think the court would sentence him to death? If you shot him before the police arrived and he died in your house, would you feel better?

These are not questions we can answer for you. It will depend upon the totality of the circumstances. The threat you faced and what you needed to do to protect your life or the lives of your family, and there is no easy right or wrong answer. We want you to know what the law says, apply it to your own situation so you are able to make your case and justify your actions to the prosecuting attorney.

Minnesota is a castle doctrine state which means a person may use lethal force defensively against an intruder/attacker in "one's abode" to prevent the commission of a felony. Defense of one's "abode" removes two of the four elements; 1) "actual and honest belief that you were in imminent danger of death or great bodily harm" and 2) "Retreat is not practical." However, force may not be used against a public safety person (police officer, fireman, emergency medical personnel) who had identified themselves and was on official business. The victim must not also be engaged in criminal activity.

Minnesota's legal terminology is called "defense of dwelling." For clarity purposes, dwelling is defined as; a building used as a permanent or temporary residence (*Minn. Stat. § 609.581*). The term "abode" is also used in *Minn Stat. § 609.065* and is defined as "a dwelling maintained by an individual, whether or not owned by the individual and whether or not occupied by the individual, and includes a dwelling place owned or leased by the individual's spouse." (*Minn Stat. § 290.01 subd. 7(b)*). An abode or dwelling does not include your yard, "property" such as land, outbuildings, dog houses, and detached garages.

Unlike when out in public, defense of dwelling does not require you to have an "actual and honest belief that you were in imminent danger of death or great bodily harm". What the law does require is for you to reasonably believe that the use of force is necessary to prevent a felony from being committed in the home. But note the word "felony". The reasonable man test will be applied to your use of reasonable force in defense of dwelling and you must be able to articulate reasonable grounds for your belief that a felony was being or going to be committed. You have to infer the *intent* of the intruder from the totality of the circumstances.

Someone in your home may be innocent of everything other than making a mistake. The stranger in the bathroom or the hallway could be your teenage daughter's boyfriend, who she let in without letting you know. The man who entered your unlocked front door and standing in your darkened living room might be lost and confused. Someone running in through your front door could be fleeing from an attacker.

If the felony has already been committed and the burglar is attempting to flee, it is not lawful to use lethal force to prevent his escape or to apprehend him for the crime.

In defense of dwelling the Minnesota Supreme Court, in State v. Carothers, cited as 594 N.W.2d 897 (Minn.,1999), considered whether retreat must be considered and summed it up this way:

> A duty to retreat does not attach to defense of dwelling claims. So long as a person claiming defense of dwelling meets all [our emphasis] of the criteria for making his or her claim—that the killing was done in the belief that it was necessary to prevent the commission of a felony in the dwelling, that the person's judgment as to the gravity of the situation was reasonable under the circumstances, and that the person's election to defend his or her dwelling was such as a reasonable person would have made in light of the danger to be apprehended—the person need not have attempted to retreat from his or her home.

Note that the court used the word "reasonable" repeatedly. If you have been charged with a crime, a jury must apply "the reasonable man test" if what you did the way you did it was reasonable, and they might not conclude you acted reasonably!

In State v. Pendleton, 567 N.W.2d 265 (Minn.,1997). The Minnesota Supreme Court addressed whether the threat of imminent death or great bodily harm needed to be present when defending a dwelling. The court concluded:

> ...it is clear that one does not have to fear great bodily harm or death to justify the use of deadly force to defend against the commission of a felony in one's home....a defendant asserting "defense of dwelling" is not required to show that he or she feared death or great bodily harm to justify the use of deadly force in preventing the commission of a felony in the defendant's place of abode.

In both law and practice, the requirements for the use of lethal force in self defense are lower in the abode than in public but somebody using lethal force in the abode is still very much in danger of having to persuade a jury that their decision was reasonable.

We believe your best course of action in the case of a home invasion is to remain quiet, and to retreat with your family to a safe and defensible location. You should develop a family plan so all members understand what they are to do and where they are to go. The armed family member(s) take a defensive position in a hallway or doorway, where you can see the intruder moving towards you and you will have a clear shot. If possible have someone else call 911. Then wait for the police to show up.

- No one wants to shoot anyone and live with the consequences.
- It can be expensive to clean up the bio-hazard site you have just created.
- Your property should be insured and common items thieves like to steal can usually be replaced.
- People often learn that it is very difficult to remain living in their home after a shooting.
- Searching a home for an intruder is very dangerous. This is a job that you should leave for the police.
- A homeowner is at a serious disadvantage searching for an intruder. When in your home, you need to consider that even if it is legal to shoot an intruder, is it tactically a good idea? Under less than ideal conditions and a great amount of stress, what may happen if you miss your target? Bullets (either yours or the intruders) can penetrate drywall and go into another room where a child may be sleeping. What if another family member has gone to investigate a noise and you mistakenly shoot them thinking they are the intruder?

We strongly advise you to use lethal force only if the intruder approaches your position, you know where your loved ones are, and you are forced to protect yourself and your family members.

What is not required

You are not required to be psychic. It is the threat that you reasonably believe to be imminent if you do nothing to stop it that matters. It is imminent in relation to time and action of the attacker not that the attacker has already attacked.

You do not have to inform the attacker of your unwillingness to be attacked or any medical condition that lowers the threshold of death or great bodily harm for you.

You are not required to protect yourself. You can choose to be a victim or a survivor. It is up to you.

The aftermath

Providing you are on sound legal grounds after shooting somebody, your troubles are not over. You have to deal with the aftermath of it all and it is going to be stressful. That is the subject of the next chapter.

And remember: a gun never solves problems.

CHAPTER 6
Lethal Force and its Aftermath

If the laws about the use lethal force have not frightened you yet, or if the responsibility of carrying a gun for personal protection has not raised serious second doubts, read on.

Using lethal force in real life does not work the same way as it does on television and in the movies. Somebody who is shot is not thrown backwards several feet, or even several inches. Bullets do not go precisely where the shooter wants them under the best of circumstances. When a single bullet hits a human torso, it is unlikely to stop an attacker immediately. The impact of the bullet on the body carries no more energy than the recoil of the weapon. Remember that as the bullet travels it loses energy. The only factors you have control over is shot placement and the amount of damage done by the type of ammunition you have selected.

More importantly the justified use of lethal force may end the imminent threat, but it is only the beginning of your problems.

Again, we refer to our chapter ending warning: *a handgun never solves problems*. By now you should understand that you are only sub-stituting one set of problems for another. You are still alive. You have survived physically. The question now is whether you will survive mor-ally, legally and financially.

What is the best way for you to prove the facts of your DGU? Do you have witnesses and how do you bring witnesses forward? Proving what the attacker said after he has left the scene may be difficult. How do you refute a witness who saw only part of the attack and their story hurts your case?

We recommend using technology. Any equipment that will record audio, video or both will provide an ac-curate replay of the attack. At a minimum, the use of a small lightweight digital voice recorder will provide an audio record and a historical sequence of the events. The recorder should be recording all the while you are armed in public. We know that having an accurate record has saved the liberty of the victim. Any digital re-cording file of an attack needs to be locked down (by you) and never erased. Purchase a recorder with a file locking feature. You can make copies, just always keep the master under your control. Also consider accessorizing with a re-mote microphone. Minnesota is a "one party state" mean-ing that as long as one party (you) agrees to be recorded it is legal.

You can expect the aftermath of a justified self defense shooting to be risky. You are now entering, what will become a master's program in the American Judicial System. Most people have never been arrested, never incarcerated, photographed and fingerprinted, in short have never been treated like a criminal. You may get to experience all of this and a lot more.

Along with selecting a firearm to carry you need to find a good crimi-nal defense attorney who has experience in Minnesota's firearms and self-defense laws. Keep their name and number at hand and be absolutely sure the person who loves you the most knows how to contact them.

It is vital that you understand all of the above before you even think about carrying a handgun in public.

The description that follows reflects the progression of events from the moment the gun goes bang until you are free to go home. Hopefully your experience will go well should you ever have a DGU. It is impossible to cover every possible attack or outcome. We just want you prepared to deal with what typically happens.

Threat of force — is it enough?

You are armed and find yourself the victim of an attack. The vast majority of the time, when you draw or display a gun that action will end the imminent threat without a shot being fired. Your attacker will most likely flee.

Let's talk about what you say as well as what you do.

Talking yourself into trouble

From the moment you begin to act in self defense you have to protect yourself not only from the imminent physical consequences of being the victim of a violent crime, but from the legal system as well. Everything you say and do is of vital importance. From that moment, you are no longer "a citizen"; you are "a suspect" and it is up to you to protect your rights.

Attempting to stop an attacker by saying something out of the movies is a good way to "talk" yourself into trouble. Clint Eastwood's Dirty Harry character can say, "Go ahead: make my day," when attempting to persuade somebody not to attack him. You are not Clint Eastwood.

For the armed citizen the general rule is to communicate your need for help in a way that will establish you as a victim and invite witnesses to become attentive to your situation. You want everything you say to be accurately heard and repeated by your witnesses who may only see you, hear you, or both.

Your actions will tell a story that you want witnesses to confirm even if unknowingly doing so. Attempting to step away from the attacker is passive behavior, not aggressive. Bad guys typically run from the scene, however you are staying and managing the crime scene.

Actions and what you say taken in their totality will show you as the victim of an attack. Unfortunately, people have been programmed to understand guns are bad. Bad guys have guns and since you have a gun, you are a bad guy. Yet you are not acting like a bad guy. Witnesses will be confused. By your actions and what you say, you are creating a picture for your witnesses that they can describe accurately. Your liberty may depend on it.

Commands should be kept short, and repeated, loudly. "Stop don't hurt me; Stop don't hurt me; Stay back, stay back," are commands that instruct your attacker to leave you alone, establish you as a victim, and trigger the Good Samaritan instincts in any witnesses to help. Ideally, anything you say when confronted by an attacker is something you would want to be repeated later, even if it is overheard by somebody around the corner or inattentively doing other things.

Yelling any form of a threat that refers to death, gun, weapon, or any type of threatening phrase will trigger the witnesses "fight or flight" syndrome. They will chose flight because they believe you are putting them in danger. Witnesses will report to the police hearing you yell threatening statements and that you threatened them.

Instead of being witnesses that can help you, their reports will assist the prosecution in sending you to prison.

Chasing an attacker

An attacker's decision to flee the scene ends the imminent threat to you and also ends your right to use force and to claim justification by self defense.

While the temptation to chase somebody might be understandable, do not do it. If you give chase, you are no longer a "reluctant participant," and your use of lethal force may be treated as an attack, not a defense. In Minnesota giving chase breaks the "reluctant participant" link for you and may establish the attacker as a reluctant participant. Do not give up your justification of self defense by giving chase.

Besides, remember the witnesses. Do you want them seeing you chasing your attacker? What if a police car pulls up just as your attacker rounds the corner, running away from you, and you have a drawn handgun?

It is not unusual for an attacker to call the police on a victim. If you have given chase you have made the attackers case that you are a threat to him.

It will not be good for you. So do not chase him.

When the attacker flees

With the four elements all present, you have drawn your firearm to stop the threat. The attacker decides to flee, so let him. This is the best outcome, it is the easiest situation to handle, and the one that is least likely to cause you legal trouble.

You can encourage him to leave by making it as easy as possible. Leave an escape route open if possible. Do not place yourself between him and the nearest exit. If you happen to find yourself blocking his exit, move aside and let him go. Make it easy on yourself, you owe it to your family.

A bonus to him fleeing is knowing that at the next meeting of the robbers and assaulters union local, he will tell his buddies that there are citizens out there with guns!

Your DGU is not over. You have threatened deadly force by pointing a gun at another human being. The attacker or any witnesses may tell a very different story to the 911 operator. You do not want their version of the "truth" being the only version of the attack the police have.

You could be tempted to just walk away, but do not. You may have drawn the attention of somebody from a nearby house or passing car, and the only thing that they saw was you pointing a gun at your attacker. Who threatened who from the witnesses point of view? When they called 911, what do you think they will report?

Remember following your decision to take action, you will have to defend yourself from the legal system. This begins with your 911 call and what you say. You need to protect your rights so only provide enough information to establish yourself as the victim. Immediately call 911 and report, for example: "I just had a defensive gun use at Ninth and Elm. I defended myself and the attacker has run away. The attacker was a tall, thin white man with black hair, a blue jean jacket and tan pants. He ran down Elm to the south. No one was hurt and I'm safe now. My name is John Jones. I will file a report once I have been able to consult with my attorney." Then immediately get off the phone and call your attorney. Pointing a gun at someone is a crime and you are in trouble, at least temporarily. You need an attorney to assist you in establishing your claim of justification of self defense. Even the short 911 call tells law enforcement that there is another story to sort out. Remember the attacker may have already made a 911 call implicating you as the bad guy.

During your 911 call you may be instructed to wait there for the police. When the police arrive, they should find you with your ID and permit in hand, and your gun holstered. Your story should be very short, and entirely factual. Any deeper discussion should be avoided for the time being. You can say, "A man attacked me; here is his description. I defended myself and he ran away, I am very scared and upset, I do not consent to any search or any seizure, and I need to talk to my attorney.

Why? They'll ask. "You were the victim, right? All you have to do is talk to us. Let's just clear this up right away."

Do not start gabbing. You are in no condition to protect yourself from confusion in the investigation. You are not your best representative at this time. "I need to talk to my attorney," is all you need to say at that point, although you may have to repeat it. And then, you say nothing more. To fully understand why you must stay silent watch " Don't Talk To Police Under ANY Circumstances! Here's Why! - Prof. James Duane" (http://www.youtube.com/watch?v=VhYMFX5zrq4). This video explains what you may be up against even as a victim of an attack.

You are going through an extremely stressful experience and the police know it. Your brain wants to make sense out of the nonsense of what just happened. Again, rational thought is going to be very difficult because your brain has blocked out any information it did not feel necessary to your survival. Talking now is risky because when you are not thinking clearly you may inadvertently use words that hurt your standing rather than help it. For example, there is a great difference of meaning between saying "so I shot him," and "so I shot to stop the threat." Expect your words to be recorded and become part of the evidence against you. Admitting on tape that you "shot him" does you no good. Police have no duty to find evidence to exonerate you.

When the attack continues

The last, and most dangerous (and, thankfully, very unlikely) possibility is that you will actually need to use deadly force and shoot an attacker in order to prevent him from killing you.

The physics of a lethal confrontation

Newton's Law applies in real life. You cannot fire a shot sufficient to lift an attacker off his feet and knock him back several feet. If you could, it would have a similar effect on the shooter.

Even if your first shot stops the attack it will not be anything as dramatic as your attacker flying backward. He might appear to stumble or fall (most likely forward). It is possible that your first shot will physically incapacitate him immediately and it is certainly possible that it will change his behavior.

Or, quite possibly, he will simply continue with his attack either because he does not know he has been shot, it was not a life threatening wound or even if the wound is life threatening there is enough oxygen in his brain to maintain full voluntary function for ten to fifteen seconds.

The physiology of a lethal confrontation

Adrenaline has both physical and psychological effects, and the threat of a violent confrontation is certain to cause your adrenal gland to produce and deliver a massive amount adrenaline into your system with a huge complex of effects. When the attacker, encounters an armed citizen, he is likely to also have a large dose of adrenaline introduced into his system.

Your adrenaline charged body is now ready for battle. Several physiological effects will come into play when you go into survival mode.

Vision tends to narrow

This is the so-called "tunnel vision" effect where it becomes difficult or impossible to see anything besides the threat. This is also called "target fixation." In more than one instance this fixation has caused the victim to shoot the attacker's gun. Train yourself not to look at the weapon but at the center of mass, at whatever part the attacker presents and shoot there. Shooting center of mass will lower the likelihood of a miss.

Strength goes up

This is why light triggers on self defense weapons are such a bad idea. What feels like simply resting a finger on the trigger may result in unintentionally firing it. If your handgun has a light trigger pull, it is extremely important that you must keep your finger off the trigger until you are ready to shoot.

Dexterity drops

Your dexterity drops as does the ability to perform complex tasks. The reason dexterity drops is your body is moving the majority of your blood to your large muscle groups to aid in your fight or your flight. Lower blood flow to your fingers means less control over them.

This is why external safeties are dangerous. Heck, you may not even remember you have one and that it is engaged. Easy-to-operate, uncomplicated handguns are better for self defense.

The perception of time changes

This is known as the tachypsychia (literally, the speed of mind) effect. Things may seem to happen in slow motion, or to speed up. This is one of the many reasons not to be too quick to talk to police afterwards. You might honestly say that a confrontation took two or three minutes when it really only took a few seconds. Police officers and prosecutors are not always very sensitive to the difference between an honest misstatement and a misrepresentation. A digital voice recorder will give the actual duration of the attack.

Auditory exclusion

Most hunters will report not noticing the loud report of a rifle when they shoot a deer. The same is likely to be true during a violent confrontation. However, that same report will often be uncomfortable even with hearing protection on the range. The sound of your firearm is the same. Your mind is processing that information differently.

The ability to feel pain drops.

Pain is irrelevant to survival and is commonly suppressed until sometime later. In order to be a factor, pain first must be perceived, and second, it must cause an emotional response. Ronald Reagan did not even know he was shot by Hinkley until he was in the car and being examined by a secret service agent.

Psychological splitting

You may have an "out-of-body" sensation. You can still direct your body and its functions, but you are watching events as an outside observer.

Physiologically, when under attack, your body will engage your "fight or flight" survival patterns. Your will resort to your most basic survival skills and your training.

Remember Maslow's Hierarchy of Human Needs, that after our need to maintain life (breathing, eating, and maintaining body temperature) is our need to be safe.

Your response to an attack will be as automatic a response as you may ever experience.
Your training of what to do to survive an attack will take over. So, the more you train, the better your response to an attack will be.

Rational thought becomes difficult

According to Artwohl and Christensen[5], your cognition also changes when you are under attack and in what they call a "high-arousal state":

"Experiential thinking is the kind of thinking that will

---

[5] Dr. Alexis Artwohl, Loren W. Christensen, Deadly Force Encounters: What Cops Need to Know to Mentally and Physically Prepare for and Survive a Gunfight at 45-46 (Paladin Press, 1997).

automatically kick in whenever you perceive a threat and your body is flooded with natural drugs that induce the high arousal state. Under threat conditions, experiential thinking will dominate and reduce or even eliminate your ability to think in a rational, creative, and reflective manner. It is effortless, automatic, lightning quick, action-oriented, and much more efficient (but not necessarily more accurate) than rational thinking. It is experienced as much more compelling than rational thinking...

Experiential thinking is also what you do when you follow your gut instinct. There is nothing mystical about gut instincts, sixth sense, or intuition. Our brain is an incredible computer constantly analyzing subtle bits of information to reach conclusions, information that may not be obvious to our conscious awareness. You know your conclusion is right, but you can't explain exactly how you know that (of course, your conclusion could also be wrong).

Experiential thinking does not follow a step-by-step process to reach a conclusion but reaches it quickly without your knowing how it got there. You must rely on this type of thinking when you do not have enough time or information to reach a carefully reasoned, logical conclusion."

Having the "four elements" so well engrained into your psyche as to influence your experiential thinking will allow you to recognize when the four links of the chain are present very quickly. You must rely on this type of thinking to keep you out of prison, therefore, the better trained your mind is the more likely you will be successful.

All of these effects apply to both the victim of the attack and the attacker, and must be taken into account. The sort of pain that would normally stop somebody in their tracks may well have no immediate effect on a determined attacker. This is why defensive measures like pepper spray are much more effective on volunteer test subjects than real-life attackers.

It is entirely possible for either the attacker or the victim, or both, to continue fighting even after being seriously, and perhaps even fatally, wounded. Shear emotion such as rage or hate can keep a grievously injured person fighting. Humans will have enough oxygen remaining in the brain for full voluntary function for ten to fifteen seconds after being shot in the heart.

This is why the legal principle that lethal force is justified until the threat ends is so important.

If the attacker continues the attack, even if the wounds he has already received will later prove fatal, until the threat ceases it is not only lawful to continue shooting, it is necessary.

The right to use lethal force ends when the attacker stops attacking, but the event does not end until the attacker no longer represents a threat of death or great bodily harm. If it becomes necessary to shoot an attacker, it is justified to continue shooting until the attack stops, or any one link of the chain of the four elements breaks.

It may take one shot for that to happen, or it may take many shots.

You may not even see the shots landing. On a well-lighted pistol range, a sharp hole against a target will be easily visible at close range, but violent confrontations rarely take place in well-lighted areas. Even in good light, a wound may be hidden by the attacker's clothing. Rather than look for a wound, watch for a change in behavior of the attacker. This is likely to be the first and best indication that the attacker is no longer a threat.

The physical effects of a shooting

There is no way to discuss the effects of a shooting without discussing some awful facts.

The most important one is that shooting somebody in order to physically stop an attack requires doing a lot of damage to another human being, damage that is likely to be fatal.

Handguns are damaging but not necessarily incapacitating. If the first shot stops the attacker it is more likely because he has changed his mind, not because he is unable to continue. This should be indicated by a change of behavior to break off the attack.

A single shot can be reliably counted on to immediately incapacitate an attacker if it severs the upper spinal cord. If that happens the nerves will be unable to carry information below the cut or break and the attack will stop.

The second way to immediately incapacitate an attacker is a shot to the brain which is also very difficult. Sufficient damage to an attacker's brain will end his ability to continue the attack. The skull is thick and the head is a small target under the best of circumstances, you will literally be unable to concentrate on the handgun's sights, focusing instead on the attacker.

Also, the attacker may be moving from side to side. There are a lot of important body parts in the chest, the heart and lungs, for example. Shots to the torso, may incapacitate the attacker, but this will take more time.

This is why instructors teach that defensive shots should be aimed at the attacker's center of mass or the largest potion of whatever is presented as the target and that you should continue to fire until the threat ends.

Shooting center of mass also has other advantages. If your handgun fits you correctly it is easy with training, to make tight shot groups in targets at five to ten feet (which are typically self defense distances) without using sights. When under attack and with your adrenaline pumping and eyes fixed on the attacker, it is unlikely your sights will be useful. This is another reason training and practice is so important.

A center of mass shot increases the likelihood you will hit the attacker. It is hard to think about this while in fear of your life, but you do have to consider where your bullets might go if you miss. A missed shot can travel a long way, and can easily hurt or kill an innocent person.

Remember physical consequences of a justified self defense shooting are just the beginning of your problems. Now we must deal with the aftermath, it is going to be long and uncomfortable, and there is just no way to avoid it.

After a lethal confrontation

The immediate problem of being murdered by the attacker ends when he either flees, surrenders, or is no longer able to attack because he has been sufficiently incapacitated but other problems are just beginning.

As soon as you take out a firearm in a DGU, much less actually press the trigger, you have become a suspect, and are going to remain one at least until the investigation is concluded. Provided your claim of self defense stands, you may avoid being a defendant in a criminal case and in a civil lawsuit.

If you have injured or killed somebody in self defense, there is a legal obligation to see that first aid is rendered. Your failure to do so may become a chargeable offense even if your claim of self defense was justified.

The information given the 911 operator should be kept short and factual. "I have had a defensive gun use at (the address or location) and need the police and an ambulance." There is no need to have your excited adrenaline driven babbling report of the details of the shooting preserved as evidence on the 911 recording. Your do not talk alarm should be loudly ringing. "Anything you say can and will be used against you in a court of law" no matter to whom you have spoken.

This requires a firm intention because the 911 operator will instruct you to stay on the line. That is what they are trained to do. You should use the dispatcher as your conduit for communicating with responding officers and that can be a good thing. Communicating with the responding officers through the dispatcher may keep you from getting shot and apprise the officers that the scene is safe. The more information police and emergency services have, the better they can do their jobs. Unfortunately the more information you provide the greater the likelihood it will used against you. Remember, an important part of the job of the police is to collect and preserve evidence for your prosecution. Follow their directions, but keep the chit-chat to a minimum.

You should remain at or as close to the scene as is reasonably safe. A wolf (attacker) will run from the crime scene which is what witnesses would expect. By remaining at the scene you are not acting like a wolf which may confuse the witnesses. You are evidence and part of the crime scene, so leaving the scene of a shooting may be taken by police, prosecutors, and courts as a sign of guilt.

You should protect all the evidence you can. You cannot and should not alter, change, move, discard, destroy, lose or in any other way mess with evidence. It is not only illegal it is bad strategy. Protect the evidence but also, leave the evidence alone.

When the police arrive

There are several principles involved in being prepared for the arrival of the police. You need to avoid being shot by the police when they arrive on the scene. Ask the 911 operator to describe you to the responding officers and tell them you are not a threat to them and you will cooperate with all of their commands.

After using or threatening deadly force, the police are not your friends. That is worth repeating. After using or threatening deadly force, the police are not your friends.

They will not see themselves as your friends either. It may suit an investigator to portray himself as sympathetic to you in order to draw out information and to get you to talk about what happened. They will be coming into the situation cold, knowing nothing more than that they have been summoned to the scene of a shooting or an attack. Police routinely see the aftermath of violent crimes and few of them are done in self defense.

At a crime scene police are trained to do certain things and considering you as a victim is not one of them. As the adage says, "when hearing hoof beats, think horses not zebras."

When police are summoned to a shooting, they first think about a man with gun, assault and attempted murder, not a justifiable defensive gun use. The same is true when they hear about somebody pointing a gun at somebody. It is understandable. From a police officer's point of view, an armed criminal, assault, robbery, attempted murder, and murder are the "horses," and defensive gun uses are the "zebras." You are a victim, a zebra.

It is important to be as non-threatening to the police as possible when they arrive on the scene. If it is safe to do so, if the attacker is unable to resume the attack, or has fled, the gun should be holstered. If not, it is important to remember to keep it pointed in a safe direction, with your finger off the trigger. If possible, somebody else should be sent to meet the police when they arrive, to tell them there is no present danger, to describe the victim, "She is a small, black woman wearing a white coat, and she is the victim." The attacker is lying on the ground." Repeat that there is no longer a present danger.

Remember your hands. Police officers love to see hands. At this point, your hands should be visible and empty, if at all possible.

Most of what you should do is just common sense. Follow police directions as to what to do. Cooperate immediately, communicate what you are doing, and make no sudden movements that can be misinterpreted.

When it comes to action, as opposed to discussion, compliance is mandatory. Be as calm as you can, polite and cooperative. After all, you have called the police to come to preserve evidence you will need in your defense.

It is necessary to protect yourself from the legal system, and that largely consists of two things: saying as little as possible and immediately consulting with a good attorney who is experienced in criminal matters.

As an aside, how you are treated by the police is very likely to be directly proportional to the age and experience of the first officers on the scene. Older and more experienced officers will be able to assess your situation using their years of experience. They also have refined interrogative experience. As the scene is assessed, senior officers (especially beat officers) will figure out what happened fairly quickly. If a "wet behind the ears" rookie is running the scene, be ready for by-the-book treatment. Record names and badge numbers if necessary and deal with any mistreatment later.

Establishing victimhood

What you say to the police when they arrive is critical. As said before, police are trained to see you as a suspect. You need to get them to report you as the victim. Most important is that you do not say too much. They are going to need some very basic information and this is your opportunity to point out evidence they may overlook. Once you have worked through the four statements it is time shut up. It is time to exercise your right to remain silent. It is not the job of the police to determine your guilt or innocents, it is their job to collect and preserve evidence.   A guide to help you communicate with police and yet not say too much was developed by Massad Ayoob.

> Massad F. Ayoob is an internationally known firearms and self defense instructor. He has taught police techniques and civilian self defense to both law enforcement officers and private citizens in numerous venues since 1974. He was the director of the Lethal Force Institute (LFI) from 1981 to 2009, and he now directs the Massad Ayoob Group (MAG). Ayoob has appeared as an expert witness in number of trials.
>
> Ayoob has authored several books and more than 1,000 articles on firearms, combat techniques, self defense, and legal issues, and has served in an editorial capacity for Guns Magazine, American Handgunner, Gun Week, and Combat Handguns.

Massad recommends making the following four statements: "He attacked me," followed by "I will sign a complaint," "there is the evidence," and "I need to talk to my lawyer". As a matter of law, a demand to consult with an attorney cannot be used as evidence of guilt. Also state that you do not consent to any search or seizure. The police will do their job and search you and probably seize you as well. Just do not give them your permission.

By limiting your comments to police, using Massad's four statements you may improve your case. Your goal is to have the police report to reflect you as the victim (not a wolf), include evidence to support your position as the victim and your willingness in prosecuting the attacker while preserving your rights.

"He attacked me"

It is not a problem to say that you were attacked. It does not, in and of itself, admit the use of deadly force, but it is an important part of the justification for it. Justification is what is called in law an "affirmative defense." When claiming "he attacked me" you are inferring that you have absolute standing as a reluctant participant. You did nothing to provoke, precipitate or participate in the altercation.

Going beyond "he attacked me" to "so I shot him" is an admission that, if you need to make it, you can make it later on the advice of an attorney.

It is best not to start talking. You might not be able to stop and will likely do yourself more harm. Understand that the possibility of arrest is about the same as the sun coming up tomorrow. If you cannot limit your comments to Massad's "He attacked me" then do not talk.

There is no advantage, and much disadvantage, to discussing any of the details of the incident then and there. Anything you say about the exact details of the attack can and will be examined for possible vulnerabilities and compared with later statements, and can easily be used to suggest that you have changed your story rather than that you have said the same thing in different ways. If you tell what happened then but leave out an important element, it is likely that you will be accused of "conveniently" remembering it later or that you are lying. Here the digital voice recorder will allow you accurately recall and retell the attack. You should not make a statement right then and there. It needs to be done later with your attorney's assistance.

And there are questions you cannot answer without the answers being used against you, like "Were you angry at him?" If you say yes, then it can be argued that you shot him because you were angry at him. If you say no, then you are a liar—how could anybody not be angry at somebody who tried to kill him.

The simple way to avoid any possibility of either misinterpretation or being accused of lying is to say as little as possible.

What you do not say cannot be used against you, thanks to your Fifth Amendment right against self-incrimination.

"He attacked me" is all you need to say on that subject before talking to your lawyer. That will get the police on the right track.

"I will sign a complaint"[6]

This does not mean right now. Writing out and signing a complaint

---

[6] We are reluctant to alter Mr. Ayoob's text. However, in Minnesota, victims submit a report and the prosecutor signs a complaint.

needs the advice of your attorney. If the police officer responds by saying, "Fine, just write down what happened," the only safe response is, "I'll be happy to, just as soon as I've talked with my attorney," and repeat that as many times as necessary.

Saying "I will sign a complaint" is not a commitment to talk further. What it does is embed in the police report that you were the victim. It indicates to the prosecuting attorney that you are willing to help them put your attacker behind bars.

Realistically, the police will arrest you most of the time. The only thing they know for sure is that there has been a shooting, and they have every reason to believe that the victim has shot somebody. Whether or not it was a justified shooting is a decision they must leave to others.

"There is the evidence"

Police officers are humans, and humans can make mistakes. They can suffer from perception warps. Shell casings from the attacker's handgun can be stepped on; a knife can be overlooked; or a baseball bat, tire iron, or claw hammer might not even be seen as a weapon and not taken into evidence even though the attacker's fingerprints on it can be very important. The police were not present during your attack. It is vital from your point of view that none of the evidence be overlooked or damaged. Gathering evidence is what the police do.

Evidence is not just physical evidence. It is perfectly reasonable to point to witnesses, or to suggest that somebody in a nearby building might have overheard the confrontation. Look for cameras on buildings, in parking lots, or people with cell phones.

The behavior of the attacker may also be important evidence. Was his behavior erratic and possibly drug induced? Had he been drinking? Are there drugs on his person?

What you want to project, without going into detail, is that you were defending yourself and expect the evidence to support your claim.

"I want to talk with my lawyer"

You need to immediately declare:

> *"I need to talk to my lawyer,*
> *I do not consent to any search,*
> *I do not consent to any seizure"*

This is the most important part of the formula, and you are likely to need to repeat it. As you can see, this is a slight variation on Ayoob's four-point strategy: explicitly saying that you do not consent to any search or seizure. This fourth step is the part that cannot be skipped. Those who are concerned that if they start talking they might have trouble stopping, should just skip right to this step. "I need to talk to my lawyer and I do not consent to any search or seizure."

This is your security blanket: "I need to talk to my lawyer, and I do not consent to any search or seizure." Keep repeating it until the police allow you to speak with your lawyer. Never, ever, consent to any search or seizure. Experienced criminal law specialists advise that there is no upside to consenting.

Why not talk?

Ayoob, who trains police officers who investigate police shootings, recommends that any interview with the officer take place at a later time. An officer who has been involved in a shooting may say something, innocuous in context, or a heated exclamation showing how angry the officer is that can be used to suggest that he acted improperly.

Ayoob is not alone in this. IACP, the International Association of Chiefs of Police, strongly recommends that police officers not be interviewed immediately after a shooting:

> ...the officer can benefit from some recovery time before detailed interviewing begins. This can range from a few hours to overnight, depending on the emotional state of the officer and the circumstances. Officers who have been afforded this opportunity to calm down are likely to provide a more coherent and accurate statement. [emphasis added]

Realistically, there is nothing you (an armed citizen) can do to avoid the likelihood of being arrested after a shooting, and what you need to focus on is minimizing the damage anything you said might cause. The best strategy is to consider yourself under arrest from the moment you pull the trigger. Think "anything you say (or do) can be used against you in a court of law".

One common investigative technique is for an officer to portray himself as one who is sympathetic to the suspect who only needs a few questions cleared up before closing the whole matter. It is a simple play to the victim's need for security and certainty in a stressful, strange, and uncertain situation. By considering yourself under arrest, you can better control the outcome. In the wake of a shooting, talking to a policeman before consulting with an attorney is a risky proposition of dubious possible benefit.

So do not do it. Just repeat "I want my lawyer, and I do not consent to any search or seizure."

What the police will do

While physical abuse and some forms of intimidation are illegal and rare (but not unknown) there are forms of intimidation and influence that courts have not only said are completely legal, but which are part of police officers' training.

David Kopel, a leading civil rights attorney specializing in advocacy for self defense issues, points to the research of Richard A. Leo, Ph.D., J.D., Associate Professor of Criminology, Law and Society, and an Associate Professor of Psychology and Social Behavior at the University of California, Irvine.

Leo's research shows that police routinely use "techniques of neutralization" in an attempt to get you to talk and to keep you talking.

These can involve telling you that the interrogator thinks you have not done anything wrong, that the attacker deserved what happened: that you have committed a crime, but only a minor one, say, that your attacker was just slightly injured and is, even at this moment, being booked, and that all the investigator needs is for you to write out and sign a complaint.

Any or all of that could be true.

Any or all of that could be false.

You do not know.

You should not talk.

The investigator could think that you have committed murder and wants to get more evidence. He may believe that the person you shot deserved it in a moral sense, but you are still guilty of a crime for having shot him. And it is entirely possible that the hypothetical attacker, instead of now being booked, is lying dead in the morgue and the police are gathering evidence that will be used to prosecute you and would love for you to help them with that.

There is no way to know, and until your lawyer tells you otherwise, you simply should not say anything except, "I want to speak to my attorney, and I do not consent to any search or seizure." If you find that you have to keep repeating that, fine.

The relationship between police and suspects is disproportionate in favor of the police. While citizens are not permitted to lie to the police, the police, in fact, are permitted to lie to suspects and frequently do. They can, with utter impunity, say that if you talk to them you will not be arrested, and then arrest you after you talk.

The police may explain that it is in your best interest to get your side of the story on the record without getting lawyers involved ("It'll look bad if you do not talk now, Bob") and that letting you explain what happened is something they are doing as a favor to you, even though they know it is not.

If they have two suspects they can put both of them in the back of a police car and leave them alone to talk to each other with the hidden video camera in the front of the car taping the conversation. Or, separate the suspects and pit one against the other.

These are a couple of examples of investigative techniques an investigator can use. It is the job of police investigators is to get as much information as possible to support a charge and conviction for the prosecutor to sort out.

There is another dynamic to the investigation. To the extent that an interrogation is a battle of wits, the opponents are not equal.

The police investigator is experienced at this. He interrogates people on a daily basis and may have been doing it for decades. You have gone through your entire life without being the subject of a police interrogation at all.

This is like somebody who has never picked up a tennis racket going out on the court against a professional tennis player, except, in the case of a police interrogation, there is a lot more to lose than a tennis match.

It is actually much worse than that. When you go into a tennis match you are not frightened half out of your wits. The minutes and hours after you have been forced into a defensive gun use is not a time when you can coolly and calmly answer questions or explain yourself, and it certainly is not a time when you will be thinking about all the implications of the various laws involved.

Realistically anybody involved in a defensive gun use will need the help of an experienced criminal attorney and must not talk with the police, except as above. There is no way you can avoid the necessity and cost of a good lawyer. Any attempt to "do it yourself" is just going to cost you money (if you are lucky) or years of freedom (if you botch the job). Leave your defense to the professionals!

If it turns out that a police interview is in your interest, the attorney can and should participate in the interview. Many criminal attorneys will simply refuse to have their clients take an interview at all and submit a sworn statement instead.

Finally, your attacker is unlikely to consider whether your lawyer will be immediately available when he attacks you. It is possible that your attorney will be in court, at a dinner party, playing golf or at the kid's hockey game. If you are attacked late in the evening, call the "person who loves you the most" and who will move heaven and earth to get you representation immediately. Being represented by someone familiar with the legal system and whose head is much clearer than yours is the important thing.

When are you under arrest?

If police officers have said, "I'm placing you under arrest," it is fair to assume that you are. But, even if they have not formally made that statement, you might be.

Take a hypothetical case: you are sitting in a room at a police station, behind a table, with two plainclothes detectives on the other side of the table between you and the door. A third, uniformed officer is standing in front of the door. Are you under arrest, or are you voluntarily chatting with the police and free to leave at any time?

Asking, "am I under arrest? " is the obvious thing to do, but it will not do any good. Feel free to try it.

"Why, should you be under arrest? Have you done something wrong?" is the standard comeback and both an attempt to change the subject and an invitation to talk. Ask, "am I free to leave?" If not, assume that anything you say can and will be used against you.

If you are under arrest you have the right to talk to your lawyer. The police must make a telephone available for you to call him or her, and cannot question you further after you have demanded to talk to your lawyer unless you choose to waive that right, something they will be only too happy to let you do. Remember, if you still have your recorder keep it running.

If you are not under arrest or not the subject of a "Terry stop" you are free to leave. However, the police do not have to do anything to help you because you are free to walk out the door. If you stay, the court will take anything you say as a voluntary consensual conversation.

Can you walk out that door?

There is only one way to make your custodial status clear: try to leave.

In that situation, if you get up and quietly but firmly say, "I'm going to leave now," and walk toward the door, perhaps saying, "Excuse me, I need for you to step aside so I can leave" to the officer standing in front of the door, one of two things will happen: either you will be allowed to leave or you will be informed that you are under arrest, in which case you still must continue to demand to speak to your attorney, and never consent to any search or seizure.

Not talking is not just for you

Not talking to the police does not just apply to you as the victim. The prosecutor may subpoena anyone with whom you have spoken. Certain family members, your spiritual leader and your attorney may avoid answering questions.

If the victim and the attacker knew each other, the police will proceed on the assumption that there was a previous history of problems between the two and attempt to find out details about it. Anything said by a family member for example regarding you and your attacker once having harsh words can be used as evidence against you. Family members should be instructed that they are not to open the door to policemen who do not have warrants, and to always explain that:

1. They will be happy to have a conversation with any investigators as soon as they have talked to their attorney, and
2. They do not consent to any search or seizure.
3. They must not talk further until their attorney tells them otherwise.
4. Do not talk with the news media, even if they offer you anonymity.
5. Stay off the internet, especially blogs regarding the incident.

This is advice your attorney should give you. If they do not tell you to sit tight and let them handle it, get a different attorney.

Most of the time a law-abiding citizen, regards the police as allies. They are the folks you call when you hear a suspicious sound in the alley outside your house at night. When you encounter a policeman working overtime at the local supermarket, you know he is there to protect the supermarket and you probably give him a smile and a nod. Even when a police officer stops you for having a turn signal out or a minor traffic violation, he is doing his job, and it is just not a big deal, so you do not treat the police officer as somebody who is endangering your freedom.

This is our relationship with police most of the time and under ordinary circumstances. But after using or threatening deadly force, everything changes. To the police officer, you are no longer an ordinary citizen.

You are a suspect, and, once again; the police are not your friends.

This may sound paranoid to some, but for anyone who has been the subject of a police investigation, paranoia like this has become good policy. The risks of talking are huge, and offer few benefits. We do keep repeating this, and we hope we are not boring you, but this is so important that it probably can not be repeated too often; "I want my attorney"

We like Massad's four statements and you should be sure that you can follow them. They help to position you as the victim. But do remember that the fourth point; the request for your lawyer, the refusal to consent to any search or seizure, and not talking after—is the most important part of it.

After a nonlethal confrontation

The same principles apply to the majority of defensive gun uses in which no shot is fired. If anything, these situations can be more complicated. Unlike the case of a successful defensive shooting, the attacker is able to spin the situation to his advantage, if the attacker has simply fled or is still on the scene, uninjured, when the police arrive.

The following is a case from another state, the names have been changed.

Bob carried a handgun daily to protect the large sums of cash that his business requires that he carry about with him.

One day, he was involved in a small traffic accident in which the driver of another car backed into him, causing no serious damage to his car, but jamming him up against the curb. The other driver came out of the car with a tire iron, saying, "I'm going to beat your head in," and added some colorful expletives as he moved toward Bob.

Believing, reasonably, that he was in immediate danger of having his head beaten in, and retreat not being practical, Bob drew his handgun and pointed it at the attacker at which point the attacker broke off the attack, retreated to his own car, and drove off.

Bob, thinking that the incident was over, simply drove home. There was, shortly, a knock on his door, and two uniformed police officers asked if they could come in to talk to him, which he agreed to. They asked him some details about the incident, which he answered thoroughly and honestly, if somewhat heatedly, at which point they asked if he could produce the gun that he had been carrying and the permit to carry under which it was legal for him to carry it.

He produced both; the policemen seized both, and promptly arrested him on felony charges, at which time he finally contacted an experienced criminal attorney. After some negotiation with the prosecutor's office, his attorney managed to get the charges reduced to a misdemeanor, provided he pled guilty, surrendered his permit to carry, and made no attempt to have his handgun returned to him.

Bob made several mistakes and was fortunate enough to have gotten off so easily.

His first mistake was not immediately calling the police to report the DGU. It is an understandable reluctance but a critical error. Bob had a defensive gun use and had drawn a gun and pointed it at somebody. But his reluctance to call the police allowed the attacker time to get the first report into the police thereby framing the "facts" of the altercation. It is called "the race to the courthouse," and he let his attacker win by default.

His second mistake was not calling his lawyer.

His third mistake was to let the police into his home and talk with them. This was a particularly bad idea. An interview with the police should be on Bob's terms and conducted with his attorney present.

Bob had no obligation to open the door to the police or to answer their questions. Producing his handgun and permit was misrepresented as required. Bob should have required the police to produce a search warrant and made contact with his attorney before answering officer's questions. He got suckered into an interview that had significant risk and little chance of reward.

When the four elements are present and you decide to produce a firearm, even if you do not pull the trigger, the most important things to do are:

1. Call the police
2. Call your lawyer
3. Refuse to consent to any search or seizure
4. Remember Massad Ayoob's four statements
5. Say nothing more until after talking with your attorney.

Financing a Defensive Gun Use

Armed citizens know that the need to shoot someone is a low probability and high consequence event. Although you may never have needed to use a gun in self defense, we know that low probability is not the same thing as zero probability. Threats to your personal safety have increased over time, pushing the odds higher in the future that you will need to use your gun someday to protect your life. The world is becoming a more dangerous place to live every day.

So, are you going to bet everything you own and maybe your future earnings that you will never need to use your gun? Have you considered how you will pay for an attorney and possible damages should you ever have to use a gun to save your life? Most armed citizens find out at the worst possible time that they could not afford to use their gun. Just ask George Zimmerman. After three years, and over $3,000,000 spent on attorneys, the Government has finally given up looking for a way to prosecute him for a righteous shooting. This is in addition to the cost of his defense during the criminal trial. Zimmerman is millions of dollars in debt now. Saving his life financially ruined Zimmerman, but you don't have to be ruined financially with a little planning.

We are not selling insurance nor are we paid any money to tell you about this. We want you to know where to look for coverage in your current Homeowner's policy if it is there, or what questions you will need to ask your current insurance agent if it isn't. It may turn out that you will have to change your insurer your agent or both, for you to become properly insured. This coverage is either in your policy or it isn't. Your Homeowner's policy cannot be endorsed to add back this coverage, which is why your changing insurer and/or agent may be necessary.

Several organizations do sell stand alone "self defense" or "gun use" "policies". Some of these are nothing more than pre-paid legal plans or very limited liability policies. Before you buy one of these, obtain a specimen policy and ask your insurance agent to review it for you. Unlike your Auto insurance or Homeowner's policies which are "pay on your behalf" policies, many of these "self defense" or "gun use" type policies are an "indemnification" policy. What is the big difference you may be thinking? Well, a "pay on behalf" policy literally stands in your shoes and pays all your defense costs for you. An "indemnification" policy will expect you to pay for everything yourself first, and then they may "indemnify" or reimburse you for covered expenses they approve when everything is settled. If you are found guilty at all, some will just void their policy with you. Unless you have an available source of a huge line of credit or several million dollars in the bank, how are you going to pay everything over several years until the case is settled and wonder if your insurance company will decide to reimburse you? You may want to carefully consider buying a

Homeowners "pay on behalf" policy instead.

Some insurers are very comfortable offering Homeowners or Renters policy's that provide liability coverage for the use of intentional but reasonable force when protecting people (and sometimes property). Other insurers refuse to cover any intentional use of force even if it is used in your self defense. Will your insurer cover intentional acts of self defense?

First, all liability policies exclude harm you intentionally inflict on others. Some policy's stop there, while other's will agree to exclude this exclusion if you were using "reasonable force" to protect yourself or others. This coverage grant important because the insurance company will also pay an unlimited amount for your defense costs. How much money will you need should you injure an innocent bystander or two because your shots missed your intended target and hit someone else?

Let's look at an insuring agreement from an actual liability section in a Homeowner's policy.

Liability Coverages

PRINCIPAL COVERAGES -- LIABILITY AND MEDICAL PAYMENTS TO OTHERS

Coverage L -- Personal Liability -- "We" pay, up to "our" "limit", all sums for which an "insured" is liable by law because of "bodily injury" or "property damage" caused by an "occurrence" to which this coverage applies. "We" will defend a suit seeking damages if the suit resulted from "bodily injury" or "property damage" not excluded under this coverage. "We" may make investigations and settle claims or suits that "we" decide are appropriate. "We" do not have to provide a defense after "we" have paid an amount equal to "our" "limit" as a result of a judgment or written settlement.

Coverage M -- Medical Payments To Others –

"We" pay the necessary medical expenses if they are incurred or medically determined within three years from the date of an accident causing "bodily injury" covered by this policy.

Sounds pretty good, right? But there is an exclusion that removes coverage for intentional acts in the policy. This exclusion needs to be excluded and provide coverage for justified acts of self defense. Here is how it's done.

Exclusions That Apply To Coverages L and M -- This policy does not apply to:

"bodily injury" or "property damage":
1) which is expected by, directed by, or intended by an "insured";
2) that is the result of a criminal act of an "insured"; or
3) that is the result of an intentional and malicious act by or at the direction of an "insured".

This exclusion applies even if:
1) the "bodily injury" or "property damage" that occurs is different than what was expected by, directed by, or intended by the "insured"; or
2) the "bodily injury" or "property damage" is suffered by someone other than the person or persons expected by, directed by, or intended by the "insured".

However, this exclusion does not apply to "bodily injury" or "property damage" that arises out of the use of reasonable force to protect people or property.*

***This sentence is called a coverage grant.** It brings back coverage for your specific use of reasonable force in self defense.

If you find a similar sentence as bolded above in your homeowners policy, your use of reasonable force (fists, 2x4, or a gun) for self defense is a covered occurrence including the cost of your defense. Now re-read this not as an exclusion, but how you could be **insured for your liability and defense costs.**

And we have learned most people who switch their insurance to self defense friendly insurers, actually pay an average of about **$200 per year less** for their insurance. Your premiums will vary based upon your underwriting criteria and claims history. Because armed citizens are "certified good guys", insurers recognize this in their underwriting and often charge us lower premiums.

Please call your insurance agent today to find out if you are properly insured or not! If it turns out you are not properly insured and your agent can't seem to help you, please contact an LTI instructor or LEOSA Trainers, Inc., and we will be very happy to help you find an agent.

Timing is important. Waiting until after your gun goes bang will be too late. Take care of this important matter while you are waiting for your permit to arrive in the mail.

Finding an attorney

When you need an attorney is not the best time to be looking for one. Know who you are going to call before the handgun goes bang and your defensive gun use is now in the aftermath stage.

Interview a number of attorneys, who practice criminal defense law. Skip the attorney that wrote your will, helped you buy your house or did your divorce. This is about your liberty and you need an attorney that understands criminal defense, the weapons laws of Minnesota, and the laws of justification and self defense. It would be better if the attorney has a Minnesota permit to carry and carries on a regular basis. The Shooters Bar (www.theshootersbar.org), Jews for the Preservation of Firearms Ownership www.jpfo.org/filegen-a-m/attorney.htm or Legal Match www.legalmatch.com are national registries of attorney's who specialize in DGU cases and permit to carry law.

And remember: A gun never solves problems.

Anne Kitzman / Shutterstock.com

CHAPTER 7
Routine Police Encounters

Most people who carry a handgun will never encounter a deadly threat or be involved with the police in a serious criminal matter. Realistically, unless on the range, most permit holders will not touch their guns other than to put them on and put them away. And that is of course a good thing.

Permit holders will encounter police officers from time to time as everybody does. Whether it is the police officer on overtime at the local drugstore, the one who has pulled you over for an out-of-order turn signal, or sitting nearby at a restaurant having lunch.

This chapter deals with ordinary police encounters, ones where issues of deadly force, police investigations, and the threat or reality of arrest are not involved.

It is important to know that the Minnesota Personal Protection Act provides for a statewide computerized registry of permit holders that is available to law enforcement officers for official use only. In Minnesota a permit to carry (and appropriate ID) must be presented to a law enforcement officer upon request. Failure to present a permit is a $25 petty misdemeanor.

Do not argue

Times and places to argue with police are nearly nonexistent. The roadside is not one of them, nor are other routine encounters. Not arguing does not mean agreeing. Keeping any interaction with police on a pleasant and professional level makes any encounter go better for the officer and you.

Police are human beings. They come to work wanting to go home alive and well. Officers are now being challenged to interact with law abiding armed citizens. They must develop or refine their skills of determining who is a wolf and who is a fellow sheepdog. For some, this is not going to be difficult. For a few this will be an uncomfortable adjustment.

When to display your permit

Under the MPPA, a permit holder has no general obligation to inform a police officer if you are armed, unless asked. If asked, there is no option: you must display your permit and photo identification and disclose whether you are armed or not.

While people new to carrying a handgun assume that everybody has X-ray vision and can spot the gun immediately that is simply not the case. If the contact is casual and amounts to no more than an exchange of pleasantries then displaying your permit to an officer is not necessary.

If the contact is based on official business, you have the choice of voluntarily displaying your permit to the officer before he asks. We have found that informing the officer demonstrates your concern for the officer's safety and comfort. Chalk it up to living the "Golden Rule". You could be pleasantly surprised at the outcome. Informing the officer is also a good idea should the contact involve the discovery of your handgun. Surprising an officer on duty Christmas morning with coffee and a donut is one thing. Surprising an officer at the mall with the handgun he did not expect to see is another matter. If your contact is heading anywhere near your handgun just say; "I have a permit to carry and I am armed." The officer may ask further questions or may just say "thanks for letting me know."

Here is a tip. Learn to carry your permit to carry and ID opposite from your handgun. You will lessen the concern of accessing your permit if it is not next to your handgun.

Be polite

Consider the concern that a police officer may have when he or she has rarely if ever encountered a law-abiding armed citizen. Some officers are going to be nervous, and while there is no need to be overly familiar, simple politeness will help to reassure the officer that you are not going to be a problem, whether the handgun issue comes up or not.

In many ways, the success of Minnesota's carry law is in understanding and appreciating the issues of all involved. Permit holders do not deserve or want to be harassed. Law enforcement officers want and deserve to be safe in the company of permit holders. The general public expects that permit holders and law enforcement officers both respect the law.

Obey all instructions promptly

This should be obvious but, if you are confused, politely ask for clarification. When you are obeying instructions, say what you are doing, "I'm getting my wallet out now" for example. Make it clear that you are cooperating with the officer's commands.

The instructions you will be obeying have to do with physical actions. Providing information (ID, permit to carry, proof of insurance) necessary for the business at hand can and should be produced.

It is important to understand the difference between consensual police contact, lawfully detaining you temporarily, and arrest.

- Consensual contact allows you to walk away at any time.
- Lawfully detaining contact for investigative purposes is a Terry stop, which requires the officer to have an articulable suspicion based upon the totality of the circumstances that a crime has been, is being, or is about to be committed. Although you are temporarily not free to leave, you are not required to answer questions beyond providing identification if asked.
- Arrest is when you have lost your liberty. You are not free to leave. Loss of liberty does not necessarily begin when you are told you are under arrest. It can begin well before you are read your Miranda rights.

Maintain control of your weapon

Almost invariably when a police officer decides to take possession of your handgun the officer will choose to retrieve it himself. That is what they are trained to do. If you are asked to relinquish control of the handgun kindly decline by saying, "I don't consent to any seizure." The officer can take possession of your handgun under a Terry stop. The MPPA is silent regarding when and how to return the handgun to the permit holder, it will likely be based on the facts of the situation. Without any evidence or facts tying the permit holder to the "reasonable articulable suspicion" that is the basis for the Terry stop, the firearm should be returned once the contact is complete.

Do not offer to turn over your handgun before the officer asks you to do so, because you do not want to give up your Fourth Amendment rights by "consenting" to a search or seizure.

Should your gun be seized, the law requires that a receipt be issued for any property seized. Be sure that you request a receipt.

Keep your hands in plain sight

This should be largely common sense. The idea is not to make the police officer nervous, and they can, even in ordinary confrontations, become very nervous about things like quick movements and hands in pockets. As they say, "cops love to see hands."

Do not consent to a search or seizure

Police officers will, from time to time, ask your permission to search you or your car. Proactively inform officers that you do not consent to any search or seizure. As a general rule do not answer police questions with a "yes" or "no." "You don't mind if I look in your car do you?" This question is phrased so it cannot be answered by a simple yes or no without giving your permission. That does not mean, of course, that you will not be searched: just do not consent to one.

Legally speaking, a full search is different from being "patted down" or a "pat-down search." A pat-down search is just what it sounds like: the police officer pats on your clothes attempting to see if you have a weapon. They do not get to stick their hands inside your clothes or pockets unless they feel a weapon through the garment.

Often police officers want to search people they stop, even for minor traffic offenses. But if there is not "an articulable suspicion based upon the totality of the circumstances that a crime has been, is being, or is about to be committed" they cannot even pat you down —unless they ask you for permission and you say "yes." So do not. Just politely say, "I do not consent to any search or seizure." Do not consent to a search of your car, either. Many people we know have refused consent, and the police officers simply turned to other matters. They knew that saying no was a matter of right and were not offended.

If you are asked to consent to a search and you refuse the officer may not be happy. He may tell you that he can make you wait there until he gets a search warrant or they may call a dog to sniff the car. Most likely that will not happen. The fact that you do not give permission for him to search your car is not enough evidence to persuade a judge to issue a search warrant.

Most likely, he will finish writing the ticket and send you on your way.

When a routine encounter becomes something else

It is possible what began as a routine police encounter becomes something more. This can happen without any warning and without you necessarily having done something wrong, or done anything at all.

When a routine encounter becomes non-routine, it is necessary for you to immediately transition into a defensive mode and behave just as you would after a situation where you had used, or threatened to use, deadly force.

When the encounter turns sour immediately lawyer up. Do not wait, there is no downside to immediately saying, "I need to talk to my lawyer, and I do not consent to any search or seizure."

At the end of the day

Over time police officers have learned that armed citizens pose no threat to them, we are some of their biggest supporters and strongest allies. All armed citizens have a mutual responsibility to practice the "golden rule" when dealing with law enforcement.

And remember: a gun never solves problems.

CHAPTER 8
Choosing a Carry Gun

This chapter is like writing an advice for the lovelorn column. No matter what your problem is, or the advice we may offer, there will always be someone who thinks our advice is wrong or that they have the better answer for you. That is just the nature of this subject. Quite frankly because there are so many different people it is also the reason why there are so many different types and sizes of handguns.

Our objective in this chapter is not to tell you what handgun you should or should not buy, but to instruct you how to determine for yourself what is the best handgun for you.

We would like to offer at least several unvarnished universal truths about the handgun you decide to carry, no matter what make or caliber it is, or if it is a semiautomatic or a revolver.

- Every time you press the trigger, it must go bang.
- The performance of any cartridge is dictated by physics and apply equally to any bullet while in flight.
- Penetration is dictated by bullet weight, impact, velocity and expanded diameter. Generally, when different bullets penetrate to the same depth those moving faster and exhibit the largest expansion will damage the most tissue.
- A gun will not get lighter as the day goes on.
- If a handgun does not fit you, you cannot competently shoot it.

The most important characteristic for a good choice in a handgun that you will carry to protect your life, is that it must be reliable in order to protect your life. Reliable and expensive are not interchangeable terms, but it is likely that a reliable quality handgun will cost more than one that is not so reliable. To determine your budget, ask yourself how much money are you willing to spend on a handgun that will be expected to save your life?

If you have done any prior internet research about what is a good handgun to carry, you are probably more confused now than when you began. It is difficult to ask ten people about what they think would be a good carry gun and expect any two answers to be even close to the same advice. So if you do not typically ask your friends or a total stranger to help you decide what shoes you should buy, our advice is stop asking others what handgun you should buy as well. Just like shoes, you need to decide what is the right handgun for you based upon how often you will wear your handgun, how it fits your own body, how comfortable it is to use, how it will work with your wardrobe, how much it will cost, how you intend to carry it and other personal factors.

First, from a purely mechanical standpoint you can choose between either a revolver or a semiautomatic. Although there is other technology available such as a derringer, they are not as well suited for your personal protection as they are for poker players in old western movies. Revolvers and semiautomatics both have advantages and disadvantages which we will discuss. Your job is to decide for yourself which type of handgun will suite you the best.

We would like to remind you that your carry gun will be a working gun. It is going to live with you and go wherever you go. It will soon show some wear and tear and you can expect it to get dirty and dusty and rusty just from your wearing it all the time.

You should also search for holsters that are commercially available for the handgun that you would like to carry before you decide to spend a substantial amount on your new gun, only to learn there are only a few holsters available that it will fit. Custom holsters can be made for any gun, but they will generally be much more expensive than one that is commercially made. No matter where or how you decide to carry your handgun, for your safety it must always be carried in a holster! No exceptions.

Revolvers

Revolvers have been compared to mans' best friend, a dog. Revolvers are reliable, they bark when you press the trigger every time. They are not complicated pieces of machinery and are certainly not high maintenance. They are not fussy about the ammunition that you feed them, but they generally have a more limited supply of ammunition. Revolvers shoot ammunition that is normally more powerful than semiautomatics so fewer shots may be needed to stop a threat (it is still shot placement and the amount of tissue destroyed that matters the most to stop a threat). However,  because revolvers do not use any of the recoil to operate, you will feel all of the recoil of the more powerful rounds against your hands and arms, which can make them more uncomfortable for you to shoot.

Because revolvers can be more challenging to use, they are generally carried by the more experienced shooters. The wider physical size of the cylinders and/or the revolvers larger grip can make them a bit more difficult to carry concealed when carried on your hip. A solution to carrying a physically larger handgun concealed may be to buy a shoulder holster which will tuck your handgun more closely to your body and under your arm.

Small frame .38 Special revolvers are commonly carried in a front pocket. If you buy a revolver to carry in a pocket, be sure it has an enclosed hammer which will enable you to draw it from your pocket without the hammer snagging on your clothing or catching on your key ring.

Small frame revolvers are also a good choice to carry as a backup gun in an ankle holster. You could carry either your pocket revolver or a revolver

with an exposed hammer in an ankle holster.

Advances in metallurgy have made it possible to manufacture very strong but lightweight handguns. The fall of the Soviet Union has allowed firearms manufacturers access to Scandium which comes from areas that were once behind the iron curtain, which when added to aluminum, makes it suitable for use in handguns.

The main application of scandium by weight is in aluminum scandium alloys for minor aerospace industry components. These alloys contain between 0.1% and 0.5% of scandium. They were used in the Russian military aircraft, specifically the MiG-21 and MiG-29.

Some sports equipment which relies on high performance materials such as baseball bats, and bicycle frames have been made with scandium-aluminum alloys. Lacrosse sticks are also made with scandium-titanium alloys to take advantage of the strength of titanium.

Smith & Wesson produces revolvers and pistols with frames composed of scandium alloy and cylinders of titanium chambered in .38 Special and .357 Magnum. These lightweight handguns are considerably more comfortable

and more accurate to shoot when using lower pressure ammunition instead of full pressure magnum rounds. With scandium alloy light weight revolvers, it is very important to buy ammunition made specifically for these guns. Although they will shoot full pressure ammunition, you will not appreciate the results. Because scandium is a very rare metal, the price of a handgun that is made with it will be much more than a similar model made from steel.

A newer caliber of .327 Magnum has been designed as an alternative to the more challenging .357 Magnum. The advantages of this revolver

are that the ballistics of a .327 Magnum are very similar to that of a .357 Magnum, however the revolver handles much more like a less powerful .32 Magnum. It delivers the punch you need without the pain (to you anyway).

Because the grip does not also have to contain the ammunition within it, a revolver offers a much wider array of options to properly size to your hand. A large grip may be replaced with a smaller grip or a smaller grip may be replaced with a larger grip on the same revolver.

Semiautomatics

Semiautomatics are more like cats than dogs. They are more complicated pieces of machinery, and they are more susceptible to failure to fire at the worst possible time. They can and will jam.

Like a cat, a semiautomatic may not like the ammunition you feed it,

although most do have a higher ammunition capacity than a revolver. Semiautomatics do require more maintenance more often to keep them working.

Most people do prefer to carry a semiautomatic instead of a revolver. Even a higher caliber semiautomatic such as the .45 ACP, is easier to shoot than a smaller caliber revolver. First, the recoil of a semiautomatics smaller cartridge is less than a revolver cartridge and secondly, the semiautomatic absorbs some of the energy from the recoil to operate itself and prepare itself for the next round to be shot (this why the term "semiautomatic" is used to describe these handguns). We train new shooters to shoot with a semiautomatic and people then become comfortable with this technology from the early stages of their shooting experience. We are all creatures of habit and people often stay with what they are familiar with and comfortable using.

Ammunition is generally less expensive for semiautomatics, which makes the cost of regularly practicing with them more affordable for the average person. There is also a vast assortment of ammunition in each caliber to appease those finicky semi automatics. We would caution you against choosing a caliber such as a 10mm or .357 Sig because ammunition for these calibers is not as commonly available as .380 ACP, 9mm, .40 Cal and .45 ACP ammunition at retailers or gun ranges.

Have you ever wondered why some handguns seem right for you and others are very difficult to shoot or do not operate for you as you expect? Have you ever shot a handgun knowing you were aiming dead center of the target and your shot ended up to either to the left or right of the bulls eye? Have you experienced your shots hitting the target far from where you thought you were aiming? Has a friend loaned you their gun to shoot that they were very proficient shooting but you could not hit the broad side of a barn from the inside with it?

People are inclined to blame the gun for these issues and if you did, you would be half right. The other half of the blame is your hand. These issues happen when the gun does not fit your hand correctly and therefore you cannot operate the handgun correctly. This is what we refer to as a classic train wreck of a relationship. If you happen to own a handgun that you cannot shoot correctly because it is the wrong gun for you, sell it because the gun is not going to change its size and neither is your hand. This is also the primary reason that well intended advice which gun you should buy from everyone else fails for you, unless you happen to get the advice from someone who is exactly the same physical size as you are. The same is true if there is one handgun in your home and you share it with someone else, unless you are the same size one of you will not be equally competent using the same handgun.

How well a handgun fits you is really as important as reliability. Even if your handgun fires every time you press the trigger but all of your shots miss your intended target, you are in big trouble. Shooting innocent people because you cannot control your handgun is unacceptable and very expensive. Failing to stop your attacker could cost you your life.

Do not expect the guy behind the counter at the gun store to be very helpful. Gun store people are usually very knowledgeable about the technical features of a good number of firearms, but most of them are not trained to know how to fit a gun to you correctly.

As we have mentioned, fitting handguns and shoes are very similar. They both need a correct width (grip) and length (frame) to fit you properly. For example if a shoe is too short or too narrow for you, it is too small and you cannot put it on or if you do your foot will soon hurt you. If it is too long or too wide, it is too large and your foot will float around inside your shoe and your foot will develop blisters. Neither your feet nor your shoes will ever adjust their size to each other so your shoes will never fit you comfortably. Wearing the shoes more often will not resolve the problem just like practicing with a gun that does not fit you will not correct your shooting problems either. Make sense?

To perform a handgun fitting procedure you may need a mirror or a trusting friend to help you determine the fit of your handgun selections.

<u>Before you do anything with a handgun, perform a clearing procedure to verify that it is unloaded.</u>

The first measurement you need to make is the grip. Every time you pick up a handgun, your strong side (shooting hand) knuckles should automatically land directly below the trigger guard. No adjustment should be necessary to align your knuckles where they belong. If your knuckles are off to the side of the trigger guard, this means the grip is either too large or too small for your hand.

Some firearms do have grip options you can try to help you adjust the grip size however the magazine well on a semi automatic is not adjustable. If the gun still does not fit your hand by changing to another grip option, the grip will never fit you correctly. You are holding the wrong gun. Try again with another handgun. Keep track of the price of each handgun you try out that does not fit you. This is the running total of the money you are saving.

Once you have found a handgun with a correct grip size for you, the second measurement and an equally important one is the length or frame size. To determine this measurement, with the action at rest (firearm verified as unloaded, hammer not cocked, the safety off and the muzzle pointed in a safe direction) gently touch the trigger but do not press it. Every time you touch the trigger, your trigger finger should always land on the trigger half way between the tip of your finger and first joint. No adjustment should be necessary. If your finger cannot reach in far enough, this means the frame is too large. If your finger goes in too far and the trigger is near the first joint of your finger, this means the frame is too small. If your finger does not land half way between the tip and first joint, you will either push or pull the barrel every time you shoot because your finger does not land correctly on the trigger. Correct finger placement on the trigger is very important because when your finger touches the trigger correctly, when you press the trigger it will come straight back and not change the direction of the barrel as you shoot the handgun.

This fitting process is identical for both a revolver and a semi automatic handgun.

Once you know a particular handgun correctly fits your hand, measure the distance between the top knuckle directly below the trigger guard of your shooting hand and the bottom of your trigger finger as you touch the trigger. You can mark this distance with a pen or a pencil. You just need to know the distance. Once you have this information you can pick up any handgun and if the grip size is correct, you can easily measure the frame size and immediately tell if the handgun you are holding fits you and will shoot correctly for you or not.

A gun that does not fit you correctly cannot be shot by you accurately, just like shoes that do not fit you correctly cannot be worn by you comfortably.

Okay, by now there should be a pile of handguns in front of you that all fit you. If you touched enough guns at the gun store, you might realize that one consideration is of little importance when fitting a handgun, caliber. But the caliber is still an important part of your decision when choosing the right handgun for you.

In fact, you may have a variety of calibers from which you can choose. Make a list of

the make and model of all these guns and take your list to a range where you can rent these guns before you decide which one to buy. You will be deciding what is the correct caliber for you at the gun range. You need to buy some ammunition for each gun that you have determined fits you so you can see how competent you are shooting it. The right caliber for you will be the largest caliber that you can accurately shoot center of mass (within the largest middle area) of a silhouette target set at 21 feet, without using the guns sights. This is called point shooting and is what you will naturally do when you are under an attack. All your shots must be placed on the silhouette, with no shots missing the target completely or in the white paper area around the silhouette. You want to buy the handgun that you achieve the best grouping of rounds with the largest caliber.

> Here is a shooting tip to help you tighten your shots into a smaller group; push forward with your shooting hand as you pull back with your non-shooting shooting hand and clamp the handgun in your palm. The harder you clamp the gun, the less the gun will move and your shots will be closer together.

We do not know which handgun(s) will be right for you. What is important is that you will know which handgun(s) will be right for you when you are finished shooting. You may learn that you are equally competent with more than one handgun. That is okay. If your budget allows, give them all a good home.

And remember: A gun never solves problems.

CHAPTER 9
The Legalities of Everyday Carry

We would like to take another opportunity to remind you that although we will be discussing legal issues and the laws in general, we are not attorneys and we are not giving anyone legal advice and our discussion should not be taken as legal advice. If you have a specific need for legal advice, you need to talk to your attorney.

In this chapter, we will be discussing various laws that all touch in one way or another on the topic of carrying a handgun in public. The primary law we are governed by is *Minn. Stat. § 624.714* which we call the Minnesota Personal Protection Act, however there are other state and federal laws we will also discuss and which you need to understand and follow.

Minnesota law generally prohibits people from carrying loaded firearms in public places, unless the person possesses a valid Minnesota permit to carry or a permit issued by another state recognized by Minnesota (we are intentionally not discussing lawful hunting or sport shooting activities).

Minnesota's laws prohibit any person, other than a peace officer, from carrying, holding, or possessing a pistol in a motor vehicle, snowmobile, or boat, or on or about the person's clothes or the person, or otherwise from being in possession or control of a pistol in a public place, without first having obtained a permit to carry (or has a permit recognized by Minnesota). *Minn. Stat. § 624.714; 624.7181; 97B.045.*

Minnesota does not generally prohibit persons, who are not otherwise prohibited by law from possessing firearms, from possessing or carrying a firearm within the person's own dwelling and its immediate surrounding property.

Minnesota's law does not authorize state or local public officials and governing bodies to post or otherwise regulate or prohibit the general possession or carrying of firearms by permit holders within or upon public properties (e.g., buildings, facilities, nature areas, parks, etc.). *Minn. Stat. § 471.633.*

This is also a good time to dispel the myth that Minnesota has a "concealed carry" law. It does not have such a law today, nor has Minnesota ever had a law that required you to carry a gun concealed. The law is silent about how you choose to carry your handgun. It is (and should be) determined by your good judgment and common sense, based upon where you are going and what you are doing.

You will also need to consider the way that you are perceived by others while carrying a firearm. Perhaps make an adjustment to what may otherwise be a perfectly legal manner to carry a gun, while at the same time, a very stupid manner to carry a gun. For example, it is totally legal to carry a AR-15 down Nicollet Mall and into your favorite department store to buy a new tie, however common sense suggests that doing so would not be a smart thing to do.

We should also point out there is a big difference between the terms "carrying" a handgun and "transporting" a handgun. Anyone who is allowed to legally possess a handgun my also transport it if the handgun is unloaded and properly encased without the need for a permit to carry. When we refer to "carrying" a handgun, we mean a loaded handgun somewhere on your body while you are out in public.

Your "permit" is not the card the sheriff sent to you. Your "permit" actually consists of both your government issued photo ID (what you submitted to the sheriff with your application , a driver's license or state identification card, or a US passport) and the card the sheriff sent to you. Minnesota law requires a permit holder must possess the permit (the permit card and a valid ID) while carrying a handgun in public.

Should either your permit card or ID be stolen or lost, it is best to replace it before carrying a handgun in public. Under the law, police officers may give you a petty misdemeanor citation not to exceed $25 for a first offense if you are noticed to be armed and without your permit. The police may not take your handgun from you. The citation must be dismissed if you demonstrate in court or in the office of the arresting officer that you had a valid permit at the time of the alleged violation.

You do not have to disclose to anyone that you have a permit to carry other than to a law enforcement officer if you are asked. If asked you are also required to disclose if you are armed at the time. If there is any question of your credentials, the officer may ask you for your signature, which they will compare to your driver's license (or other ID). Otherwise, permit holder data is considered private information and may not be made public (except in cases such as a DGU and you become newsworthy to the public).

Most laws are usually written to prohibit behavior that was otherwise permitted. For example, Adam and Eve had the do not eat from the fruit tree law. That was it and everything else was allowed. From the times of the Garden of Eden, many laws have been written to restrict or change what behavior had been allowed or tolerated. Some laws force us to do things we would not otherwise do willingly. As you will see, the Minnesota Personal Protection Act rolled back a number of State laws that had been written over time that restricted our ability to carry a gun in public, although even the "official" name 624.714 CARRYING OF WEAPONS WITHOUT PERMIT; PENALTIES. is a reminder why laws are written. Some restrictions still do apply.

Another Minnesota law preempts all local governmental authority to regulate firearms and ammunition except that local governments may regulate the discharge of firearms within their borders and they may enact local zoning laws to determine where a shooting range or gun shop may operate. Otherwise, local firearms ordinances must be identical to state law. *Minn Stat. 471.633, 624.717*

Long Guns

Why I the world would we talk about long guns in a carry book? Well, there are a couple good reasons. You might just need a long gun with a C-Mag during a civil riot or disturbance from people with hurt feelings as we witness from time to time, and there is too much misinformation circulating by supposed "experts" about what they claim you "legally can do" that could land you in a heap of trouble.

Do not be surprised if some bar room gun nut tells you that Minnesota's permit to carry law allows you to carry a deer rifle or evil black rifle or Tommy gun. It really does not do that. A different law does.

Even self-declared firearm "experts" either do not read or clearly understand firearms laws that quite frankly may have been enacted decades apart from each other, but they somehow believe should work seamlessly as though they were all enacted by the same legislators at the same time. That is not how these laws happen, and the more laws we have, the more difficult it is to eliminate conflicts so they work together as desired. For these reasons, Minnesota firearms laws can be confusing.

The three laws that directly or indirectly address possession, carry or transportation of long guns are:

Minn. Stat. § 624.714 CARRYING OF WEAPONS WITHOUT PERMIT; PENALTIES

Minn. Stat. § 624.7181 RIFLES AND SHOTGUNS IN PUBLIC PLACES

Minn. Stat. § 97B.045 TRANSPORTATION OF FIREARMS

Let's look at each law so this makes sense:

Under Minn. Stat. § 624.714 , CARRYING OF WEAPONS WITHOUT PERMIT; PENALTIES - Minnesota's "carry" law:

Only pistols are regulated, not the carry or transportation of long guns.

Under Minn. Stat. § 624.7181 RIFLES AND SHOTGUNS IN PUBLIC PLACES :

"carry" does not include:

(1) the carrying of a BB gun, rifle, or shotgun to, from, or at a place where firearms are repaired, bought, sold, traded, or displayed, or where hunting, target shooting, or other lawful activity involving firearms occurs, or at funerals, parades, or other lawful ceremonies;

(2) the carrying by a person of a BB gun, rifle, or shotgun that is unloaded and in a gun case expressly made to contain a firearm, if the case fully encloses the firearm by being zipped, snapped, buckled, tied, or otherwise fastened, and no portion of the firearm is exposed;

(3) the carrying of a BB gun, rifle, or shotgun by a person who has a permit under section 624.714;

(4) the carrying of an antique firearm as a curiosity or for its historical significance or value; or

(5) the transporting of a BB gun, rifle, or shotgun in compliance with section 97B.045.

Under Minn. Stat. § 97B.045 TRANSPORTATION OF FIREARMS.

Subdivision 1.Restrictions. A person may not transport a firearm in a motor vehicle unless the firearm is:

(1) unloaded and in a gun case expressly made to contain a firearm, and the case fully encloses the firearm by being zipped, snapped, buckled, tied, or otherwise fastened, and without any portion of the firearm exposed;

(2) unloaded and in the closed trunk of a motor vehicle; or

(3) a handgun carried in compliance with sections 624.714 and 624.715.

Subd. 2.Exception for disabled persons. The restrictions in subdivision 1 do not apply to a disabled person if:

(1) the person possesses a permit under section 97B.055, subdivision 3; and

(2) the firearm is not loaded in the chamber until the vehicle is stationary, or is a hinge action firearm with the action open until the vehicle is stationary.

§ Subd. 3.Exceptions; hunting and shooting ranges. (a) Notwithstanding provisions to the contrary under this chapter, a person may transport an unloaded, uncased firearm, excluding a pistol as defined in paragraph (b), in a motor vehicle while at a shooting range, as defined under section 87A.01, subdivision 3, where the person has received permission from the lawful owner or possessor to discharge firearms; lawfully hunting on private or public land; or travelling to or from a site the person intends to hunt lawfully that day or has hunted lawfully that day, unless:

(1) within Anoka, Hennepin, or Ramsey County;

(2) within the boundaries of a home rule charter or statutory city with a population of 2,500 or more;

(3) on school grounds; or

(4) otherwise restricted under section 97A.091, 97B.081, or 97B.086.

(b) For the purposes of this section, a "pistol" includes a weapon designed to be fired by the use of a single hand and with an overall length less than 26 inches, or having a barrel or barrels of a length less than 18 inches in the case of a shotgun or having a barrel of a length less than 16 inches in the case of a rifle:

(1) from which may be fired or ejected one or more solid projectiles by means of a cartridge or shell or by the action of an explosive or the igniting of flammable or explosive substances; or

(2) for which the propelling force is a spring, elastic band, carbon dioxide, air or other gas, or vapor.

Pistol does not include a device firing or ejecting a shot measuring .18 of an inch, or less, in diameter and commonly known as a "BB gun," a scuba gun, a stud gun or nail gun used in the construction industry, or children's pop guns or toys.

So, by homogenizing the three laws, what we have is that a permit holder (Minn. Stat. § 624.714) may carry a an uncased and loaded rifle or shotgun (Minn. Stat. § 624.7181), but must generally unload and case it when transporting it in a vehicle (Minn. Stat. § 97B.045).

Permitted places

Generally speaking that which is not specifically prohibited is permitted. You will not need to look for a sign that welcomes armed citizens, although that would be nice. A permit holder can carry a handgun anywhere in public across the state unless it is a location that is specifically prohibited by law or is a posted private establishment (or private residence).

Locations Where Permit Is Not Required

A permit to carry is not required to:

- Keep or carry a pistol about a person's place of business, dwelling, or on the premises or land possessed by the person;
- Carry a pistol from a place of purchase to the person's dwelling or place of business, or from the person's dwelling or place of business to or from a place where a pistol is repaired;
- Carry a pistol in the woods or fields or on Minnesota waters for the purpose of hunting or target shooting in a safe area; or
- Transport a pistol in a motor vehicle, snowmobile, or boat if the pistol is unloaded, contained in a closed and fastened case, gunbox, or securely tied package.

Minn. Stat. § 624.714, subd. 9.

Prohibited places

Minnesota state laws and the US Federal Code prohibits permit holders from carrying in some places and anyone who violates them runs the risk of severe legal penalties.

Permit holders are expected to know that they are prohibited from carrying in the following locations, even if there is no sign to warn them. Ignorance of the law is no excuse.

1. Grades 1-12 schools and licensed child-care centers.

School Zones: Federal law prohibits knowingly possessing a firearm at a place that the individual knows, or has reasonable cause to believe, is a school zone. The law defines "school zone" as an area that is: "in or on . . . or within 1,000 feet of . . . the grounds of a public, parochial or private school." Exceptions include possession on private property that is not part of the school grounds; possession for use in an approved school program; possession of a firearm that is unloaded and in a locked firearms rack in a motor vehicle; and possession by a law enforcement officer and an authorized school contractor (e.g., a security guard). *18 U.S.C. §§ 922(q); 921(a)(25).*

Schools: Buildings, Busses, Improved Property, and Licensed Child Care Centers: Minnesota law generally prohibits any person from knowingly possessing, storing, or keeping a firearm on school property, including in any school building, bus, or facility temporarily under the exclusive control of a school, where signs give actual notice. This law defines school to mean any public or private elementary, middle, or secondary school building or its improved grounds, whether owned or leased by the school. The law also prohibits firearms possessions in a licensed child care center during the time that children are present. A violation of any of these prohibitions is a felony.

The law also prohibits a person who is knowingly on school property from: (1) using or brandishing a replica firearm or BB gun; and (2) possessing, storing, or keeping a replica firearm or BB gun. A violation of the first is a gross misdemeanor, and a violation of the second is a misdemeanor.

Prohibitions involving schools do not apply to:
- Active licensed peace officers;
- Military personnel or students participating in military training, who are on duty, performing official duties;
- Persons authorized to carry a pistol under *Minn. Stat. § 624.714*, while in a motor vehicle or outside of a motor vehicle to directly place a firearm in, or retrieve it from, the trunk or rear area of the vehicle;
- Persons who keep or store in a motor vehicle pistols in accordance with *Minn. Stat. § 624.714* or *624.715*, or other firearms in accordance with section 97B.045;
- Firearm safety or marksmanship courses or activities conducted on school property;
- Possession of dangerous weapons, BB guns, or replica firearms by a ceremonial color guard;
- A gun or knife show held on school property;
- Possession of dangerous weapons, BB guns, or replica firearms with written permission of the   principal or other person having general control and supervision of the school or the director of a child care center; and
- Persons who are on unimproved property owned or leased by a child care center, school, or school district unless the person knows that a student is currently present on the land for a school-related activity. *Minn. Stat. § 609.66, subd. 1(d)*.

What about Postsecondary educational institutions?

Any public postsecondary educational institution may establish policies restricting the carrying or possession of firearms by its students or its staff while on the institution's property. Public postsecondary educational institutions are not authorized to generally prohibit the lawful carrying or possession of firearms by members of the public who are neither their students nor their employees. *Minn. Stat. § 624.714, subd. 18(b)*.

Higher educational institutions cannot prohibit the lawful carry or possession of firearms by anyone in or on a parking facility or parking area. *Minn. Stat. § 624.714, subd. 18(c).*

2. Federal courthouses.

Federal law prohibits citizens, even those with permits to carry, from carrying guns in federal courthouses and this is not superseded by Minnesota law. There is no case law as to whether adjacent parking lots are also prohibited, but a conservative approach is best: park outside of the parking lot and secure your handgun in your car before going in.

3. Courthouse complexes.

Minn. Stat. § 609.66, subd. 1(g), prohibits permit holders from carrying in courthouse buildings, unless the sheriff is notified. Once the sheriff is notified, it is legal to carry in a courthouse building (but not into the courtroom or hearing rooms).

A notification should be sent by certified mail to a sheriff, return receipt requested, if you want to go armed in a courthouse and you should keep a copy of the letter and the return receipt.

A sample letter is shown below which you may personalize with your own information to use:

Date

Sheriff
County Courthouse
Address
City, MN 55555

VIA Certified Mail

Dear Sheriff,

Minn. Stat.609.66, Subdivision 1g (a)(1) specifies that a person who "possesses a dangerous weapon, ammunition, or explosives within any courthouse complex;" is guilty of a felony, except for several classes of persons, including "persons who carry pistols according to the terms of a permit issued under Minn. Stat. 624.714 and who so notify the sheriff as appropriate." (Minn. Stat. 609.66, Subd 1g, (b)(2))

As long as I possess a valid permit issued under Minn. Stat. 624.714, please consider this letter as the required notification, securing for me the exemption specified in Minn. Stat. 609.66 Subd 1g, (b)(2).

Enclosed, please find a copy of the front and back of my current:

> Permit to carry a pistol; and
> Minnesota Drivers License

Thank you.

Very truly yours,

Bob Smith
1234 Anywhere Street
Anytown, MN 55555
MN Drivers License X-XXX-XXX-XXX

4. The state capitol and buildings in the "capitol complex."

Minn. Stat. § 609.66 subd. 1(g) also prohibits carrying handguns in the state capitol building, its grounds, and nearby buildings in the "capitol complex," with some exceptions. In 2015, the Minnesota legislature removed the requirement for permit holders to give written notice to the Commissioner of Public Safety that you intend to carry on the capitol grounds. Permit holders may carry while visiting the Capitol.

5. State correctional facilities.

Minnesota law prohibits bringing, without the consent of the facility's chief executive officer, a firearm into or onto the grounds of a state correctional facility or state hospital. There is an exception for law enforcement officers carrying a firearm in the line of duty, but there is no exception for a person carrying under the authority of a state-issued permit to carry. This prohibition also applies to the transporting of firearms. *Minn. Stat. § 243.55.*

6. State hospitals

7. Federal buildings and security areas.

Federal law prohibits the possession and carrying of firearms within any federal facility that is conspicuously posted as prohibiting firearms (e.g., federal courthouses, federal prisons, federal hospitals, federal administrative buildings, national park buildings including visitor centers, and virtually all other federal buildings including Post Office facilities and parking lots). The law also prohibits firearms possession within most designated security areas (e.g., the security areas of airports, many military bases, certain sensitive governmental industrial sites, and other governmental security areas).

The term "federal facility" means a building or part thereof that is owned or leased by the federal government, where federal employees are regularly present for the purpose of performing their official duties.

There are exceptions for qualified federal, state, and local law enforcement officers, authorized members of the armed forces and, in some cases, members of the public carrying a firearm incidental to hunting or other lawful purposes. *18 U.S.C. § 930.*

Notwithstanding the firearms ban in most federal facilities, beginning in 2010, federal law specifically authorizes the carrying of personal firearms into all but a few national parks and wildlife refuges, provided it complies with the laws of the state(s) in which the park or refuge is located. However, firearms may not be carried into any posted federal buildings within the park or refuge. *(Credit Card Accountability Responsibility and Disclosure Act of 2009, § 512, Pub. L. No. 111-24).*

Carry at work

There is nothing in Minnesota law that prohibits a permit holder from carrying his or her handgun at work.

The law does authorize public and private employers who wish to establish policies that restrict the carrying or possession of firearms by its own employees while they are acting in the course and scope of employment. *Minn. Stat. § 624.714, subd. 18(a).*

Permit holders may not carry at their place of employment if it is a specifically prohibited place like a 1-12 public or private school or a correctional facility.

The employer/employee relationship is a different one than that of a store owner and their customers. The law permits employers to set policies about employees' behavior in the workplace. Such policies should be explained to employees when hired or when new policies are adopted or policies are changed.

While there are no pending court cases as of this writing, it is possible that an employer who disarms his or her employees while in the workplace, assumes the responsibility for maintaining the safety of all employees. Employers have very broad latitude to determine acceptable behavior while the employee is "acting in the course and scope of that employment."

Parking lots

With the exception of federal property such as the post office, the owner or operator of a private establishment may not prohibit the lawful possession of firearms in their parking facilities. Parking lots and ramps are considered public spaces, even if they are owned by an employer. Employers are specifically prohibited from forbidding permit holders

from storing a firearm in their vehicle in a parking lot or parking area on their property or within their control.

A public postsecondary institution regulated under Chapter 136F or 137 may establish policies that restrict the carry or possession of firearms by its students and employees while on the institution's property however a postsecondary institution may not prohibit the lawful carry or possession of firearms by anyone in a parking facility or parking area.

Minnesota courts have ruled that a church may prohibit firearms from its property, including parking facilities and parking areas owned or operated by the church, and may notify its employees and the public in any manner it chooses. *Edina Cmty. Lutheran Church v. State of Minnesota, (A07-0131), 745 N.W.2d 194 (Minn. App. 2008)*. This ruling does not prohibit any other church that disagree with the Edina Community Lutheran Church, from welcoming their armed worshippers.

Posting

This might sound silly at first, but most permit holders like the signs that ban guns. They are a constant reminder to the sheep that sheepdogs are nearby. Signs are also a constant reminder to the wolves a sheepdog may be nearby as well.

Only a private establishment may post which is defined as a building, structure, or portion thereof that is owned, leased, controlled, or operated by a nongovernmental entity for a nongovernmental purpose. By definition, governmental entities or entities operating for governmental purposes are not allowed to post.

It is not necessary for a private establishment to post a sign to prohibit the possession of a firearm. If the operator of an establishment sees you and asks you to take your firearm outside, even if there was no sign, it may still be a reasonable request and you should comply. On the other hand, you may be asked to leave just because an employee may not like your firearm, but there is not a corporate prohibition against your being armed on the premises, so sorting this out can get a bit tricky.

It is not a crime to walk past a sign that bans guns on the premises in a private establishment simply because the sign has been posted. The law recognizes a property owners right to set limitations on what people can do on their property. Someone who has been asked not to bring a gun into the building, either by direct verbal notice or by the posting of 11 x 17 inch signs at each entrance saying "[Operator of the establishment] BANS GUNS ON THESE PREMISES," may well find himself being asked to leave. A proper notification requires that you be personally informed of the private establishment's policy that firearms are not allowed and then asked to leave. This is the exclusive criteria to notify a permit holder when otherwise lawful possession of a firearm is not allowed in a private establishment.

If you do not leave when told to do so, the police can be summoned, and you can be charged with a petty misdemeanor trespassing violation, with a $25 fine.

If you are told to leave, and it is a legitimate and proper request, just leave. Unlike trespass where you can be prevented from returning for up to a year, once you have complied with the request to leave, you are free to return. Most people elect not to return because their firearms and their wallet are connected together. Go shop where they are both welcomed.

Minnesota courts have ruled that a church may prohibit firearms from its property, including parking facilities and parking areas owned or operated by the church, and may notify its employees and the public in any manner it chooses. (*Edina Cmty. Lutheran Church v. State of Minnesota, (A07-0131), 745 N.W.2d 194 (Minn. App. 2008)).*

Besides governmental entities, there are other entities who are not allowed to post premises, although the law does not provide a penalty for those who wrongly violate your rights. One of the more popular offenders are owners and landlords of shopping malls. The law specifically prohibits a landlord (or their representatives) from restricting the lawful carry or possession of firearms by tenants or their guests. A private enterprise (a business) located within a mall or leased office building may post the area over which they have exclusive control.

Although the owner of a private establishment may post their premises, they may not prohibit the lawful carry or possession of firearms in a parking facility or parking areas.

The posting requirement does not apply to residences. The lawful possessor of a private residence (this does not include the common space of a multi unit residence) may prohibit firearms and provide notice thereof in any lawful manner. Lawful notice from a possessor of the residence can be a simple verbal request to remove the firearm.

Airports and flying

There is no "official" count, however we believe there are somewhere around 25,000,000 armed citizens in the United States. Many of these people travel by air. Airports and airlines have met enough people who travel with a firearm, that it is no longer an "event" at the airport.

If you are just dropping off someone at the airport, there is nothing you need to do unless you plan to go into a secured area of the airport. The same is true if you are meeting someone who has arrived and you are picking them up. The baggage claim area is in an unsecured area of the airport, so you can park, go in and help carry their luggage if necessary.

If you are the traveler, things change a lot. From the TSA website:

Travelers may only transport UNLOADED firearms in a locked, hard-sided container in or as checked baggage.

All firearms, ammunition and firearm parts, including firearm frames and receivers, are prohibited in carry-on baggage. To avoid issues that could impact your travel and/or result in law enforcement action, here are regulations to assist you in packing your firearms and ammunition:

- All firearms must be declared to the airline during the ticket counter check-in process.
- The firearm must be unloaded.
- The firearm must be in a hard-sided container that is locked. A locked container is defined as one that completely secures the firearm from being accessed. Locked cases that can be pulled open with little effort cannot be brought aboard the aircraft.
- If firearms are not properly declared or packaged, TSA will provide the bag to law enforcement for resolution with the airline. If the issue is resolved, law enforcement will release the bag to TSA so screening may be completed.
- TSA must resolve all alarms in checked baggage. If a locked container containing a firearm alarms, TSA will contact the airline, who will make a reasonable attempt to contact the owner and advise the passenger to go to the screening location. If contact is not made, the container will not be placed on the aircraft.
- If a locked container alarms during screening and is not marked as containing a declared firearm, TSA will cut the lock in order to resolve the alarm.
- Travelers should remain in the area designated by the aircraft operator or TSA representative to take the key back after the container is cleared for transportation.
- Travelers must securely pack any ammunition in fiber (such as cardboard), wood or metal boxes or other packaging specifically designed to carry small amounts of ammunition.
- Firearm magazines and ammunition magazines must be securely boxed or included within a hard-sided case containing an unloaded firearm.

- Small arms ammunition, including ammunition not exceeding .75 caliber for a rifle or pistol and shotgun shells of any gauge, may be carried in the same hard-sided case as the firearm, as long as it follows the packing guidelines described above.
- TSA prohibits black powder or percussion caps used with black-powder.
- Rifle scopes are not prohibited in carry-on bags and do not need to be in the hard-sided, locked checked bag.

Unless you are a frequent flyer and already know each airlines rules, we suggest that you ask if firearms are permitted on the airline(s) you will be flying before you purchase your ticket. Also ask about any limitations on transportation of ammunition you want to take along on your trip. Are there any other limitations you should be aware? Airlines are charging for everything these days, so ask if there is any additional charge for you to fly with a firearm.

You need to first declare the firearm when at the ticket counter and it has to be unloaded and locked in a hard or metal gun container inside of your checked luggage. Since your firearm, spare magazines, speed loaders, and ammunition are locked in your checked baggage, you might as well put your holster in your baggage too. Keeping a holster on your body will only cause you problems with hypersensitive TSA agents.

You can never ever walk through a security checkpoint while you are in possession of a gun. It does not matter if it is unloaded and secured in a locked box. This also applies to spare magazines, speed loaders, and ammunition, as well.

You should make it a habit to check all your pockets and bags before leaving for the airport so you are ready when you arrive to check your bags and go through security. You can avoid missing a flight because you forgot that you had locked your gun in your briefcase, or need to figure out what to do with a spare magazine or speed loader. Taking the time to check to be sure your firearm and accessories were properly stored, is a small inconvenience when compared to being arrested. Besides civil fines, security violations may also lead to felony criminal charges in federal court.

You also need to know how you will handle layovers, particularly if you will be changing airlines or staying overnight. It is best if the airlines can move your checked luggage to your next flight without the need for you to take possession of it. If you must take possession and leave the airport and go to a hotel for the night, avoiding trouble in places that severely restrict the possession of firearms like New York can be very difficult. It is best that the airline retain possession of your checked luggage. Your carry on luggage should contain what you need for an overnight stay whether planned or not.

Post offices

Federal facilities are governed by the United States Code of Federal Regulations. Entering post offices should be avoided when armed. The signs posted at post offices quote two sections of federal regulation.

1. United States Code (USC) 18 USC 930 (which deals with federal facilities in general), and
2. Code of Federal Regulations (CFR) 39 CFR 232.1 (i).

However United States Code (USC) 18 USC 930 does not apply to postal facilities because 39 USC 410 exempts Post Offices from 18 USC 930 (except for theft of mail, robbing a post office, stealing postal money orders and so forth).

39 CFR 232.1 which rises from 39 USC 410 however, does govern conduct on postal property and clearly prohibits guns while on post office property. The **bolded** sections of 39 CFR 232.1 below needs your attention. By merely entering postal property, you give up your Fourth Amendment rights against search and seizure.

(a) Applicability. This section applies to all real property under the charge and control of the Postal Service, to all tenant agencies, and to all persons entering in or on such property. This section shall be posted and kept posted at a conspicuous place on all such property. This section shall not apply to:

(i) Any portions of real property, owned or leased by the Postal Service, that are leased or subleased by the Postal Service to private tenants for their exclusive use;

(ii) With respect to sections 232.1(h)(1) and 232.1(o), sidewalks along the street frontage of postal property falling within the property lines of the Postal Service that are not physically distinguishable from adjacent municipal or other public sidewalks, and any paved areas adjacent to such sidewalks that are not physically distinguishable from such sidewalks.

(b) Inspection, recording presence.

(1) Purses, briefcases, and other containers brought into, while on, or being removed from the property are subject to inspec-

tion. However, items brought directly to a postal facility's customer mailing acceptance area and deposited in the mail are not subject to inspection, except as provided by section 274 of the Administrative Support Manual. A person arrested for violation of this section may be searched incident to that arrest.

(2) Vehicles and their contents brought into, while on, or being removed from restricted nonpublic areas are subject to inspection. A prominently displayed sign shall advise in advance that vehicles and their contents are subject to inspection when entering the restricted nonpublic area, while in the confines of the area, or when leaving the area. Persons entering these areas who object and refuse to consent to the inspection of the vehicle, its contents, or both, may be denied entry; after entering the area without objection, consent shall be implied. A full search of a person and any vehicle driven or occupied by the person may accompany an arrest.

(3) Except as otherwise ordered, properties must be closed to the public after normal business hours. Properties also may be closed to the public in emergency situations and at such other times as may be necessary for the orderly conduct of business. Admission to properties during periods when such properties are closed to the public may be limited to authorized individuals who may be required to sign the register and display identification documents when requested by security force personnel or other authorized individuals.

(c) - (k) omitted (not related to firearms)

(l) Weapons and explosives. Notwithstanding the provisions of any other law, rule or regulation, no person while on postal property may carry firearms, other dangerous or deadly weapons, or explosives, either openly or concealed, or store the same on postal property, except for official purposes.

(m) – (o) omitted (not related to firearms)

(p) Penalties and other law.

(1) Alleged violations of these rules and regulations are heard, and the penalties prescribed herein are imposed, either in a Federal district court or by a Federal magistrate in accordance with applicable court rules. Questions regarding such rules should be directed to the regional counsel for the region involved.

(2) Whoever shall be found guilty of violating the rules and regulations in this section while on property under the charge and

control of the Postal Service is subject to fine of not more than
$50 or imprisonment of not more than 30 days, or both. Nothing
contained in these rules and regulations shall be construed to
abrogate any other Federal laws or regulations of any State and
local laws and regulations applicable to any area in which the
property is situated.

(q) Enforcement.

(1) Members of the U.S. Postal Service security force shall exercise the powers of special policemen provided by 40 U.S.C. 318
and shall be responsible for enforcing the regulations in this section in a manner that will protect Postal Service property.

(2) Local postmasters and installation heads may, pursuant to 40
U.S.C. 318b and with the approval of the chief postal inspector
or his designee, enter into agreements with State and local enforcement agencies to insure that these rules and regulations are
enforced in a manner that will protect Postal Service property.

(3) Postal Inspectors, Office of Inspector General Criminal Investigators, and other persons designated by the Chief Postal
Inspector may likewise enforce regulations in this section.

*[37 FR 24346, Nov. 16, 1972, as amended at 38 FR 27824, Oct. 9,
1973; 41 FR 23955, June 14, 1976; 42 FR 17443, Apr. 1, 1977; 43 FR
38825, Aug.*

*31, 1978; 46 FR 898, Jan. 5, 1981. Redesignated and amended at 46 FR
34330, July 1, 1981; 47 FR 32113, July 26, 1982; 53 FR 29460, Aug.
5, 1988; 54 FR 20527, May 12, 1989; 57 FR 36903, Aug. 17, 1993; 57
FR 38443, Aug. 25, 1992; 63 FR 34600, June 25, 1998; 70 FR 72078,
Dec. 1, 2005]*

Prosecutors like to add on other charges such as disorderly conduct
and disturbing the peace for example, just to up the ante of charges
against you so be mindful of the consequences.

This is a long way to say it, but if armed stay off postal property. Park
your vehicle on the street or another area that is not controlled by the
post office. Disarm and store your firearm in your vehicle before leaving
your vehicle and enter a post office.

Non-postal Federal facilities

So, for non-postal facilities, Title 18, United States Code, Sec. 930.— Possession of firearms and dangerous weapons in federal facilities applies and is very clear (the emphasis is added):

Sec. 930. Possession of firearms and dangerous weapons in Federal facilities.

(a) Except as provided in subsection (d), whoever knowingly possesses or causes to be present a firearm or other dangerous weapon in a Federal facility (other than a Federal court facility), or attempts to do so, shall be fined under this title or imprisoned not more than 1 year, or both.

(b) Whoever, with intent that a firearm or other dangerous weapon be used in the commission of a crime, knowingly possesses or causes to be present such firearm or dangerous weapon in a Federal facility, or attempts to do so, shall be fined under this title or imprisoned not more than 5 years, or both.

(c) A person who kills any person in the course of a violation of subsection (a) or (b), or in the course of an attack on a Federal facility involving the use of a firearm or other dangerous weapon, or attempts or conspires to do such an act, shall be punished as provided in sections 1111, 1112, 1113, and 1117.

(d) Subsection (a) shall not apply to:

(1) the lawful performance of official duties by an officer, agent, or employee of the United States, a State, or a political subdivision thereof, who is authorized by law to engage in or supervise the prevention, detection, investigation, or prosecution of any violation of law;

(2) the possession of a firearm or other dangerous weapon by a Federal official or a member of the Armed Forces if such possession is authorized by law; or

(3) the lawful carrying of firearms or other dangerous weapons in a Federal facility incident to hunting or other lawful purposes.

(e) (1) Except as provided in paragraph (2), whoever knowingly possesses or causes to be present a firearm in a Federal court facility, or attempts to do so, shall be fined under this title, imprisoned not more than 2 years, or both.

(2) Paragraph (1) shall not apply to conduct which is described in paragraph (1) or (2) of subsection (d).

(f) Nothing in this section limits the power of a court of the United

States to punish for contempt or to promulgate rules or orders regulating, restricting, or prohibiting the possession of weapons within any building housing such court or any of its proceedings, or upon any grounds appurtenant to such building.

(g) As used in this section:

    (1) The term "Federal facility" means a building or part thereof owned or leased by the Federal Government, where Federal employees are regularly present for the purpose of performing their official duties.

    (2) The term "dangerous weapon" means a weapon, device, instrument, material, or substance, animate or inanimate, that is used for, or is readily capable of, causing death or serious bodily injury, except that such term does not include a pocket knife with a blade of less than 2 ½ inches in length.

    (3) The term "Federal court facility" means the courtroom, judges' chambers, witness rooms, jury deliberation rooms, attorney conference rooms, prisoner holding cells, offices of the court clerks, the United States attorney, and the United States marshal, probation and parole offices, and adjoining corridors of any court of the United States.

(h) Notice of the provisions of subsections (a) and (b) shall be posted conspicuously at each public entrance to each Federal facility, and notice of subsection (e) shall be posted conspicuously at each public entrance to each Federal court facility, and no person shall be convicted of an offense under subsection (a) or (e) with respect to a Federal facility if such notice is not so posted at such facility, unless such person had actual notice of subsection (a) or (e), as the case may be.

Many people have seized upon (d)(3) to justify carrying a gun in a federal facility, by using the argument that they have a permit to carry and their carrying of a firearm is an "other lawful purpose" so they are exempt from the prohibition.

The problem with relying on 18 USC 930(d)(3) is that this section in no way empowers anyone to carry a gun in a federal facility; rather, that section simply states that 18 USC 930 does not apply to someone lawfully carrying a gun incident to some lawful purpose. Unless specifically prohibited by Minnesota statutes, the state generally leaves the regulation of federal property to others. The MPPA does not specifically authorize the lawful carry into a federal facility either.

It is never lawful to carry into a federal court facility; that is illegal except for law enforcement officers and certain members of military while on active duty.

But does Title 18, Section 930 mean that it is legal to carry into, say, a federal office building? That is what the exemption in the law seems to say for somebody with a permit to carry and being in the building for "other lawful purposes".

Because it is a gray area, we advise you to stay out of gray areas. Test court cases are expensive and the outcome is never certain. If you wish to make this your fight, start by contacting your members of Congress to change the law.

Carrying and being impaired

Although the MPPA is very specific about carrying and drinking, we can sum it up by saying DO NOT CARRY IF IMPARED. Carrying while "under the influence of alcohol or a controlled substance" is prohibited.

Minnesota does not have a zero tolerance policy however. Instead it has an "impairment prohibition". The MPPA sets the legal limit for tolerated blood alcohol content (BAC) of .04 (four hundredths of one percent) while remaining legally armed. If your BAC exceeds .04 but is less than .10 the punishment is a petty misdemeanor and results in a suspension of your permit. Going armed with a BAC of .10 or more as a misdemeanor and results in a suspension of your permit in addition to a fine or jail time.

Realistically, none of this should be a problem for a responsible permit holder. Even a relatively small man or woman can drink one beer, a single glass of wine, or a single shot of whiskey without going over a BAC of .04, and most people's BAC will drop at about .02 per hour after they stop drinking.

However, if you decide to drink while armed and have a DGU, the real risk is you have given the prosecuting attorney the reason necessary to let a jury decide if your decision to draw your gun or to shoot someone was justified or not, rather than making that call.

One permit holder we know elected to ignore our advice not to mix drinking and guns, and went out drinking with some friends and got impaired enough to have the bouncer toss him from the bar. Upset at the bouncer, he went to his vehicle and returned with a handgun and decided to shoot up the place. He was arrested for attempted murder. His instructor was called by the sheriff's office on behalf of the prosecuting attorney to testify that he was instructed in class not to drink while armed and that he was instructed about the legal use of lethal force, at the former permit holder's trial.

Please consider this as your one and only warning not to carry and drink or you may find your instructor will be called and asked to help the prosecution put you in prison for a very long time also.

When it comes to mixing drinking and carrying, you can control this behavior. If you want to relax with a drink or two, unload your gun and lock it up where it is safe before drinking and do not retrieve it until you are no longer impaired!

Traveling outside of Minnesota

If you happen to be one of those people who has lived your life close to home, you will be surprised should you decide to take a trip around the country. Besides sightseeing new terrain you will find that some states treat armed citizens very well, but you may also be surprised to find other states or cities are not so friendly.

The authority to manage the lawful carry of firearms is the responsibility reserved to each state and there is little consistency in the carry laws from one state to another. There is no (thankfully) Federal regulation governing permit holders. If there ever was a Federal law that set uniform standards all across state lines you might think that would make life better. However, the trade-off for consistent carry laws is the risk of unnecessary federal conditions placed on every armed citizen or an anti-rights President overturning the rights of millions of people across the entire country. We prefer to deal with differences in laws from state to state than to hand the federal government overwhelming power over an individual's right to maintain their constant state of peace.

Whether or not another state honors a Minnesota permit to carry is entirely up to the that state's legislature or perhaps a bureaucrat of that state. If the law passed by the legislature states they will recognize all other states permits, the legislature has made the decision. On the other hand, if the legislature has authorized the state's Attorney General or another person, to determine based upon a set of criteria, which states permits they will honor, a bureaucrat may interpret those instructions from the legislature narrowly or broadly, depending upon their personal political beliefs.

Minnesota carry law is similar to other states in many ways but there are also some differences. The laws are subject to change at any time by the legislatures, and you should learn about the current law in a given state before carrying a gun there. For example, some states forbid carry in bars, Minnesota allows it. Most states require that permit holders carry concealed, Minnesota allows permit holders to carry openly or concealed, and in some states there are serious penalties for even accidentally displaying or showing the outline of a firearm.

Generally speaking, it is lawful to travel with an unloaded gun, ammunition stored separately, locked in a case in the trunk or the rearmost area of a vehicle, if one is simply traveling through a state, rather than staying overnight or longer. The McClure-Volkmer act also known as the Firearm Owners Act of 1986 (FOPA) deals with this. Title 18 United States Code section 926A provides:

> "Notwithstanding any other provision of any law or any rule or regulation of a State or any political subdivision thereof, any person who is not otherwise prohibited by this chapter from transporting, shipping, or receiving a firearm shall be entitled to transport a firearm for any lawful purpose from any place where he may lawfully possess and carry such firearm to any other place where he may lawfully possess and carry such firearm if, during such transportation the firearm is unloaded, and neither the firearm nor any ammunition being transported is readily accessible or is directly accessible from the passenger compartment of such transporting vehicle: Provided, That in the case of a vehicle without a compartment separate from the driver's compartment the firearm or ammunition shall be contained in a locked container other than the glove compartment or console."

The protection afforded under federal law while traveling will not be helpful should you stop traveling and stay overnight. It is not legal to possess a handgun even if it is unloaded and locked in a case in the trunk of a car, while remaining in certain places such as New York City or the District of Columbia. The same principles that apply to entering the security zone of the airport apply in these places. Forgetting that you have a gun with you does not constitute an excuse should you decide to stay overnight.

The best practice is to know if you will be entering places on your trip that you need to be concerned about before you leave home. If you want to travel with your firearm consult the Attorney General's offices of the states and ask about the metropolitan areas through which you will be traveling or be staying overnight. A good resource is the website www.handgunlaw.us for reliable information about carry and who to call to get your questions answered in the fifty states.

The National Rifle Association also publishes a guide on the interstate transportation of firearms which is available from http://www.nraila.org/gun-laws/articles/2010/guide-to-the-interstate-transportation.aspx

Traveling outside the United States

When traveling outside of the United States by air, you need to be aware of the laws of your destination. Just because you may be able to get a firearm on board an airplane while in the United States, how are you going to deal with it when you arrive in another country? Is any license or permit necessary for you to possess a firearm in another country and if so, can you get one or do you have one? Have you considered if you will be allowed to return to the United States with a firearm aboard a foreign airline? What about stops and layovers during the trip? Can you travel with your favorite hollow point ammunition or are there any ammunition restrictions? Are certain types of firearms restricted or prohibited? Do you have the needed paperwork to prove you possessed the firearm and ammunition in the United States before you left home.

If traveling by land, Mexico for example is easy, the country severely restricts the importation of firearms and ammunition. Leave your firearms and ammunition at home. An exception is possible if you are bringing a firearm into Mexico for hunting purposes accompanied by a Mexican hunting guide, but you should contact your Mexican outfitter for help and information on import requirements.

Canada forbids US citizens from entering the country with handguns. Canadian Customs will permit a visitor to Canada to declare and check in guns at the border, and then retrieve them when returning to the United States. The guns should be unloaded, in a locked case, and the ammunition should be stored separately.

Canadian law prohibits the possession of hollowpoint ammunition, and if that is what you have brought with you it is important check in your ammunition as well.

The Canadian Customs station will hold the guns for up to forty days. Upon leaving Canada, you just stop at the same Customs station and produce your photo ID and the receipt. They will give the guns back to you.

You should then keep the guns cased and unloaded while proceeding down the road to US Customs. Importation of firearms or ammunition into the United States requires a permit from the Bureau of Alcohol, Tobacco, Firearms and Explosives unless the traveler can demonstrate that the firearms or ammunition were previously possessed in the United States. One way to do this is by completing Customs and Border Protection (CBP) Form 4457 with your local CBP office before leaving the United States. A bill of sale or receipt showing transfer of the items to the traveler in the United States may also be used.

In the United States you have constitutional protections both against unreasonable searches and seizures and against compelled self-incrimination. Although the authorities may search anywhere within your reach without a search warrant after a valid stop, they may not open and search closed luggage without probable cause to believe evidence of a crime will be found, particularly when it is in a locked storage area or trunk of a vehicle, unless you consent. You have a right not to consent. Furthermore, although you may be required to identify yourself and produce a driver's license, vehicle registration, and proof of automobile insurance, you have a right to remain silent.

Know the local laws of your destination.

The most important rule is to be sure, in advance, that you can lawfully possess the firearm at your destination. Specifically, know whether the specific firearm, magazines and ammunition may be lawfully possessed. State legislatures have been known to change firearms possession laws at the whim and fancy of whatever the current political reason de jour happens to be. Check early and often for any changes in the law at your destination.

And remember: a gun never solves problems.

CHAPTER 10
The Mechanics of Everyday Carry

If you have already decided not to carry a gun, you can just skip this chapter.

Much of this chapter will be devoted to what you may think of as common sense. But for some reason when it comes to guns, common sense is not an innate sense, it must be learned and then put into practice.

For example, you likely insure possessions that if stolen, lost or destroyed would be too expensive for you to repurchase in cash. Or you may buy insurance for occurrences that you cause, such as an auto accident that could be too costly for you to just write a check for the damages. So, armed citizens need to plan how to pay the legal and other possible costs of having a defensive gun use.

Pointing a gun at someone is a crime. So is shooting someone. Proving to a prosecuting attorney, a judge or a jury that you were legally justified in pointing a gun at or shooting someone is not something you should tackle without the help of a good criminal defense attorney. You need an attorney to help you extract yourself from this legal entanglement and they are expensive and no attorney will begin working for you until they know how you will pay for their services and any other costs necessary such as expert witnesses, to build your defense. Legal fees and other defense costs can easily amount to several hundred thousand dollars.

What if your DGU did not go perfectly? The rest of your life is at stake.

The best made plan always changes after the first shot. How much money will you need if one or more of your shots happen to miss your intended target and you shoot the wrong person? Now it is just a question how many comma's and zeros will follow the first number after the dollar sign. A professional firearms instructor who is interested in your personal and financial safety will be sure to help you understand how to finance a defensive gun use including your defense costs before you take a loaded gun out in public.

This chapter is also about the social graces of going armed responsibly in public. Besides the physical aspects of holsters, and where to put a gun on your body and such, armed citizens need to consider how we can blend in to a mainly unarmed society as well. This is much different than just thinking about what might be "legal" to do. Armed citizens have an unwritten agreement to behave in a socially acceptable manner. What is considered socially acceptable or not while armed is viewed from the eye of the public. We need to be aware of the conflict between what is legal behavior and ill-advised behavior as perceive by others. There will be times when you are totally legal in what you may wish to do, such as openly carry around downtown Minneapolis, but common sense should suggest to you that doing so will cause a commotion, maybe scare the women and horses and leave a bad impression of all armed citizens on others. Although open carry is legal in Minnesota, that does not make it a smart thing to do in all places. The legislature can always change the law when there is enough disruptive behavior brought to their attention.

This chapter is also about the considerations of carrying a firearm. Two fundamental rules apply no matter how or where you decide to carry a gun. First, you must always maintain control over your gun. When you leave home with a gun, it must return home with you at the end of the day. Second, you must never carry a gun without it being in a holster.

Attitude

It is not cool to carry a gun. The reason people choose to carry a gun is to maintain their constant state of peace. They are not cops or vigilantes.

A gun on their hip does not provide a force field around anyone that keeps harm from finding them any more than carrying a spare tire in the trunk will prevent having a flat tire. No one thinks it is cool to carry a spare tire and for the same reasons it is not cool to carry a gun either. Just like a spare tire, a gun can be helpful to keep us traveling down life's journey should we ever need to use it.

Your attitude about carrying a firearm needs to reflect the legal and social responsibilities of being an armed citizen.

Headline Maker

If you ever have a defensive gun use, you will become instantly infamous. You should know this about your gun, it is an instant headline maker. That is not necessarily a good thing because the media will seek out everyone who is related to you, ever dated you (and you know how kind an x-significant other may be to you), and all your co-workers to learn everything they can about you. Although you are truly the victim, because the media considers a gun bad, and you obviously have a gun then you, by default, will be treated by the media as the bad guy, not the victim. Your case will be tried in the court of public opinion because the court of public opinion cares little about the facts. Do not participate in interviews, internet chat forums or respond to internet articles. You need to instruct others who know you and may be tempted by momentary fame, not to talk or write either. Even an innocent comment your mother makes about a fight you once had as a kid, could be misconstrued against you. Your interest is to adjudicate your case in the only court that matters, a court of law.

When should I carry?

It is up to each person when their handgun should leave home with them. If asked "when should you have a home fire extinguisher nearby?" the answer might be all the time, just in case a fire is caused by an electrical short or for some other reason. Fires rarely give an advance notice so it is smart to keep it handy instead of out in the garage underneath the kids bikes and sports gear. If attacked and your handgun is not handy because you left it at home in the safe, it will not be of any use to you. For the same reasons, being prepared means being prepared all the time because random acts of violence are random.

Everyone has to make their own decisions about when to carry. This is why we say being prepared is being prepared all the time.

Do not touch the gun

There is a tendency of someone who is new to carrying a gun, to be constantly checking and touching the firearm or holster through the covering garment to make sure the gun is still there. We call this "pistol petting." Do not do that because it is annoying and looks really stupid.

Avoid unintentional display

Some states have a "concealed carry" law but Minnesota is not one of them. In those states with a concealed carry law, citizens are forced to carry their firearm concealed or risk arrest if the gun becomes visible, even if you did not intend to expose your firearm.

Minnesota has a "permit to carry" law. The word "concealed" is not in the law anywhere which was deliberate. In Minnesota, should any part of your concealed firearm become visible to anyone else for any reason or for any length of time, you have not broken the law.

Printing is also a term that applies to firearms, but it means something completely different than the printing term you are most familiar. The "printing" of a firearm happens when your cover garment is tightly stretched over your firearm and the outline or "print" of the firearm becomes visible through your clothes. Although this is not illegal in Minnesota, it does tend to defeat the purpose of keeping others from knowing that you are armed.

Sometimes it may be necessary to adjust or move the firearm from one place on your body to another. Please be discrete in doing so. If this is something that you know will be a frequent occurrence in your life, practice transferring your gun from your primary carry location to your alternate carry location at home until you become proficient in making the transfer. Remember, clear your firearm before you practice transferring it around on your body.

A gun in a hip holster may unintentionally be exposed if you sweep your jacket back as you normally would do to retrieve your wallet. This can be resolved with just one minor adjustment. Never carry your wallet and your gun on the same side of your body. When you reach for your wallet, your hand is nowhere near your gun. This practice of separation will be helpful for you during a routine police encounter as well.

When wearing a jacket during cool weather, it is a good idea to fasten the bottom of the jacket so a breeze or a gust of wind will not catch your jacket and accidentally expose a firearm.

Most unintentional displays of a firearm can be avoided with a little planning and practice.

Carry methods

Just as there are many different types of people who live a wide variety of lifestyles, there are many different methods used to carry their guns.

There is one carry method we strongly advise against, off body carry. Off body carry is any form of carry where your gun is not under your immediate control, such as leaving it in your vehicle, in a purse, or the pocket of a coat you hung up in a restaurant.

There are several good basic carry methods which include: hip holster, shoulder holster, pocket holster, and deep cover.

Each of these methods of carry have advantages and disadvantages, and we will review each one in turn. Because of both the physical and social differences between men and women, the subject of carry for women has some special considerations, and those will be covered as well.

A handgun must always be carried in a holster for your safety. All holsters must cover the trigger guard completely, and support the gun in the same position.

Hip holsters

One of the more popular carry methods because it combines both security and quick access is the hip holster, which holds the gun on the outside of the hip by a belt. Hip holsters are typically worn on the "strongside" hip (the right hip for right-handers; the left hip for lefties), at or behind the hip joint. Another benefit of a hip holster is a gun may be easily carried openly or covered by some form of garment to carry it concealed. While most hip holsters allow a shirt to be worn over them you need to take notice if your garment prints the outline of the gun or if there is a noticeable bulge.

As long as you are wearing a covering garment that can be quickly brushed aside, this keeps the gun reasonably available and well-concealed. On the other hand, a gun in a hip holster that is under two sweaters and a zipped-up parka during winter will not be quickly accessible. The changing climate is something you need to think about and perhaps make some seasonal adjustments.

There are all sorts of hip holsters. Some feature retaining devices such as "thumb break" snaps, to help to keep the gun in the holster.

Holsters vary dramatically both in configuration and quality. We recommend buying the best holster you can afford. Buy a well-made holster designed for the gun it is carrying that also fits you correctly. A good holster is also a good investment and will last for many years if properly cared for.

Hip holsters also come in high-tech plastics. Plastic is less expensive and needs less care than leather and are also called Kydex holsters after the type of plastic used in their manufacture.

To work well a hip holster must be accompanied by a good belt. The belt should be ridged and wide enough to fill the belt slots of the holster.

Inside the waistband

Another popular type of hip holster is the "inside the waistband," or IWB, holster. Instead of riding on the outside of the belt, this holster is slipped inside the waistband of the pants and is secured to the belt, which presses the holster and handgun into place.

The covering garment does not need to extend past the bottom of the holster, because everything is concealed inside the trousers. Nothing but a strap is visible on the belt line, and somebody seeing the strap will not understand what it is. The importance of the stiffness of the belt is diminished, since the belt is used to compress the holster up against the body rather than supporting the entire weight of the gun. And if it becomes necessary to remove the primary cover garment, you can pull your shirt or blouse out and over the holster, providing decent concealment.

As always, there are trade-offs. Unless you already have pants that fit loosely around the waist, you will be required to buy new slacks with an additional inch or two in the waistband.

When selecting an IWB holster, buy one that provides the most comfortable contour to your body and holds the firearm with equal amounts of the gun above and below the belt. Although inside the waist band is a great way to carry a gun finding a comfortable IWB holster will require trying more than just one or two.

Some IWB holsters are soft-sided, and the mouth of the holster will collapse when the gun is removed, making holstering a complicated, two-hand operation that might require undoing the belt. This is not a problem for someone who keeps their gun in their holster all day, but presents ongoing difficulties for people who have to take the gun out to store it before going into a prohibited place.

Shoulder holsters

Shoulder holsters have some advantages, but they do require a covering garment, which must also cover the straps across your back and shoulders as well. If you want to take off your jacket or vest but do not want to expose your holster and firearm, you will need to remove your shoulder holster and gun and store it all in a lockable briefcase or bag.

There are two basic types of shoulder holsters worn by armed citizens as shown below, a horizontal shoulder holster which points the gun at everyone behind you;

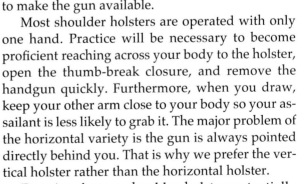

And a vertical shoulder holster which points the gun toward the ground.

Men tend to have arms that are shorter relative to their shoulder width so it is difficult for men to reach under the armpit and retrieve the gun.

Shoulder holsters can be uncomfortable. If the straps are narrow, they tend to cut into the shoulders. Shoulder rigs with wider straps are more difficult to conceal, and more expensive.

On the positive side, by carrying the handgun on one side and spare magazines or speedloaders on the other side, shoulder holsters balance well and keep the handgun reasonably available while seated or driving. A jacket or coat does not have to be completely unzipped or unbuttoned to make the gun available.

Most shoulder holsters are operated with only one hand. Practice will be necessary to become proficient reaching across your body to the holster, open the thumb-break closure, and remove the handgun quickly. Furthermore, when you draw, keep your other arm close to your body so your assailant is less likely to grab it. The major problem of the horizontal variety is the gun is always pointed directly behind you. That is why we prefer the vertical holster rather than the horizontal holster.

Drawing from a shoulder holster potentially means sweeping a large area where other people are located before the gun can be trained on the attacker. You need to be aware of who and what is in the area from 270°-90° in front of you where the muzzle of the gun will likely sweep before it will be leveled at the target. Everything and everyone is an unintended target as the firearm moves towards the assailant.

There is a valid purpose for using shoulder holsters but our recommendation is that if you have suitable alternatives, shoulder holsters should be thought of as special-occasion holsters and not be used for day-to-day carry.

Pocket holsters

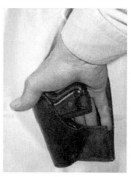

Pocket holsters are a terrific choice for many people, and they have a distinct advantage over other forms of carry that it enables you, in a stressful situation, to get your handgun in your hand without committing yourself to drawing it or displaying it at all. Pocket holsters also have the advantage of being able to move from the pants pocket, to a coat pocket, or to the pocket of a parka. However there are limitations to pocket holsters. A larger framed gun will not carry well in a pocket. And tight trousers make it very obvious there is a gun in your pocket. Tight trousers also makes it difficult to reach into the pocket and get a good grip on the handgun and remove it.

The price of a good pocket holster tends to be lower than for other types of holsters. The cost can be as little as $10 or $15 and increase from there. For guns that are going to be carried in a coat or jacket pocket more often, the purchase of a more rigid pocket holster is a good investment. These are going to be more expensive but they are still very affordable when compared with belt holsters.

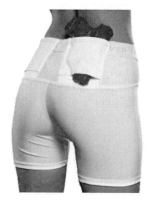

Deep cover

There are a variety of "deep cover" carry options and we want you to know about them. Like a shoulder holster, these should be considered a special occasion carry method.

One type of holster in this category is what's called the "belly band." This is a broad elastic bandage with an attached holster, and it is worn underneath a shirt. It does conceal very well, but it is necessary to either unbutton the shirt or yank it up in order to get at the gun.

Perhaps the strangest "deep cover" carry method is the under-the-pants pouch, sold by the brand names of Thunderwear™ or Thunderbelt™. The gun is carried in a breathable plastic or denim pouch on the front of the waist just over or slightly to the side of the crotch, with the butt either under the belt or the belt resting on the butt of the gun.

The real problem with Thunderwear™ and similar holsters is safety. Either holstering or retrieving the gun requires pointing it at your crotch, and that violates the safety principle of "never point a gun at anything you are not willing to destroy."

Almost everybody who uses one of these devices finds the whole process somewhat nerve-wracking. We want to caution you that such holsters should only be used after much practice with an unloaded firearm.

Carrying for women

Women have special issues when it comes to carrying self defense handguns for cultural, physiological and physical reasons. Rather than attempt to discuss this as though we knew first hand all about a woman's needs, we will demonstrate through pictures, some of the creative ways a woman could carry.

A woman should choose her own carry gun not only because she needs it to fit her hand, but because of the style of carry she may want to use.

As a historical matter, most belt holsters were designed for men. Because of generally different shapes in the hip area, and where the waist of women's slacks or skirts are relative to men's, a handgun carried in a typical belt holster will leave the muzzle pushed out by the swell of a woman's hip. This also tilts the gun so that the butt digs into a woman's side and can be uncomfortable.

For police service holsters for women this problem has been solved by adding spacers, which hold the top of the holster further out from the hip. That is a fine solution for uniformed women police officers but does not help women who want to carry concealed. The butt of the pistol sticks out significantly, and that is the sort of bulge that will be noticed under any covering garment. For women carrying openly spacers will work fine. For women while wearing jeans or slacks and a jacket or vest, a belt and holster combination is every bit as practical as it is for men.

We still need to address the question about how to carry a concealed handgun when wearing a dress or a skirt and blouse. In both cases, the typical belts are usually rather thin, and a covering garment of some sort

Behind the back   Compact belt hip   Inside the waist band

is usually worn. Similarly, for those women who wear suited skirts and similar attire, the matter of the where to put a holster can be handled by proper selection. In this case wearing a holster on a belt may not be the best option.

Shoulder holsters or a concealment shirt with a holster built under the arm are a practical solution when worn under a covering garment. Women's arms are longer in relation to the width of their shoulders, so it is usually easy for a woman to reach across the chest and grip a pistol in a shoulder holster.

Some limitations apply because these types of holsters must be covered by some garment. Women who wear sufficiently loose blouses or shirts, could wear a holster under their blouse or shirt.

Womens underwear can also multi-task for those who carry a handgun. If you are wearing underwear anyway, why not make more use of it?

For those times when it is just easier to put one somewhere else on your body we can offer several good choices to consider.

One place many women consider to carry a handgun is in a purse or the equivalent, and some manufacturers do make purses with concealed pockets specifically for handguns. We recommend against this type of carry for many good reasons. Even the most situationally alert people occasion-

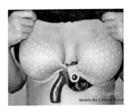

ally lapse in attention for just a moment, and if your purse is snatched, you will also lose control over your handgun to a criminal. If you are attacked, it is much more difficult and time consuming to locate and use a handgun if it is stored away in a purse. During the day at work, it will be necessary to lock the entire purse in a desk drawer, leaving it available to anybody who has the key to the desk and inaccessible to you should you need your handgun quickly. Any time a purse is resting on a counter, a shopping cart, or anywhere it is away from you, you have violated the

contract with society to maintain immediate control over your handgun.

We strongly recommend on body carry for women. As the photos illustrate, there are many different options available to work with most any wardrobe.

Miscellaneous carry methods

Some miscellaneous carry methods have been around for a while. An ankle holster is one which does have some advantages, particularly as a method to carry a back-up handgun. Some believe the main problem with ankle hol-sters is that they put the gun as far away from the hand as it can be and still be on the body. While that is true while standing, if your at-tacker knocked you to the ground and you were in a fetal position to protect yourself, having another gun on your ankle may very well be the best place for you to access a gun.

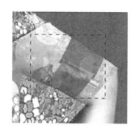

Also in the miscellaneous carry category are the various "fanny packs" specifically designed for guns. There is usually a concealed compartment, closed either by a zipper or Velcro fastenings, which keeps the gun separate from other things being carried. The gun is reasonably accessible, and the fanny pack is also useful for things like keys, wallets, change and cell phones. All of the major holster manufacturers make some form of these holsters.

Carry without a holster

Do not carry a handgun without it being in any holster at all. The holsters primary job is to protect the trigger against being pressed resulting in a discharge. A holster is used for the safety of everyone, particularly the owner of the handgun who owns all bullets from the time they leave the guns barrel until they stop moving.

The bathroom

One problem that those who carry a handgun in public will have to deal with at some time is using a public rest room. We are not going to get involved with the familiar here, but the unfamiliar.

In the case of single-user rest rooms with a lock on the door, there is no problem. You simply remove the handgun from the holster, perhaps place it on a counter top or an edge of the sink, and use the facility. When you have finished, you readjust your clothing and replace the handgun in the holster. The only possible pitfall is your forgetting the handgun in the bathroom, do not do that.

If you find yourself in a public bathroom without that level of privacy, you need to become more aware of those who may also be using the facility around you. We suggest that you always use a stall to provide the maximum amount of privacy for you. Do not allow the handgun to be placed on the floor and risk the person in the next stall seeing it even if it is still in a holster. Part of carrying a handgun is not to scare those around you with an unexpected viewing. The clunk of a handgun hitting the floor, if still in the holster or after having fallen out, will draw unwanted attention.

Obviously, this is not such a problem for those using shoulder holsters. For those who carry via a belly band or Thunderwear™, the solution is easy: the belly band or Thunderwear™ can simply be left in place, and the clothing adjusted before leaving the stall. Similarly, for pocket carry, it is just a matter of making sure, when lowering the trousers that the holster or handgun does not show.

With belt holsters, the problem needs more planning. You should never hang the holster or the handgun itself on the hook of the stall. For one thing, this removes the handgun from your immediate control, if only by a few feet. Thieves have been known to reach over the top of restroom stalls and steal purses and other bags, and it is hard to imagine any good coming out of one stealing a handgun under that sort of circumstance.

A little planning will help. It is possible to bring a briefcase or other bag into the restroom stall, keep it between your feet while using the facility, and put the handgun in that, with the trousers or slacks arranged to conceal the holster.

Or you could arrange your lowered trousers or slacks to cover the handgun, while it remains in a belt holster, and this is something that takes only a little practice. If necessary, the pistol can be removed from the holster and placed in a pants pocket, the cradle of your trousers or kept in your lap while using the toilet. Do not play with your handgun as you finish your primary objective. A porcelain toilet does not deserve to die and the muzzle blast at a few inches from your thigh leaves some very tender areas of your body very burned. You will also make the 6pm and 10pm news.

The bottom line on carrying and using the bathroom is: develop a procedure, based upon your style of carry, that allows you to safely control the firearm, keep it from view, prevent its' theft, or from being left behind. Use your procedure consistently to prevent accidents (with the firearm) and to avoid accidentally leaving the handgun in the restroom.

Storing when carrying

There are times when it may be necessary to store a gun while away from home: you may need to go to a Post Office, enter a public school or attend a school sponsored event, perhaps you may not be able to carry at work, decide to go out for a few beers with a friend, or any of a myriad of other things. When the gun must be securely stored it is important that you have planned in advance how you are prepared to do that.

We recommend securing the gun in a lockable metal container inside

your locked car. If you will be drinking alcohol, we also recommend that you unload the gun before locking it up.

The goal is not to take a handgun where it is prohibited or possession is not allowed and to prevent the gun from being stolen while it is not under your immediate control. Simply leaving it in a car is a bad idea. All cars can be broken into in just several seconds by experienced thieves, and the lock on a cars' glove compartment is typically plastic and easy to break open. A lockable metal box that can be hidden under the seat and attached with a strong cable is much better than relying upon the cars storage areas.

The trunk was once a good place for storage, but today most cars come with a trunk-opening latch or button in the passenger compartment so the trunk of the car is no longer secure. A gun stored in the trunk must also be in a locked container.

You can get a specially made gun box to bolt into your car. These are not expensive when compared to the value of maintaining your ownership of your handgun. They can be installed in either the passenger compartment of the car or the trunk. Some of these lockboxes come with a push button lock combining reasonable security with reasonably quick access.

When traveling, stay at hotels with in-room safes or bring a gun safe. When you are carrying a handgun in public, maintaining control over it is your perpetual responsibility. It needs to be either on your person, or secured.

Carrying openly

Minnesota law is silent about how anyone may carry. This simply means that a permit holder is allowed to either carry openly or concealed. The decision of how to carry is left up to your good judgement and common sense.

Number and type of guns carried

Minnesota law does not limit the number of handguns a permit holder can carry at the same time, or at different times. It is perfectly lawful to carry a dozen guns at once. This is where the common sense we began discussing at the very beginning of this chapter should be exercised. Carrying a handgun is not only a huge responsibility, it physically can be a pain so at most, you may want to carry a primary firearm and one for a backup.

Handguns vs. long guns

In terms of carrying a gun, Minnesota laws do distinguish between handguns and long guns. The "Carry Law" (*Minn. Stat. § 624.714*) deals with pistols.

Minn. Stat. § 624.7181 makes it illegal for most people to carry a rifle, shotgun, or BB gun in public, however, it also expressly excludes permit holders: a permit holder can carry a rifle or shotgun anywhere that he or she can carry a pistol or revolver. The sole exception is a permit to carry does not authorize the transporting of a loaded, unloaded or uncased long gun in the passenger compartment of a motor vehicle. Long guns must always be transported unloaded and encased.

Carrying your shotgun over your shoulder to go shopping is legal but please do not do it. The police would, no doubt, find some legal reason to stop you that you could have easily avoided. In practice permit holders understand their responsibilities to the public and exercise common sense. We do not carry rifles or shotguns around in public for "personal defense".

Loaded guns and children

Minn. Stat. § 609.666 subd. 2 makes it a crime for someone who "negligently stores or leaves a loaded firearm in a location where the person knows, or reasonably should know, that a child is likely to gain access, unless reasonable action is taken to secure the firearm against access by the child."

While there is no specific law on the storage of unloaded firearms, any negligent storage may leave a gun owner subject to other criminal penalties, such as child endangerment, or to civil charges if somebody misuses one of the guns.

What is "reasonable action"? We do not know for sure. The people who wrote the law intended for it mean either securing all firearms, or teaching gun safety to children who are old enough but there are no appellate cases where the question has been decided if safety instruction is enough.

Minnesota law is no more stringent than the requirements of good gun safety principals and people who resolutely follow sound safety practices will not find themselves at risk.

And remember: a gun never solves problems.

CHAPTER 11
Gun Safety, On and Off the Range

Safety is a vital component of LTI's training and this book's orientation. The safety rules are simple, practical, and in some cases elegant. Following the safety rules can save you from having a very bad experience with your handgun. When you practice these rules regularly they will become second nature to you, and greatly lessen the chance of making what could be a very regrettable mistake. Armed citizens especially need to make a firm commitment to obey all the rules, all the time. If you make following the rules a habit all of the time, the odds that you will ever unintentionally hurt someone with your handgun is close to zero.

Our attention is typically focused on handguns however there is a simple fact that applies to all firearms: after a bullet leaves the barrel, there is no way to call it back. You own the bullet from the time it leaves the muzzle until it stops moving. Your best defense against causing legal harm to yourself or unintentional harm of any kind to others is to make sure no bullet is ever fired from your gun unless you intend for it to happen. You always need to control the muzzle of your gun so that even if a bullet is fired unintentionally, it will be in a direction that will cause the least amount of harm or damage possible.

The safety rules are designed to support these objectives. No one should get hurt and nothing should get destroyed so long as you make a habit of living the four basic safety rules.

Basic safety rules

The four basic safety rules are straightforward but may look different than the firearms safety rules you have learned before. Armed citizens have to look at safety in a different order than hunters or sport shooters who clear and store their firearms when they are finished with them, because our guns are always loaded. We must assume all guns are loaded when we pick it up so we must learn when touching any firearm, it must always be pointed in a safe direction. We practice the rules in the order in which they become necessary to perform.

1. Always keep your finger outside the trigger guard until you are ready to shoot

People seem to have more trouble with this rule than any other because of the ergonomics of handguns. The very function of a handgun requires they be designed for the trigger finger to naturally want to land on the trigger. This is why you must train and make a habit of keeping your finger outside of the trigger guard until you have a target acquired and are ready to shoot.

It is extremely important to keep your trigger finger pointed straight forward and parallel with the barrel. It is important that you keep your finger off the trigger, even when the gun is pointed at a target, until you are actually ready to shoot.

This rule has benefits beyond safety in a defensive shooting situation. Keeping your finger along the frame allows the finger to act as an aiming aid. Your eyes are on target. Your finger is naturally pointing where your eyes are focused. With your finger resting parallel with the barrel of the handgun, the gun will shoot where your finger is pointed and where you are looking. By pointing your trigger finger at the target, you improve your accuracy. Your hand-eye coordination replaces using your sights for aiming.

A second additional benefit to keeping your finger outside of the trigger guard is that it gives you an opportunity to make the final shoot-no-shoot decision. Under the stress of an attack, once you put your finger on the trigger, it is highly likely you will fire the gun. Keeping your finger off the trigger until the last possible moment allows for a better decision to shoot or not.

2. Keep your firearm pointed in a safe direction

Whenever you are holding a handgun, make sure the muzzle never points at anything you are not willing to destroy. Even when holstering a handgun, do it without pointing the muzzle toward any part of your own or anyone else's body.

Muzzle control has to be done consciously at first. Imagine that you are holding an unloaded handgun with it pointed in a safe direction when somebody walks in front of it. You must take the responsibility to make sure it does not point at that person. The moment you perceive the muzzle may be pointed near the person walking, you need to move the muzzle to a new safe direction. This must be actively practiced until it becomes second nature. Muzzle awareness can become so habitual that you will automatically know to reposition a muzzle even when distracted by a conversation.

So what is a safe direction? There are two ways to discern a safe direction. First, an unsafe direction is one in which you would not intend the firearm to be fired (discharged). You recognize something or someone in the possible path of the bullet that you do not want to destroy or injure. Second, a safe direction is any direction that should the firearm discharge at that moment, the least possible amount of damage would occur. A safe direction can be a matter of degree. Unless the firearm is aimed downrange at a shooting range, rarely is there a 100% safe direction. So a determination must be made as to the safest direction available at that moment.

3. Every firearm is loaded until proven unloaded

Negligent discharges are a failure to do what a prudent individual would have otherwise done. The handgun went bang when you did not expect it to go bang. The main cause of a negligent discharge is someone assumed that the handgun was unloaded and failed to do a clearing procedure. If you make it a habit to perform a clearing procedure every time you handle a handgun, even when you are certain that you unloaded and cleared it already you will not have a negligent discharge. It is impossible for a firearm that was proven to be unloaded to be shot. Otherwise, one or more safety rules would need to be broken.

It is a negligent discharge whether or not someone was injured or something got damaged. The degree of damaged caused is a function of how many other safety rules were broken.

Accidental discharges are a mechanical failure of the firearm or ammunition and not a failure of the operator to follow the safety rules. Accidental discharges are very rare.

Since LTI's primary focus is self defense training, we know that all self defense handguns are always treated as though they were loaded. Therefore, we alter this rule to say that *Every gun is loaded until you prove it is unloaded.* To do this, you perform a clearing procedure (more on that in a moment).

4. Always know your target and what is beyond it

From a defensive gun use standpoint, there is no reason to ever draw your handgun without a clear understanding of your target. It is impossible to satisfy the law regarding any justification to use lethal force without a clearly identified threat and therefore an identified target. Even with an identified target that does not mean you can start shooting. You must satisfy the tactical issues, one of which is to know what is beyond your target. The shoot-no shoot decision requires you to consider, if you can, will a bullet shot at the target go through or if you miss your target entirely, injure an innocent bystander?

In the real world when it comes down to saving your life what is beyond your target is not going to matter. You have to shoot. Add to this the fear and stress of having to defend yourself and, all of a sudden, how well you have psychologically prepared yourself, how well you have trained with your handgun, and how competent and poised you have become will make owning the results of shooting someone more survivable.

Rules for handling guns

You cannot practice the basic safety rules without handling a firearm, so the next topic we will explore are the rules for handling firearms.

New gun owners need to learn what experienced gun owners have made a habit. Every time a handgun is picked up a clearing procedure must be performed by opening the action and checking the firearm. The well trained gun owner is not being forgetful or nervous, they are just practicing good handgun safety. Even if you have just handed an unloaded gun to your best friend, he should perform a clearing procedure verifying that the handgun is unloaded. The moment the gun is handed back to you, you must open the action and verify it is unloaded. Although this appears redundant developing the habit of performing a clearing procedure every time you touch a handgun is fundamental to safely living with firearms. Your proving whether a handgun is loaded or not trumps all the other safety rules in preventing a negligent discharge.

Revolver clearing procedure

For revolvers, release the cylinder and swing it out at which point the revolver cannot be fired even if the chambers are loaded. Look into each chamber of the cylinder and if the chambers contain a casing, use the ejector rod to remove the casing. It can be easy to determine whether the chambered case is a live round or a spent case by looking to see if  the primer has been struck or not. A dimple in the primer from the firing pin does not guarantee the round is spent but it is more likely it is spent than one without any dimples. Although simple, opening the cylinder and emptying the chambers is a two-step clearing procedure and gravity can assist you. Be sure to consult the owner's manual for instruction on the operation of your revolver.

Semiautomatic clearing procedure

Semiautomatics are more complicated because they can have rounds in the magazine, in the chamber, or both. It is important to follow all the steps, in this order, every time:

1. First, remove the magazine, and set it aside.
2. Second, rack the slide three times. Pull the slide all the way back and let it go. Do not worry about doing it gingerly; the gun can handle it. If a round is ejected after the first racking, check to see if you failed to do step one. If so, remove the magazine and rack the pistol three more times.
3. Third, pull the slide all the way back, and if so equipped, lock the slide in the open position. Inspect the chamber to be sure it is empty.
4. Fourth, close the slide and make the action inert by pointing the pistol in a safe direction and pull the trigger with chamber empty.

This is the same semiautomatic clearing procedure taught to air marshals, federal flight deck officers (armed pilots), and other federal law-enforcement officers. It works for them. Make it work for you, too.

Be sure to consult the owner's manual for instruction on the operation of your semiautomatic.

Handing a handgun to another person

Before you hand a firearm to someone else, always verify that the gun is unloaded and the action is open.

A revolver with an empty cylinder swung out, or a semiautomatic with the slide locked back and the magazine removed, can be handled safely because it cannot be fired at that moment. The base of the grip should be pointed at the person receiving the handgun with the barrel pointed in the safest possible direction.

When handing a firearm to somebody else, always do it just like this. In addition to being the safest way to hand off a firearm, it also shows consideration and respect for the recipient.

If somebody wants to hand you a firearm: Ask them to unload it and open the action first. There are very few situations when this rule and the rule above may not apply.

Do not leave firearms unattended, loaded or not

The reasons for this are obvious. Firearms that are not under your immediate control should be secured. If they are not being kept for self-protection, they should be unloaded as well. Many states, Minnesota included have laws against leaving a handgun assessable to minors. You have an obligation to society to always maintain control over your firearm.

Think before you act—take your time

If you are at the range, and your handgun has failed to fire when you have pressed the trigger, there is no reason at all to rush to take the next shot. Keep the handgun pointed down range and wait at least fifteen seconds before attempting to clear the misfire. If you are concerned or unsure about what to do next, call the range officer or a knowledgeable friend. Safety trumps everything else at the range.

Safety when shooting

A firearm has never on its own, done something stupid. Negligent discharges are caused by poor decision making by a human, a failure to follow one or more of the basic safety rules. Beyond gun handling are issues around actually shooting. Most shooting of course, should and will take place on the range.

Wear hearing protection

Loud sharp sounds can severely damage your hearing. Be sure to have your hearing protection in place before you step out on the range. Hearing protection can consist of specially made earplugs or headsets that clamp over the ears. When shooting for an extended period of time, perhaps with several other shooters or when shooting larger caliber firearms, wearing both types of hearing protecting is advisable.

There are also very effective electronic sound-canceling headsets that use high-tech computer circuitry to cancel out loud sounds while letting ordinary sounds like conversation through. These headsets offer the best of both worlds so you may be able to converse with another shooter and still protect your hearing.

Wear eye protection

Lead particles or flying hot brass can be bad for your eyes. For those who do not wear glasses normally, eye protectors are necessary. For those who do, eye protectors that fit over glasses add protection and are strongly recommended.

Be sure you know where your bullet will go

The range is the place to find out if your firearm shoots where you point it. Before selecting a particular handgun for carry, be sure it points well for you. For example, if a particular revolver shoots to the right of where you point it, you want to find that out at the shooting range and not in the street.

Formal ranges have massive backstops behind the target area. At indoor ranges note that the ceiling above the target is often marred by bullets that did not go where they were supposed to go. This indicates sloppy shooting and likely to irritate the range owner. Outdoors, it can be much worse. A round that is fired above the backstop can go a long distance while most well-designed outdoor ranges have a large enough "dead area" behind the backstop, that is often not the case with informal ranges. Be sure that you know where your bullet is going to go, not only if you hit the target, but if you miss it.

Do not shoot when impaired

An afternoon at the range, followed by dinner and a few drinks with friends is a fine thing. It is the order that is important. Reverse the order, drink before shooting and you are asking for trouble. Guns and alcohol just do not mix, and that includes when cleaning guns as well as shooting them.

The same warning obviously applies to any prescription or nonprescription drugs that affect your judgment or perception. Mixing firearms and recreational drugs is not only illegal, it is stupid. Any medication with the warning "do not operate heavy equipment" anywhere on the bottle should be a clue that you should stay away from your firearms while using that medication. If in any doubt, do not go shooting until you have consulted a physician or pharmacist.

When done shooting

The first task when your are finished shooting is to --- perform a clearing procedure and secure the firearm and the ammunition. Do this before leaving the shooting point. Uncased firearms behind the shooting point are almost always pointed in an unsafe direction.

Wash your hands

The chemical components that make up modern propellants are not toxic, but they are not intended for human consumption either. The lead in bullets is very definitely toxic. After shooting, be sure to wash your hands thoroughly before doing anything else.

Cleaning guns

For whatever reason, negligent discharges and cleaning a gun just seem to go together. In every case one or more the four basic safety rules were violated (most likely a failure to perform clearing procedure).

When it is time to clean your firearm, be sure to consult the owner's manual for instruction on how to disassemble your handgun and review the manufacturer's recommendations for cleaning.

Do not ignore safety rules when cleaning a firearm, make sure it is unloaded and remove any ammunition from the immediate area.

Cleaning a firearm is a great time to introduce children to your handgun. They can look at components normally hidden, better understand how each part makes the handgun work and ask you questions. If you are lucky, they will help you clean the handgun.

Storage at home

Firearms that are not being kept for self defense should be unloaded and secured, with the ammunition stored separately. For those owning a lot of firearms, make it easy on yourself by owning a gun safe. Buy the biggest safe you have room for because as soon as it is home and installed it will be too small. For those with only a few guns (at least for now), buy good individual gun cases (preferably lockable) and store them in a locked closet.

When it comes to self defense weapons, storage options are less obvious and require some careful thought. Self defense firearms need to be stored loaded. Your specific household circumstances will determine your options. Accounting for kids in your life is the foremost concern. If you do not have kids to worry about, leaving your handgun on the nightstand becomes an option. A self defense handgun is a "working gun" when it is in its holster and being carried. A stored self defense handgun is a working handgun that is "off-the clock". So, the trick is to store your handgun so it can be easily retrieved and get "back on the clock" as quickly as possible if needed. If a handgun is needed, it is needed now.

There is a Texas saying, "I live by the eight foot rule. I'm never more than eight feet from a loaded gun". Storing several firearms throughout your home is a good way to go. Making them accessible for you and not for others again requires the proper storage equipment. Quick access handgun safes, bed rail mounted shotgun racks, under the bathroom sink lockboxes, under the towel rack and behind the towel, handgun storage wall clocks, hollow books, lockbox inside of the lazy boy or behind a suitable curtain are all storage ideas that work. Firearms can be discretely stored for quick access and with the safety of children in mind.

As a matter of safe gun handling, every time you remove the handgun from the box always verify to yourself whether or not it is loaded. Yes, you will treat it as loaded regardless, but you do need to know its condition, do not rely on your memory and never assume you know the condition of a gun.

Gun safety and children

For those with children, the most important part of gun safety is education. Teaching your children the gun safety rules for children is essential.

The NRA "Eddie Eagle" program recommends teaching children to do the following if they see a firearm:

STOP!
DO NOT touch.
LEAVE the area.
TELL an adult.

We recommend the NRA "Eddie Eagle" program very strongly. With hundreds of millions of firearms in tens of millions of households in the US, it is important for all children to know what to do if they see a firearm: Stop! Do not touch. Leave the area. Tell an adult. This training will be useful not only in your own home, but can save a life should your children visit the home of someone who pays less attention to safety than you do.

Teaching children about the proper handling of firearms under an adult's supervision is certainly a good idea. Take your children to the range and teach them range rules. Having kids observe adults shooting provides the opportunity to point out good behavior and occasionally less than good behavior. Children experiencing the sound of shooting and watching the recoil will impress upon them the power of firearms. Finally, letting them shoot an appropriate caliber firearm for their age, size, and experience will properly begin a positive and respectful lifelong relationship with firearms.

And remember, a gun never solves problems.

CHAPTER 12
Shooting, on the Range and on the Street

When you take your permit to carry course from an LTI instructor, shooting should be a relatively small but a very important part of your training. The reason is simple, what is important about the responsibilities of a permit holder are the day-to-day things like staying out of trouble, avoiding conflict, and so forth. We hope most permit holders will never have to take out their handgun "for real" and that is just fine.

But if you are going to carry a self defense handgun, you must know how to shoot it on the street as well as the range. While we are going to discuss some of the details of that here, you really do need some one-on-one instruction if you are not already very familiar with handguns. Even then, more instruction is a good idea.

There is a very big difference between shooting at a willing target hanging in front of you at the range (the focus of much other training) and a self defense shooting on the street, which is the concern of LTI permit to carry training.

Target shooting vs. self defense shooting

Target shooting is, among other things, fun. At a range, you stand behind a shooting bench in a well-lighted area shooting at a target that is anywhere from 5 to 25 yards down range. You take your time settling into whatever position you like, take a breath and let half of it out, focus carefully on the sights and gently press the trigger until the gun fires. If you have done it right, there is a nice round hole in the paper target, or perhaps you have knocked over a tin can, or vaporized a stale cookie into a cloud of rapidly expanding crumbs. You are under no serious stress of a life or death situation, and your brain has not gone into survival mode. The lighting is good and there are no unexpected or unforeseen obstacles to think about. You know what is behind your target and shooting someone by mistake is nearly impossible.

The point is that when target shooting you can manage everything as you want it. It is pretty much stress free shooting and the target is not shooting back at you.

A self defense shooting is going to be different in almost every respect. Most self defense shootings take place within a distance between victim and attacker of no more than ten feet and under low-light conditions. The bad guy will be moving and other people may unexpectedly get between you or behind your target. Your brain will go into survival mode and rational thinking will be difficult. You will resort to doing what you have trained to do. At ten feet or less shooting the attacker center of mass will not require sights. Self defense shootings happen very quickly, often within ten seconds or less. Do not be surprised if your best made plans always change after the first shot. If you have a lot of time to think about it, you have probably got enough time to escape.

The stress of a life-threatening situation causes physiological changes that have serious implications. It is not possible to duplicate the actual stress of a life-threatening event on the shooting range.

What is possible to do is teach self defense shooting, as opposed to target shooting. We start with how you stand, moving to how you hold your firearm and finally, to how you aim (point) your firearm, and we emphasize point when shooting in self defense.

Studies of actual DGU's have shown that under the stress of a life threatening situation police and armed citizens use what is known as an Isosceles stance combined with point shooting.

The Natural Isosceles

The Isosceles is instinctive. You face the target squarely. You may

find yourself taking at least a half step backwards. This is a natural reaction to a threat. In fact, moving backwards, or any other direction, will make you a more difficult target for your attacker. Moving backwards indicates your desire to get away and any witnesses will more likely recognize you as the victim.

The handgun is thrust out using both arms equally, either at chest or eye level, as though using the gun to push the threat away.

A violent confrontation is physiologically different than shooting on the range. A massive adrenaline dump and the sudden stress of close personal violence makes it almost impossible for most people to use the sights or focus on anything other than the threat.

If your attacker is also moving taking an accurate shot becomes even more difficult. You will have control over stopping momentarily when you shoot, but your attacker is not going to be that cooperative.

Leveraging the body's natural response to a threat makes your response easier. So integrating this natural response with your training at the range makes your response to the threat more fluid, faster, and automatic. Do not mistake this as an excuse not to train. We are just being smarter about it

Colonel Rex Applegate, who spent much of WWII training OSS agents, argued over many years that, "most shooters, no matter how well trained in other stances instinctively revert to the Isosceles when faced with life threatening situations".

Videos of police shootings bear this out. Police are, by and large, *not* trained to step back, and they are trained to use their sights. Nevertheless, in video after video, you can see that the officers are stepping back and focusing on the attacker instead of their sights.

This is why we emphasize that your carry handgun must *point* well for you. *Point shooting is aimed shooting.* You are just using your body, hand eye coordination, and stance to aim at the target rather than the sights of your gun.

The late Julio Santiago of Burnsville, Minnesota, a veteran of the US Army and twenty-five years as a Deputy Sheriff, was one of the first trainers to note this. He spent much of his life teaching the importance of

point shooting, particularly in low-light situations where the sights are not be useful.

Most self defense shootings take place at very close distances where point shooting works. Take a look around your home. Unless your house has very large rooms, it is difficult to envision a situation where you could be more than twenty or so feet away from an attacker.

This is why self defense firearms training takes place at very close distances. Many LTI trainers do all their shooting training and qualifications between fifteen and twenty-one feet which, in terms of real-life self defense distances, is fairly long.

You should regularly plan range time, at least once a month. Shooting skills are depreciable skills so regular practice is important. Using good formal or informal instruction is a good idea. Practice using the isosceles stance.

To assume an isosceles stance, grip the handgun with your strong hand (finger off the trigger) and support it with your weak hand. Bring it up to chest level and thrust it straight out toward the target, as though trying to push it away with the muzzle of the firearm. Look at the target and not your sights. You should be square with the target, your feet at shoulder width or a little more.

If the pistol fits your hand correctly when you shoot, a hole will appear near the middle of the target - the center of mass of an attacker. If you keep firing in this way, a number of holes will appear near the center of the target.

Although point shooting is natural and the Isosceles stance is what you will do in a DGU, there are two other legacy shooting styles you will see from time to time. These are not defensive shooting stances. They are what your father was taught.

The Weaver

In the Weaver stance, the body is turned slightly away from the target as the pistol is brought up to eye level so that the sights can be used in a two handed grip, with the strong arm flexed and the weak arm flexed more. The strong arm pushes out on the pistol, while the weak arm pulls back, creating an isometric clamp on the handgun that helps the shooter quickly return the pistol to the same position after each shot. It feels a little awkward at first, but with some practice it is possible to quickly fire multiple accurate shots at a target.

The Chapman

The Chapman stance, or Modified Weaver, is similar. The main difference is that the strong arm is kept as straight as possible, ideally with the elbow locked. In effect, the strong arm becomes a human rifle stock. Again, the strength of the upper body is used to bring the sights back on target, and the target is not faced quite directly.

With either the Weaver or the Chapman stance, the torso is at 60 to 90 degrees away from the target and head is usually turned slightly to the side to bring the dominant eye in line with the sights.

There is no question that mastering either of these stances requires a lot of time and effort. The problem is that many people (we think almost all) who have been thoroughly trained in either of these stances simply will not use it when under the stress of an attack.

What could go wrong?

Failure to train

If you have not trained sufficiently, when you are under the stress of an attack you will have nothing on which to resort. Confusion reigns and an effective response is unlikely. The consequences of not training increases the likelihood of making very serious mistakes. Mistakes that prevent you from articulating "why you did, what you did, the way you did it" which will land you in prison. Commit to regular practice and practice correctly leveraging your natural response to a threat and the shooting skills taught by your instructor.

Have the wrong gun

What if you have a handgun that does not fit your hand? Either you bought the wrong gun or someone gave you the wrong gun. Sell it and buy a firearm that fits you correctly. Point shooting requires a handgun that fits your hand. There will not be time for "grip or trigger finger adjustment" in the middle of an attack.

Flinching

If you flinch your shots, they will be wildly off target. Stop anticipating the recoil. Focus on the trigger press.

Too many shots

Most people will instinctively take up a stance similar to the Natural Isosceles stance, with the handgun thrust out at chest level, and that is how you should practice. Fire two center of mass shots and a third to the hip area and assess. If there is no change of behavior (the attack continues), fire a second set of three rounds to stop the threat.

When you are under stress you will resort to your training. Remember, rational thought is difficult if you train to fire three rounds and evaluate this is what you will do on the street. You are shooting to stop the threat and only the minimum number of rounds necessary to stop the threat is considered reasonable force. Too few and the threat continues. Too many and its murder. The difference between going home and going to prison can be nothing more than how many times you pressed the trigger.

Practice often.

And remember: a gun never solves problems.

CHAPTER 13
Training

If you have decided to obtain a Minnesota permit to carry, you need training. Obtain training that is certified by the Minnesota Department of Public Safety which will include both classroom training and a shooting qualification. After you pass the course, you will be presented with a certificate of training making you eligible to apply for a Minnesota permit.

Where to get training

Under the MPPA a sheriff can accept any training they wish, but all sheriffs must accept LTI training. LTI's curriculum has also been accredited by a number of states and/or their respective Law Enforcement organizations.

What training includes

LTI believes that training to carry lethal force for personal protection requires much more than knowing the skills and drills of firearms. Our job is to provide the instruction necessary for you to survive an attack physically, morally legally, and financially. Frankly other training will not do all of this for you.

We would like you to consider this as the beginning of your training, not the end. Armed citizens need to be aware of changes in the law in Minnesota as well as many other states.

Proposed changes to state or federal laws may be desirable for us, and then again may be an erosion of our rights. As more armed citizens decide to add their voices together, we become one of the largest lobbying forces in every state, clearly outnumbering other groups by tens of thousands of people. So training includes learning how to think as fully actualized citizens who now exercise all ten of their protected rights, not just nine out of ten.

CZ and Blue say sheepdogs must continually train.

And remember: a gun never solves problems.

Chapter 14
Out-of-State Permits

Out-of-state licenses *for* Minnesota Residents

Getting additional out-of-state licenses may allow you to carry in states that do not yet recognize your Minnesota state permit.

Many other states have agreements regarding recognition (one state automatically honors another's licenses) or reciprocity (each state must recognize the other for the licenses to be valid in the other state) allowing citizens with home state licenses to carry in states with such agreements. On a rare occasion, a state may terminate recognition of another states license. Consult www.handgunlaw.us or the Attorney General's office of the state of interest.

Several states will allow you to apply for a non-resident license or permit by mail. The four best options are Florida, Pennsylvania, New Hampshire, and Utah. To remain timely, we again want to refer you to www.handgunlaw.us for application details for non-resident permits.

And remember: a gun never solves problems.

Chapter 15
What to Do After You Have Your Permit

First of all practice situational awareness and conflict avoidance to *stay out of trouble*. Look at it this way: most if not all people who get their permits to carry have already lived their entire lives without needing to point a gun at another human being, and it is best to keep it that way.

We sincerely hope you have learned from the experience of others after reading the chapters about the use of lethal force and what happens after using a handgun. The consequences are serious and real even if you just have to point a gun at someone without pressing the trigger. As happens, politicians who oppose your rights to be safe may try to make political points from your defensive gun use even if what you did was perfect. Should your name ever become a verb, your life is pretty much ruined.

The permit to carry simple allows you to carry a concealed weapon in public. It certainly does not make you bulletproof, attack-proof, arrest-proof, or lawsuit-proof or a junior G-man. And of all the many things it is not, the foremost among them is it is not a reason to go looking for trouble.

Spend time at the range with your carry handgun

A handgun is a tool which your body and mind must both become trained to become proficient to operate when you are under a great amount of stress. Repetition can be your friend if your training is more than draining bullets from one magazine after another. As with most tools, the more you use it, the more poised and competent you become with it, and the more likely that, even under stress, you will use it properly. Particularly at first, you should plan on making regular trips to the range and practicing point-shooting at close targets. Practice with silhouette targets to shoot center of mass as if you were in a real DGU, take three shots and quickly evaluate. In a real DGU, you are looking for a change in behavior from the bad guy. Did the attack stop? If so, you must immediately stop shooting.

Clean your carry handgun

Handguns are machines, and machines need regular care and maintenance. People adopt different policies about how often and how thoroughly to clean their handguns. Some take the position that the handgun should be clean enough to "eat off of" and perform a full, detailed disassembly and cleaning of their guns after every shooting session. That is not wrong, although it might be excessive. We suggest that you read the owner's manual and follow the instructions provided there. If you bought a used firearm from a friend, you can search and find most owner's manuals on line to download.

After cleaning a handgun, we recommend to dry fire it to be sure it functions properly. Snap caps can be used to help prevent damage to the firearm.

We recommend swabbing the barrel, wiping the breach area with a lightly oiled cloth patch between full breakdown cleanings. Remember, do not over oil.

Keep up with changes in the law

There is the legislature. As Judge Gideon J. Tucker said in 1866, "No man's life, liberty, or property is safe while the legislature is in session." There are elements of the law that may someday be addressed by the legislature. Other states have had to do this. There is also the temptation of the gun control proponents to repeal the law entirely, seriously erode the law or to add massive new restrictions to your rights. Enacting the

MPPA is only another step to protecting the gains that have been made. As the political winds shift, it is very important that every permit holder keep a watchful eye on the legislature and when necessary, actively petition your elected officials for what legislation you favor or legislation oppose. It is also very important to financially support legislators who support you. This is a two way street.

Prepare to renew your permit

Since your permit is valid for five years, it is easy to forget when it is time to renew it. Renewing your permit is basically the same procedure as applying for your permit was initially, but it will cost you a little less. You will need to take a refresher course before you can submit your application.

Contact your LTI instructor for more information about the renewal process when you are within one year of your permits expiration date. You can visit www.LTI.us to locate instructors.

And, for one last time, remember:
a gun never solves problems.

GLOSSARY

ABODE

Minnesota Administrative Rules 8001.0300 RESIDENT AND DOMICILE DEFINED; CONSIDERATIONS.

Subpart. 6. Definition of abode.

An abode is a dwelling place permanently maintained by a person, whether or not owned and whether or not occupied by the person. It does not need to be permanent in the sense that the person does not intend to abandon it at some future time. However, a cabin or cottage not suitable for year round use and used only for vacations is not an abode. Additionally, quarters which contain sleeping arrangements but do not contain facilities for cooking or bathing will not generally be considered an abode.

A person who moves a domicile outside Minnesota is not considered to be maintaining an abode in Minnesota even though the person continues to own or rent a dwelling in Minnesota if the person has moved personal furnishings and belongings from the dwelling and is making a good faith effort to sell, lease, or sublease the dwelling. Also See DOMICILE, RESIDENT

ACP

An abbreviation for "Automatic Colt Pistol" which is used to denote certain ammunition such as 25 ACP, 32 ACP, 380 ACP, and 45 ACP.

ACCIDENTAL DISCHARGE

Not human error. This type of accident is caused by a mechanical failure of the firearm allowing it to fire when the shooter does not intend to fire. See also Negligent Discharge

158

ACTION

A term used to describe what happens to the hammer when the trigger is pressed. A single action firearm must first be manually cocked and the trigger simply releases the trigger to fire. A double action means when the trigger is pressed, the hammer is both cocked and then released.

AFFIRMATIVE DEFENSE

An admission or "affirmation" that the act was indeed committed, but that the actor was justified or privileged in doing what would otherwise be criminal, because they acted in self defense.

To successfully convict the actor of the crime, the prosecution must prove to the court beyond a reasonable doubt that the actor truly did not act in self defense. This sets the standard to convict the actor, at the highest level.

AIRGUN

A gun that used a spring, compressed air or other gas to propel a projectile.

AMMUNITION

Except for muzzle loading firearms, typically this will be a cartridge for pistols and rifles and shells for shotguns consisting of a case holding a primer, a charge (guncotton), and a projectile (a bullet, slug or buckshot).

ANTIQUE FIREARM

Minn. Stat. § 624.712 subd. 3.

"Antique firearm" means any firearm, including any pistol, with a matchlock, flintlock, percussion cap, or similar type of ignition system, manufactured before 1899 and any replica of any firearm described herein if such replica is not designed or redesigned, made or remade, or intended to fire conventional rimfire or conventional centerfire ammunition, or uses conventional rimfire or conventional centerfire ammunition which is not readily available in the ordinary channels of commercial trade.

Minnesota Guide for Armed Citizens

ASSAULT

Minn. Stat. § 609.02 subd. 10

"Assault" is:

(1) an act done with intent to cause fear in another of immediate bodily harm or death; or

(2) the intentional infliction of or attempt to inflict bodily harm upon another.

ASSAULT RIFLE

This is a name anti gun politicians and the media have attached to a semi automatic rifle to make it seem more lethal or dangerous than a rifle that looks more like their Grandpa's Winchester deer rifle. The military version is the assault rifle and it is a select fire rifle (semi auto and full auto) of intermediate power. The semi automatic varieties are not full auto but since they are cosmetically similar they are mistakenly called assault rifles.

Minn. Stat. §. 624.712 DEFINITIONS.
 subd. 1.Scope.
 As used in sections 624.711 to 624.717, the terms defined in this section shall have the meanings given them.
 Subd. 7.Semiautomatic military-style assault weapon.
 "Semiautomatic military-style assault weapon" means:
 (1) any of the following firearms:
 (i) Avtomat Kalashnikov (AK-47) semiautomatic rifle type;
 (ii) Beretta AR-70 and BM-59 semiautomatic rifle types;
 (iii) Colt AR-15 semiautomatic rifle type;
 (iv) Daewoo Max-1 and Max-2 semiautomatic rifle types;
 (v) Famas MAS semiautomatic rifle type;
 (vi) Fabrique Nationale FN-LAR and FN-FNC semiautomatic rifle types;
 (vii) Galil semiautomatic rifle type;
 (viii) Heckler & Koch HK-91, HK-93, and HK-94 semiautomatic rifle types;
 (ix) Ingram MAC-10 and MAC-11 semiautomatic pistol and carbine types;

(x) Intratec TEC-9 semiautomatic pistol type;
(xi) Sigarms SIG 550SP and SIG 551SP semiautomatic rifle types;
(xii) SKS with detachable magazine semiautomatic rifle type;
(xiii) Steyr AUG semiautomatic rifle type;
(xiv) Street Sweeper and Striker-12 revolving-cylinder shotgun types;
(xv) USAS-12 semiautomatic shotgun type;
(xvi) Uzi semiautomatic pistol and carbine types; or
(xvii) Valmet M76 and M78 semiautomatic rifle types;

(2) any firearm that is another model made by the same manufacturer as one of the firearms listed in clause (1), and has the same action design as one of the listed firearms, and is a redesigned, renamed, or renumbered version of one of the firearms listed in clause (1), or has a slight modification or enhancement, including but not limited to a folding or retractable stock; adjustable sight; case deflector for left-handed shooters; shorter barrel; wooden, plastic, or metal stock; larger clip size; different caliber; or a bayonet mount; and

(3) any firearm that has been manufactured or sold by another company under a licensing agreement with a manufacturer of one of the firearms listed in clause (1) entered into after the effective date of Laws 1993, chapter 326, to manufacture or sell firearms that are identical or nearly identical to those listed in clause (1), or described in clause (2), regardless of the company of production or country of origin.

The weapons listed in clause (1), except those listed in items (iii), (ix), (x), (xiv), and (xv), are the weapons the importation of which was barred by the Bureau of Alcohol, Tobacco, and Firearms of the United States Department of the Treasury in July 1989.

Except as otherwise specifically provided in paragraph (d), a firearm is not a "semiautomatic military-style assault weapon" if it is generally recognized as particularly suitable for or readily adaptable to sporting purposes under United States Code, title 18, section 925, paragraph (d) (3), or any regulations adopted pursuant to that law.

AUTOMATIC FIRE (full auto)

A firearm that can repeat the firing cycle of multiple cartridges with one press of the trigger.

BACKGROUND CHECK

This means the background search the Sheriffs' Department conducts to determine a person's eligibility for a permit to carry . The Sheriff will also run an annual background check on permit holders.

BALLISTICS

This is the science of studying moving projectiles and attention can be either focused on what happens inside a firearm, what happens after a bullet leaves the firearm or both.

BALL

This can mean a round ball projectile used in a muzzle loading firearm, or more commonly, to describe bullets that have a solid round or pointed nose.

BILLY CLUB

Either a collapsible or solid club made from wood, metal or plastic that can be used to strike another person.

BLOWBACK ACTION

What is common to all blowback systems is that the cartridge case must move under the direct action of the powder pressure, therefore any gun in which the bolt is not rigidly locked and permitted to move while there remains powder pressure in the chamber will undergo a degree of blowback.

The cycle begins when the cartridge is fired. Expanding gases from the fired round send the projectile down the barrel and at the same time applies force to the case against the breech face of the bolt, overcoming the inertia of the bolt, resulting in a "blow back" effect. The breech is kept sealed by the cartridge case until the bullet has left the barrel and gas pressure has dropped to a safe level; the inertia of the bolt mass ensures this (mass of the bolt + recoil spring, in some cases the hammer force too). As the bolt travels back, the spent cartridge case is extracted and then ejected, and the firing mechanism is cocked. The action spring then propels the bolt forward again, which strips a round from the feed system along the way.

This system is only suitable for firearms using relatively low pressure cartridges. Pure blowback operation is typically found on semi-automatic, small-caliber pistols and rifles. The most famous examples are the German 9mm P 08 Lugar used during the first and second world wars and the 45 ACP Thompson sub machine gun which was first sold with a 20 round stick magazine for $200 at a time when a new Ford sold for $400.

BOLT

The bolt carries a new cartridge into the chamber

BORE

The inside of a firearms barrel.

BRASS

Typically used to describe a used cartridge case, no matter what material it is actually made.

BREECH

The place where a bullet is inserted into a gun near the rear of the barrel. It is also called a chamber. The breech is not a part of the barrel.

BULLET

This is the projectile that comes out of the firearm.

CALIBER

The diameter of either a projectile or the bore of a firearm.

Firearms are measured from the top of the land to the top of the land diagonally across the bore. Often the name given a firearm is more typical of the ammunition it accepts than the actual measurement of the bore. For example, a 44 magnum barrel is actually .429 inch. A .357 magnum is measured from the top of the lands not the grooves so it is actually the same size bore as a .38 caliber which is measured from the groves. The .357 magnum is different because it has a longer case and more propellant, making it a more powerful cartridge. This is why a .357 magnum handgun can also shoot the shorter .38 special cartridge, but a .38 special handgun can not shoot the longer .357 magnum cartridge.

The caliber or diameter can be measured in several ways, for example; hundreds of an inch - .38, for a 38 caliber, - thousands of an inch .380, ACP, - or millimeters 9mm, typically a 9mm Lugar, 9mm Parabellum, 9mm NATO or 9x19mm. These three bullets are the same diameter but they are not interchangeable because their cases are all different.

CARBINE

Generally, this is a rifle that is chambered to shoot handgun or lower power rifle ammunition. Millions of Winchester Model 94 rifles were originally manufactured in .30-30, .32-55 Winchester, .38-55 Winchester, and .32 Winchester Special. More recently, the Model 94 rifle was chambered in revolver calibers such as the .38 Special, .357 Magnum, .44 Special, .44 magnum, .45 Long Colt, .38-40 Winchester and .44-40 Winchester.

CARRY

Means to go armed with. It may also mean you are carrying drugs, depending upon to whom you are talking.

CARTRIDGE

One complete round of ammunition.

CASE

For handguns and rifles, this is the metal part of the cartridge that holds the primer, propellant and bullet.

CCW

An abbreviation that can mean concealed carry weapon or to carry concealed weapon. It is also used to denote a permit or license to carry, even in states like Minnesota where there is not a "concealed" carry law.

CENTER FIRE

This describes a type of cartridge or shotgun shell, with the primer positioned in the center of the base.

CHAIN FIRE

This when a black powder revolver unintentionally fires several cylinders due to flashover to the other cylinders, from the cylinder intended to be fired. This causes the gun to fire more than one cylinder at a time and is very dangerous. Putting a small amount of lube on the front of the cylinder and using a prelubed wad can reduce the possibility of igniting adjacent cylinders. Another major cause of chain fire can be from using the wrong size caps or a worn gun which allows the caps to strike the frame from the recoil. The cap should fit snuggly on the nipple and not be loose.

CHAMBER

In a semi-automatic this is the opposite end of the barrel from the muzzle and is where the cartridge is located before firing. This term may also be used to describe the action of loading the firearm – to chamber a cartridge.

CHRONOGRAPH

A device used to measure the velocity of bullets fired from a gun. They function by detecting the shadow of a bullet as it passes over two sensors at a fixed distance apart. It then measures the time it took the bullet to cross over both sensors and from that information, calculates the velocity of the bullet.

CLIP

This is not the magazine that supplies ammunition to a firearm! This is a straight or round device that holds a number of cartridges together at the base. The ammunition may be stripped or pushed off the clip into a magazine to load it quickly. A round device may be used to hold revolver cartridges for quick loading into the cylinder.

COCK

To set the hammer or striker into a position so the gun is ready to fire in single action. On semi-automatic handguns, as the slide is moved back it also cocks the hammer or internal striker. Revolvers with an enclosed hammer cannot be manually cocked.

COMPENSATOR

This is also known as a muzzle brake whose purpose is to reduce the effects of recoil on the shooter. The compensator redirects the escaping gases in an opposite direction that the gun or barrel may otherwise be inclined to go.

COP-KILLER BULLET

A term used by the media to scare the women and horses. Conversely, there are no bullets that are non-cop-killer. Bullets do not exercise discretion over their targets.

CYLINDER

Sometimes referred to as the wheel of a revolver, this is the part of the firearm that holds the ammunition supply and turns as each cartridge is fired to supply another round.

CYLINDER GAP

This is the distance between the cylinder and the barrel of a revolver. It should not be greater that the thickness of a piece of writing paper. The gap between the cylinder and the frame near the firing pin should not be greater than the thickness of a business card.

CYLINDER STOP

This is a little metal device that is extended typically up from the frame in a revolver to lock the cylinder in place so the ammunition is properly aligned in the cylinder with both the firing pin to the rear and the barrel to the front of the gun.

DANGEROUS WEAPON

Minn. Stat. § 609.02

"Dangerous weapon" means any firearm, whether loaded or unloaded, or any device designed as a weapon and capable of producing death or great bodily harm, any combustible or flammable liquid or other device or instrumentality that, in the manner it is used or intended to be used, is calculated or likely to produce death or great bodily harm, or any fire that is used to produce death or great bodily harm.

As used in this subdivision, "flammable liquid" means any liquid having a flash point below 100 degrees Fahrenheit and having a vapor pressure not exceeding 40 pounds per square inch (absolute) at 100 degrees Fahrenheit but does not include intoxicating liquor as defined in section 340A.101. As used in this subdivision, "combustible liquid" is a liquid having a flash point at or above 100 degrees Fahrenheit.

DAO

This is an acronym for double action only firearms. When the trigger is pressed, the trigger first cocks the hammer, and when the trigger is pressed further, releases the hammer to strike the firing pin to discharge the cartridge. It is not possible to manually cock the hammer on this type of firearm.

DESTRUCTIVE DEVICE

This has the meaning given in 18 USC 921 (a) (4).

DGU

An acronym for a defensive gun use. If the four elements are all present, the odds of your surviving physically, emotionally, legally and financially improve greatly.

DISCONNECTOR

This is the mechanism in a semi-automatic firearm that prevents the firing of more than one cartridge with one press of the trigger.

DOMICILE

Minnesota Administrative Rules 8001.0300 RESIDENT AND DOMICILE DEFINED; CONSIDERATIONS.

Subpart. 2. Domicile; definition and presumptions.

The term "domicile" means the bodily presence of an individual person in a place coupled with an intent to make such a place one's home. The domicile of any person is that place in which that person's habitation is fixed, without any present intentions of removal therefrom, and to which, whenever absent, that person intends to return.

A person who leaves home to go into another jurisdiction for temporary purposes only is not considered to have lost that person's domicile. But if a person moves to another jurisdiction with the intention of remaining there permanently or for an indefinite time as a home, that person has lost that person's domicile in this state. The presumption is that a person who leaves this state to accept a job assignment in a foreign nation has not lost that person's domicile in this state.

Except for a person covered by the provisions of the Soldiers' and Sailors' Civil Relief Act of 1940, United States Code, title 50 appendix, section 574, the presumption is that the place where a person's family is domiciled is that person's domicile. The domicile of a spouse is the same as the other spouse unless there is affirmative evidence to the contrary or unless the husband and wife are legally separated or the marriage has been dissolved. When a person has made a home at any place with the intention of remaining there and the person's family neither lives there nor intends to do so, then that person has established a domicile separate from that person's family.

The domicile of a single person is that person's usual home. In a case of a minor child who is not emancipated, the domicile of the child's parents is the domicile of the child. The domicile of the parent who has legal custody of the child is the domicile of the child. A person who is a permanent resident alien in the United States may have a domicile in this state. The domicile of a member of the armed forces will be governed by the facts just prior to becoming a member of the armed forces unless the person takes the necessary steps to establish a new domicile.

The mere intention to acquire a new domicile, without the fact of physical removal, does not change the status of the taxpayer, nor does the fact of physical removal, without the intention to remain, change the person's status. The presumption is that one's domicile is the place where one lives. An individual can have only one domicile at any particular time. A domicile once shown to exist is presumed to continue until the contrary is shown. An absence of intention to abandon a domicile is equivalent to an intention to retain the existing one. No positive rule can be adopted with respect to the evidence necessary to prove an intention to change a domicile but such intention may be proved by acts and declarations, and of the two forms of evidence, acts must be given more weight than declarations. A person who is temporarily employed within this state does not acquire a domicile in this state if during that period the person is domiciled outside of this state. ALSO SEE ABODE, RESIDENT

DOMINANT EYE

This is the stronger or dominant one of your two eyes and in about 15% of people, is the opposite eye from their dominant hand (or shooting hand).

You can easily determine your dominant eye by pointing one finger at another person's nose. Ask them which of your eyes your finger is below and this is your dominant eye.

DRY FIRE

This is firing an unloaded gun to verify that the action works properly. It is advisable to first chamber a snap cap or dummy round to reduce the possibility of damage to the firearm.

EARS

The generic name we use to describe all forms of hearing protection.

EJECTOR

Just as a bouncer ejects some patrons when it is time to leave the bar, this little device ejects the spent case from a semi automatic's chamber to make it ready to place a fresh round in the chamber.

ELECTRONIC CONTROL DEVICE

An electronic control device or electric weapon means any device which is designed, redesigned, used or intended to be used, offensively or defensively, to immobilize or incapacitate persons by the use of electric current. It may also be used to temporarily subdue a person to create an opportunity to escape from him or her. It is unlikely this device will stop an attack by itself because that is not what it is designed to do.

ENCASED

This means enclosed in a case that is expressly made for the purpose of containing a firearm and that is completely zipped, snapped, buckled, tied or otherwise fastened with no part of the firearm exposed.

EXTRACTOR

This is a little hook that grabs the spent case and pulls it out of the chamber so the ejector can send it flying down the shirt of the person (usually a woman) standing beside you.

EYES

This is what eye protection is called and must be worn before entering the range.

FIREARM

A handgun, rifle, or shotgun that uses gunpowder or guncotton as a propellant.

FIREARM SILENCER

It is a felony to sell or possess any device designed to muffle or silence the discharge of a firearm. The maximum penalty for this offense is two years imprisonment and/or a $5,000 fine; however, if the offense is committed in or near a school, park, or public housing property, the maximum penalty is five years imprisonment and/or a $10,000 fine.   *Minn. Stat. § 609.66, subd. 1(a).*

FMJ

A lead bullet that is covered by a metal cover or coating. Same as full metal jacket.

FORMER LAW ENFORCEMENT OFFICER

Means a person who separated or retired in good standing from service as a law enforcement officer and who resides in Minnesota.

FOULING

These are carbon, lead or copper deposits that can accumulate in the barrel, chamber and other places within the gun after it has been fired. Proper cleaning will remove the fouling.

FPE

This is an acronym for Foot Pounds of Energy.

FPS

This is an acronym for Feet Per Second. It is the common measurement for the speed of a bullet.

FTF

This means a Failure to Fire. It can be the result of operator error, ammunition or a mechanical failure of the firearm.

FULL METAL JACKET

A metal jacket (usually copper) that completely covers a lead bullet. A metal jacket increases the speed of a bullet through a barrel over that of an unjacketed lead bullet of the same weight.

GAP

This is new ammunition introduced for some Glock pistols, the .45 caliber GAP cartridge is a shorter length than the more common .45 ACP cartridge.

GRAIN

This is a unit of weight equal to 1/437.5 of an ounce. There are 7,000 grains to the pound.

GRIP

This is the portion of the pistol or revolver that is held by either hand when shooting.

GRIP SAFETY

In some pistols, there is a strap running along the rear of the grip that must be depressed before the pistol will fire.

GROSS MISDEMEANOR

This is any crime that is not a felony or misdemeanor. The maximum fine which may be imposed is $3,000.

GUNPOWDER

Gunpowder is also known as black powder and is a mixture of sulphur, charcoal and potassium nitrate. Gunpowder was discovered in the 9th century by the Chinese who were searching for an elixir of immortality. This discovery led to the invention of fireworks and the earliest gunpowder weapons in China.

SMOKELESS POWDER

Smokeless powder refers to propellants used in firearms and artillery, which produce negligible smoke when fired. Older forms of gunpowder produced significant amounts of smoke.

There are several types of smokeless powder which include Cordite, Ballistite and, historically, Poudre B. Smokeless powders fall into one of three major classifications: single-base, double-base or triple-base powders.

Smokeless powder consists of nitrocellulose (single-base powders), are frequently combined with up to 50 percent nitroglycerin (double-base powders), and sometimes are combined with nitroglycerin and nitroguanidine (triple-base). The powder is formed into small spherical balls, extruded cylinders or flakes.

Double-base propellants commonly propel handgun and rifle ammunition. Triple-base propellants commonly propel artillery guns.

HALF COCKED

A position when the hammer is pulled back but before being fully cocked, that it is held in place and can not strike the firing pin.

HAMMER BLOCK

A hammer safety that keeps the hammer away from the firing pin unless the trigger is pulled.

HAMMER SPUR

The rear part of a hammer you use to cock the hammer with your thumb.

HAMMERLESS

The firearm really has a hammer, but it is enclosed within the frame.

HANGFIRE

This is an ammunition malfunction that results in either no bang or an extraordinary delay before the bang. If this happens to you, it is a good idea to keep the handgun pointed in a safe direction for 10 to 15 seconds until you know which version you have.

HARM

Minn. Stat. § 609.02 subd. 7

Bodily harm.
   "Bodily harm" means physical pain or injury, illness, or any impairment of physical condition.
Substantial bodily harm.
   "Substantial bodily harm" means bodily injury which involves a temporary but substantial disfigurement, or which causes a temporary but

substantial loss or impairment of the function of any bodily member or organ, or which causes a fracture of any bodily member.

Great bodily harm.

"Great bodily harm" means bodily injury which creates a high probability of death, or which causes serious permanent disfigurement, or which causes a permanent or protracted loss or impairment of the function of any bodily member or organ or other serious bodily harm.

HIGH CAPACITY MAGAZINE

During the Clinton gun ban era, any magazine that held more than 10 rounds was considered a high capacity magazine. This term has outlived its useful life, although gun grabbing politicians never seem to go away.

HOLLOW POINT

A bullet designed to expand to about twice its original diameter upon impact. This is a good self defense choice because it makes a bigger permanent cavity causing more trauma, and is less likely to over penetrate the bad guy and enter the wrong person.

IWB

This is a holster worn "inside the waistband" of pants or shorts for concealed carry.

JHP

This is a hollow point that has a metal jacket around the bullet.

LAW ENFORCEMENT AGENCY

(1) An agency that consists of one or more persons employed by the federal government, including any agency described under 18 USC 926C (e) (2);

(2) A state, or a political subdivision of a state;
(3) The U.S. armed forces; (4) or the National Guard that has as its purposes the prevention and detection of crime and the enforcement of laws or ordinances, and that is authorized to make arrests for crimes.

LAW ENFORCEMENT OFFICER

Means a person who is employed by a law enforcement agency for the purpose of engaging in, or supervising others engaging in, the prevention, detection, investigation, or prosecution of, or the incarceration of any person for, any violation of law and who has statutory powers of arrest.

LEO

Law Enforcement Officer or anyone with statutory arresting authority.

LEOSA

The acronym for the federal Law Enforcement Officers Safety Act enacted by Congress in 2004 and amended in 2010 and 2012, which created two general classes of law enforcement officers who could carry a concealed firearm in any state or political subdivision. The classes are "qualified law enforcement officers" and "retired or separated law enforcement officers". There are two types of laws not overridden by this Federal law. They are state laws which prohibit or restrict the possession of firearms on any State or local government property, installation, building, base, or park and Federal or State laws as respects the gun free school zones.

MACHINE GUN

Minn. Stat. § 609.67

It is a felony, with certain limited exceptions, to own, possess, or operate a machine gun which means any firearm designed to discharge, or capable of discharging automatically more than once by a single function of the trigger or machine gun conversion kit. The maximum penalty for this offense is five years imprisonment and/or a $10,000 fine.

MACHINE GUN CONVERSION KIT

Minn. Stat. § 609.67

"Machine gun conversion kit" means any part or combination of parts designed and intended for use in converting a weapon into a machine gun, and any combination of parts from which a machine gun can be assembled, but does not include a spare or replacement part for a machine gun that is possessed lawfully under *Minn. Stat. § 609.67, subd. 3.*

MAGAZINE

This is not a clip!

For pistols, this is a detachable holder for the ammunition supply. It may be a single stack which is slightly larger than the width of the ammunition, or a double stack which is wider because it loads the ammunition nearly side by side for greater ammunition capacity. These are placed in the firearm in a space inside the grip.

MAGAZINE SAFETY

Some pistols cannot be fired if the magazine has been removed. Maybe.

MAGNUM

Think super sized. More power, more kick, more damage, and may be more difficult to control. Fewer shots are needed if you hit your intended target however.

MENTAL STATE

(1) When criminal intent is an element of a crime in this chapter, such intent is indicated by the term "intentionally," the phrase "with intent to," the phrase "with intent that," or some form of the verbs "know" or "believe."

(2) "Know" requires only that the actor believes that the specified fact exists.

(3) "Intentionally" means that the actor either has a purpose to do the thing or cause the result specified or believes that the act performed by the actor, if successful, will cause that result. In addition, except as provided in clause (6), the actor must have knowledge of those facts which are necessary to make the actor's conduct criminal and which are set forth after the word "intentionally."

(4) "With intent to" or "with intent that" means that the actor either has a purpose to do the thing or cause the result specified or believes that the act, if successful, will cause that result.

(5) Criminal intent does not require proof of knowledge of the existence or constitutionality of the statute under which the actor is prosecuted or the scope or meaning of the terms used in that statute.

(6) Criminal intent does not require proof of knowledge of the age of a minor even though age is a material element in the crime in question.

MISDEMEANOR

A crime for which a sentence of not more than 90 days or a fine of not more than $1,000 or both may be imposed.

MOTOR VEHICLE

Has the meaning given in *Minn. Stat. § 168.002 subd.*18.

MUZZLE

The muzzle is the business end of the barrel from which the bullet exits.

MUZZLE BLAST

This is the concussion at the muzzle from the expansion of gasses after the bullet leaves the barrel. At very close range, with larger calibers or magnum loads, the muzzle blast can be as damaging as the bullet. This is the "close counts" factor.

MUZZLE FLASH

Rarely noticed when shooting outside during the daylight hours, this can be blinding to the shooter when shooting in the dark. It is a bright flash from the expulsion of burning propellant after the bullet exits the barrel.

MUZZLE VELOCITY

The maximum velocity of a bullet as it exits the muzzle. The bullet will immediately begin to slow down from there.

NEGLIGENT DISCHARGE

An unexpected discharge of a firearm due to your failure to follow one or more firearms safety rules, the most common of which is the failure to clear the firearm before handling it further. A firearm that is proven to be unloaded is impossible to "accidentally" fire.

NEGLIGENT STORAGE

Minn. Stat. § 609.666 NEGLIGENT STORAGE OF FIREARMS.
 Subd. 1. Definitions.
 For purposes of this section, the following words have the meanings given.
 (a) "Firearm" means a device designed to be used as a weapon, from which is expelled a projectile by the force of any explosion or force of combustion.
 (b) "Child" means a person under the age of 18 years.
 (c) "Loaded" means the firearm has ammunition in the chamber or magazine, if the magazine is in the firearm, unless the firearm is incapable of being fired by a child who is likely to gain access to the firearm.
 Subd. 2.Access to firearms.
 A person is guilty of a gross misdemeanor who negligently stores or leaves a loaded firearm in a location where the person knows, or reasonably should know, that a child is likely to gain access, unless reasonable action is taken to secure the firearm against access by the child.
 Subd. 3.Limitations.

Subd. 2 does not apply to a child's access to firearms that was obtained as a result of an unlawful entry.

History:

1993 c 326 art 1 s 18; 1996 c 408 art 4 s 11

OUT OF BATTERY

When the slide, bolt or cylinder is out of position and the firearm can not be fired.

OWB

A hip holster that is worn on the outside of the pants or shorts.

PARABELLUM

The ammunition designed to be used in the German Lugar P 08 pistol. It is now used to denote the 9 mm cartridge used in most 9mm pistols.

PETTY MISDEMEANOR

A petty offense which is prohibited by statute, which does not constitute a crime and for which a fine of no more than $300 may be imposed.

PHOTOGRAPHIC IDENTIFICATION CARD

This means one of the following, either a valid drivers license or other government issued photo identification such as a passport.

PISTOL

Minn. Stat. § 624.712 DEFINITIONS.

As used in sections 624.711 to 624.717, the terms defined in this section shall have the meanings given them.

Subd. 2.Pistol.

"Pistol" includes a weapon designed to be fired by the use of a single hand and with an overall length less than 26 inches, or having a barrel or barrels of a length less than 18 inches in the case of a shotgun or having a barrel of a length less than 16 inches in the case of a rifle (1) from which may be fired or ejected one or more solid projectiles by means of a cartridge or shell or by the action of an explosive or the igniting of flammable or explosive substances; or (2) for which the propelling force is a spring, elastic band, carbon dioxide, air or other gas, or vapor.

"Pistol" does not include a device firing or ejecting a shot measuring .18 of an inch, or less, in diameter and commonly known as a "BB gun," a scuba gun, a stud gun or nail gun used in the construction industry or children's pop guns or toys.

PRIMER

The point of contact on a bullet case where the firing pin or hammer strikes, that contains an ignition material used to set off the propellant.

PROJECTILE

This is what comes out of the barrel of any type of firearm.

RECEIVER

Also called the frame, it is the part of the firearm that holds everything (the grip, barrel, breech or chamber, slide, bolt) together.

RECOIL

For every action, there is an equal and opposite reaction. This is the force applied against the shooter from the ignited cartridge (in the case of a revolver it is also the "feel" of the maximum impact of a bullet on a target, at the muzzle).

RESIDENT

Minnesota Administrative Rules 8001.0300 RESIDENT AND DOMICILE DEFINED; CONSIDERATIONS.

Subpart 1. Resident. The term "resident" means:

A. any individual person who is domiciled in Minnesota, subject to the exception set forth in subpart 9; (Certain persons deemed nonresidents. A person domiciled in Minnesota is deemed a nonresident for the period of time that the person is a qualified individual under the Internal Revenue Code, section 911. For a person who has homesteaded the person's principal residence in Minnesota prior to leaving the country, this subpart applies only if the person notifies the county within three months of moving out of the country that homestead status should be revoked and does not file a Minnesota homestead application for any property in which the person has an interest during the period the person is a qualified individual.)

and

B. any individual person (other than an individual deemed a nonresident under the Soldiers' and Sailors' Relief Act of 1940, United States Code, title 50 appendix, section 574, or an individual eligible for reciprocity under *Minn. Stat. § 290.081*) who is not domiciled in Minnesota but who maintains a place of abode in Minnesota and spends in the aggregate more than one-half of the taxable year in Minnesota.

A person may be a resident of Minnesota for income tax purposes, and taxable as a resident, even though the person is not deemed a resident for other purposes. See Also ABODE, DOMICILE

REVOLVER

A pistol that uses a cylinder to hold the ammunition supply which rotates (or *revolves*) with each trigger press to position the next cartridge to be fired.

RIFLING

This is found inside of a barrel and consists of "lands" which are raised and twisted, and the groves between the lands. The effect is to put a spin (like a football) on the bullet as it moves down the barrel to improve accuracy.

RIMFIRE

The most common rimfire cartridge is the .22 caliber. The primer is coated within the entire rim so it does not matter where the firing pin strikes the rim.

SA

Short for single action, the trigger only releases the hammer. The trigger will not cock the hammer, you must do that manually.

SAFETY

Any mechanical device that will prevent a firearm from firing a cartridge. They sometimes fail so do not totally trust them.

SCHOOL ZONE

Property that is within 1,000 feet of the grounds of a school (property line), not from the school building itself. A persons private property that is not part of the school grounds and is located within the 1,000 foot school zone area is an exception to the school zone prohibition.

SEAR

The thing that holds either a hammer or striker cocked.

SEMI-AUTOMATIC

A firearm that requires a separate press of the trigger, to fire each and every round.

SHEEP

Generally, a good person who is incapable of violence. These people do not ever see the need for defensive weapons because they believe the police are there to protect them. To cope, sheep must live in a world of denial. To recognize reality would require them to examine and perhaps question their fundamental belief systems, and they will not allow that.

SHEEPDOG

This refers to people who are also good people, but are capable of violence if sufficiently provoked. Sheepdogs are not mean people or bullies, but they understand that random acts of violence could find them and are willing to use force stop a threat against their life if it becomes necessary.

SNUB NOSE

This is a handgun (usually a revolver) with a short barrel, usually two inches or less.

STANDARD OF PROOF

This is the standard of proof needed to convince a court that any given claim is true. The degree of proof necessary can depend upon the seriousness of the charge, the circumstances of the alleged crime, or the type of crime being charged. There are three standards typically applied in Minnesota.

1. Beyond a Reasonable Doubt is the highest standard and is most often used in criminal trials. It requires a not-guilty verdict if there is any reasonable doubt of the facts presented by the prosecution.
2. Clear and Convincing is the next highest level and is mid way between the lowest and highest levels of proof. This standard is typically used in civil trials.
3. Preponderance of the Evidence is the lowest standard of proof and is a greater than 50% threshold of guilt. It is the standard normally applied in civil trials and Grand Jury indictment proceedings.

SUBMACHINE GUN

This is a full auto firearm that typically uses pistol ammunition for close quarter shooting. The Auto Ordinance "Tommy Gun" is among the most famous submachine guns and uses .45 ACP ammunition (although it is available in a semiautomatic version which is also a lot of fun to shoot).

TRANSFER BAR

This is a safety feature found on some revolvers that rises into the firing position when the trigger is pulled. It is what actually hits or "transfers" the force of the hammer to the firing pin.

TRIGGER

When pressed, it either cocks and releases, or just releases the hammer (or striker). It may also disengage (or engage as with a transfer bar) a safety device.

TRIGGER GUARD

This is a metal guard that surrounds the trigger, usually by connecting the grip and frame, and is designed to protect the trigger from being moved backward.

WOLF

This is a person who has become an animal. They will kill other people just for the sport of it. They have no moral compass and are not concerned with the consequences of the judicial system. Wolves just need to be shot.

APPENDIX A

Selected Minnesota Statutes

609.06 AUTHORIZED USE OF FORCE.

Subdivision 1. When authorized. Except as otherwise provided in subdivision 2, reasonable force may be used upon or toward the person of another without the other's consent when the following circumstances exist or the actor reasonably believes them to exist:

(1) when used by a public officer or one assisting a public officer under the public officer's direction:

    (a)   in effecting a lawful arrest; or

    (b)   in the execution of legal process; or

    (c)   in enforcing an order of the court; or

186

(d)   in executing any other duty imposed upon the public officer by law; or

(2) when used by a person not a public officer in arresting another in the cases and in the manner provided by law and delivering the other to an officer competent to receive the other into custody; or

(3) when used by any person in resisting or aiding another to resist an offense against the person; or

(4) when used by any person in lawful possession of real or personal property, or by another assisting the person in lawful possession, in resisting a trespass upon or other unlawful interference with such property; or

(5) when used by any person to prevent the escape, or to retake following the escape, of a person lawfully held on a charge or conviction of a crime; or

(6) when used by a parent, guardian, teacher, or other lawful custodian of a child or pupil, in the exercise of lawful authority, to restrain or correct such child or pupil; or

(7) when used by a school employee or school bus driver, in the exercise of lawful authority, to restrain a child or pupil, or to prevent bodily harm or death to another; or

(8) when used by a common carrier in expelling a passenger who refuses to obey a lawful requirement for the conduct of passengers and reasonable care is exercised with regard to the passenger's personal safety; or

(9) when used to restrain a person who is mentally ill or mentally defective from self-injury or injury to another or when used by one with authority to do so to compel compliance with reasonable requirements for the person's control, conduct, or treatment; or

(10) when used by a public or private institution providing custody or treatment against one lawfully committed to it to compel compliance with reasonable requirements for the control, conduct, or treatment of the committed person.

Subd. 2. Deadly force used against peace officers. Deadly force may not be used against peace officers who have announced their presence and are performing official duties at a location where a person is committing a crime or an act that would be a crime if committed by an adult.

History: 1963 c 753 art 1 s 609.06; 1986 c 444; 1993 c 326 art 1 s 4; 1996 c 408 art 3 s 12; 2002 c 221 s 46

Minnesota Carry Law

624.714 CARRYING OF WEAPONS WITHOUT PERMIT; PENALTIES.

Subdivision 1.[Repealed, 2003 c 28 art 2 s 35; 2005 c 83 s 1]

Subd. 1a. **Permit required; penalty.** A person, other than a peace officer, as defined in section 626.84, subdivision 1, who carries, holds, or possesses a pistol in a motor vehicle, snowmobile, or boat, or on or about the person's clothes or the person, or otherwise in possession or control in a public place, as defined in section 624.7181, subdivision 1, paragraph (c), without first having obtained a permit to carry the pistol is guilty of a gross misdemeanor. A person who is convicted a second or subsequent time is guilty of a felony.

Subd. 1b. Display of permit; penalty.

(a) The holder of a permit to carry must have the permit card and a driver's license, state identification card, or other government-issued photo identification in immediate possession at all times when carrying a pistol and must display the permit card and identification document upon lawful demand by a peace officer, as defined in section 626.84, subdivision 1. A violation of this paragraph is a petty misdemeanor. The fine for a first offense must not exceed $25. Notwithstanding section 609.531, a firearm carried in violation of this paragraph is not subject to forfeiture.

(b) A citation issued for violating paragraph (a) must be dismissed if the person demonstrates, in court or in the office of the arresting officer, that the person was authorized to carry the pistol at the time of the alleged violation.

(c) Upon the request of a peace officer, a permit holder must write a sample signature in the officer's presence to aid in verifying the person's identity.

(d) Upon the request of a peace officer, a permit holder shall disclose to the officer whether or not the permit holder is currently carrying a firearm.

Subd. 2. Where application made; authority to issue permit; criteria; scope.

(a) Applications by Minnesota residents for permits to carry shall be made to the county sheriff where the applicant resides. Nonresidents, as defined in section 171.01, subdivision 42, may apply to any sheriff.

(b) Unless a sheriff denies a permit under the exception set forth in subdivision 6, paragraph (a), clause (3), a sheriff must issue a permit to an applicant if the person:

    (1) has training in the safe use of a pistol;

    (2) is at least 21 years old and a citizen or a permanent resident of the United States;

    (3) completes an application for a permit;

    (4) is not prohibited from possessing a firearm under the following sections:

        (i) 518B.01, subdivision 14;

        (ii) 609.224, subdivision 3;

        (iii) 609.2242, subdivision 3;

        (iv) 609.749, subdivision 8;

        (v) 624.713;

        (vi) 624.719;

        (vii) 629.715, subdivision 2;

        (viii) 629.72, subdivision 2; or

        (ix) any federal law; and

(5) is not listed in the criminal gang investigative data system under section 299C.091.

(c) A permit to carry a pistol issued or recognized under this section is a state permit and is effective throughout the state.

(d) A sheriff may contract with a police chief to process permit applications under this section. If a sheriff contracts with a police chief, the sheriff remains the issuing authority and the police chief acts as the sheriff's agent. If a sheriff contracts with a police chief, all of the provisions of this section will apply.

Subd. 2a. Training in the safe use of a pistol.

(a) An applicant must present evidence that the applicant received training in the safe use of a pistol within one year of the date of an original or renewal application. Training may be demonstrated by:

(1) employment as a peace officer in the state of Minnesota within the past year; or

(2) completion of a firearms safety or training course providing basic training in the safe use of a pistol and conducted by a certified instructor.

(b) Basic training must include:

(1) instruction in the fundamentals of pistol use;

(2) successful completion of an actual shooting qualification exercise; and

(3) instruction in the fundamental legal aspects of pistol possession, carry, and use, including self-defense and the restrictions on the use of deadly force.

(c) The certified instructor must issue a certificate to a person who has completed a firearms safety or training course described in paragraph (b). The certificate must be signed by the instructor and attest that the person attended and completed the course.

(d) A person qualifies as a certified instructor if the person is certified as a firearms instructor within the past five years by an organization or government entity that has been approved by the Department of Public Safety in accordance with the department's standards.

(e) A sheriff must accept the training described in this subdivision as meeting the requirement in subdivision 2, paragraph (b), for training in the safe use of a pistol. A sheriff may also accept other satisfactory evidence of training in the safe use of a pistol.

Subd. 3. **Form and contents of application.**

(a) Applications for permits to carry must be an official, standardized application form, adopted under section 624.7151, and must set forth in writing only the following information:

> (1) the applicant's name, residence, telephone number, if any, and driver's license number or state identification card number;

> (2) the applicant's sex, date of birth, height, weight, and color of eyes and hair, and distinguishing physical characteristics, if any;

> (3) the township or statutory city or home rule charter city, and county, of all Minnesota residences of the applicant in the last five years, though not including specific addresses;

> (4) the township or city, county, and state of all non-Minnesota residences of the applicant in the last five years, though not including specific addresses;

> (5) a statement that the applicant authorizes the release to the sheriff of commitment information about the applicant maintained by the commissioner of human services or any similar agency or department of another state where the applicant has resided, to the extent that the information relates to the applicant's eligibility to possess a firearm; and

> (6) a statement by the applicant that, to the best of the applicant's knowledge and belief, the applicant is not prohibited by law from possessing a firearm.

(b) The statement under paragraph (a), clause (5), must comply with any applicable requirements of Code of Federal Regulations, title

42, sections 2.31 to 2.35, with respect to consent to disclosure of alcohol or drug abuse patient records.

(c) An applicant must submit to the sheriff an application packet consisting only of the following items:

    (1) a completed application form, signed and dated by the applicant;

    (2) an accurate photocopy of the certificate described in subdivision 2a, paragraph (c), that is submitted as the applicant's evidence of training in the safe use of a pistol; and

    (3) an accurate photocopy of the applicant's current driver's license, state identification card, or the photo page of the applicant's passport.

(d) In addition to the other application materials, a person who is otherwise ineligible for a permit due to a criminal conviction but who has obtained a pardon or expungement setting aside the conviction, sealing the conviction, or otherwise restoring applicable rights, must submit a copy of the relevant order.

(e) Applications must be submitted in person.

(f) The sheriff may charge a new application processing fee in an amount not to exceed the actual and reasonable direct cost of processing the application or $100, whichever is less. Of this amount, $10 must be submitted to the commissioner and deposited into the general fund.

(g) This subdivision prescribes the complete and exclusive set of items an applicant is required to submit in order to apply for a new or renewal permit to carry. The applicant must not be asked or required to submit, voluntarily or involuntarily, any information, fees, or documentation beyond that specifically required by this subdivision. This paragraph does not apply to alternate training evidence accepted by the sheriff under subdivision 2a, paragraph (d).

(h) Forms for new and renewal applications must be available at all sheriffs' offices and the commissioner must make the forms available on the Internet.

(i) Application forms must clearly display a notice that a permit, if granted, is void and must be immediately returned to the sheriff if the permit holder is or becomes prohibited by law from possessing a firearm. The notice must list the applicable state criminal offenses and civil categories that prohibit a person from possessing a firearm.

(j) Upon receipt of an application packet and any required fee, the sheriff must provide a signed receipt indicating the date of submission.

Subd. 4. **Investigation.**

(a) The sheriff must check, by means of electronic data transfer, criminal records, histories, and warrant information on each applicant through the Minnesota Crime Information System and, to the extent necessary, the National Instant Check System. The sheriff shall also make a reasonable effort to check other available and relevant federal, state, or local record-keeping systems. The sheriff must obtain commitment information from the commissioner of human services as provided in section 245.041 or, if the information is reasonably available, as provided by a similar statute from another state.

(b) When an application for a permit is filed under this section, the sheriff must notify the chief of police, if any, of the municipality where the applicant resides. The police chief may provide the sheriff with any information relevant to the issuance of the permit.

(c) The sheriff must conduct a background check by means of electronic data transfer on a permit holder through the Minnesota Crime Information System and, to the extent necessary, the National Instant Check System at least yearly to ensure continuing eligibility. The sheriff may conduct additional background checks by means of electronic data transfer on a permit holder at any time during the period that a permit is in effect.

Subd. 5.[Repealed, 2003 c 28 art 2 s 35; 2005 c 83 s 1]

Subd. 6. **Granting and denial of permits.**

(a) The sheriff must, within 30 days after the date of receipt of the application packet described in subdivision 3:

(1) issue the permit to carry;

(2) deny the application for a permit to carry solely on the grounds that the applicant failed to qualify under the criteria described in subdivision 2, paragraph (b); or

(3) deny the application on the grounds that there exists a substantial likelihood that the applicant is a danger to self or the public if authorized to carry a pistol under a permit.

(b) Failure of the sheriff to notify the applicant of the denial of the application within 30 days after the date of receipt of the application packet constitutes issuance of the permit to carry and the sheriff must promptly fulfill the requirements under paragraph (c). To deny the application, the sheriff must provide the applicant with written notification and the specific factual basis justifying the denial under paragraph (a), clause (2) or (3), including the source of the factual basis. The sheriff must inform the applicant of the applicant's right to submit, within 20 business days, any additional documentation relating to the propriety of the denial. Upon receiving any additional documentation, the sheriff must reconsider the denial and inform the applicant within 15 business days of the result of the reconsideration. Any denial after reconsideration must be in the same form and substance as the original denial and must specifically address any continued deficiencies in light of the additional documentation submitted by the applicant. The applicant must be informed of the right to seek de novo review of the denial as provided in subdivision 12.

(c) Upon issuing a permit to carry, the sheriff must provide a laminated permit card to the applicant by first class mail unless personal delivery has been made. Within five business days, the sheriff must submit the information specified in subdivision 7, paragraph (a), to the commissioner for inclusion solely in the database required under subdivision 15, paragraph (a). The sheriff must transmit the information in a manner and format prescribed by the commissioner.

(d) Within five business days of learning that a permit to carry has been suspended or revoked, the sheriff must submit information to the commissioner regarding the suspension or revocation for inclusion solely in the databases required or permitted under subdivision 15.

(e) Notwithstanding paragraphs (a) and (b), the sheriff may suspend the application process if a charge is pending against the applicant that, if resulting in conviction, will prohibit the applicant from possessing a firearm.

Subd. 7. **Permit card contents; expiration; renewal.**

(a) Permits to carry must be on an official, standardized permit card adopted by the commissioner, containing only the name, residence, and driver's license number or state identification card number of the permit holder, if any.

(b) The permit card must also identify the issuing sheriff and state the expiration date of the permit. The permit card must clearly display a notice that a permit, if granted, is void and must be immediately returned to the sheriff if the permit holder becomes prohibited by law from possessing a firearm.

(c) A permit to carry a pistol issued under this section expires five years after the date of issue. It may be renewed in the same manner and under the same criteria which the original permit was obtained, subject to the following procedures:

    (1) no earlier than 90 days prior to the expiration date on the permit, the permit holder may renew the permit by submitting to the appropriate sheriff the application packet described in subdivision 3 and a renewal processing fee not to exceed the actual and reasonable direct cost of processing the application or $75, whichever is less. Of this amount, $5 must be submitted to the commissioner and deposited into the general fund. The sheriff must process the renewal application in accordance with subdivisions 4 and 6; and

    (2) a permit holder who submits a renewal application packet after the expiration date of the permit, but within 30 days after expiration, may renew the permit as provided in clause (1) by paying an additional late fee of $10.

(d) The renewal permit is effective beginning on the expiration date of the prior permit to carry.

Subd. 7a. **Change of address; loss or destruction of permit.**

(a) Within 30 days after changing permanent address, or within 30 days of having lost or destroyed the permit card, the permit holder must notify the issuing sheriff of the change, loss, or destruction. Failure to provide notification as required by this subdivision is a petty misdemeanor. The fine for a first offense must not exceed $25. Notwithstanding section 609.531, a firearm carried in violation of this paragraph is not subject to forfeiture.

(b) After notice is given under paragraph (a), a permit holder may obtain a replacement permit card by paying $10 to the sheriff. The request for a replacement permit card must be made on an official, standardized application adopted for this purpose under section 624.7151, and, except in the case of an address change, must include a notarized statement that the permit card has been lost or destroyed.

Subd. 8. **Permit to carry voided.**

(a) The permit to carry is void at the time that the holder becomes prohibited by law from possessing a firearm, in which event the holder must return the permit card to the issuing sheriff within five business days after the holder knows or should know that the holder is a prohibited person. If the sheriff has knowledge that a permit is void under this paragraph, the sheriff must give notice to the permit holder in writing in the same manner as a denial. Failure of the holder to return the permit within the five days is a gross misdemeanor unless the court finds that the circumstances or the physical or mental condition of the permit holder prevented the holder from complying with the return requirement.

(b) When a permit holder is convicted of an offense that prohibits the permit holder from possessing a firearm, the court must take possession of the permit, if it is available, and send it to the issuing sheriff.

(c) The sheriff of the county where the application was submitted, or of the county of the permit holder's current residence, may file a petition with the district court therein, for an order revoking a permit to carry on the grounds set forth in subdivision 6, paragraph (a), clause (3). An order shall be issued only if the sheriff meets the burden of proof and criteria set forth in subdivision 12. If the court denies the petition, the court must award the permit holder reasonable costs and expenses, including attorney fees.

(d) A permit revocation must be promptly reported to the issuing sheriff.

Subd. 8a. **Prosecutor's duty.** Whenever a person is charged with an offense that would, upon conviction, prohibit the person from possessing a firearm, the prosecuting attorney must ascertain whether the person is a permit holder under this section. If the person is a permit holder, the prosecutor must notify the issuing sheriff that the person has been charged with a prohibiting offense. The prosecutor must also notify the sheriff of the final disposition of the case.

Subd. 9. **Carrying pistols about one's premises or for purposes of repair, target practice.** A permit to carry is not required of a person:

(a) to keep or carry about the person's place of business, dwelling house, premises or on land possessed by the person a pistol;

(b) to carry a pistol from a place of purchase to the person's dwelling house or place of business, or from the person's dwelling house or place of business to or from a place where repairing is done, to have the pistol repaired;

(c) to carry a pistol between the person's dwelling house and place of business;

(d) to carry a pistol in the woods or fields or upon the waters of this state for the purpose of hunting or of target shooting in a safe area; or

(e) to transport a pistol in a motor vehicle, snowmobile or boat if the pistol is unloaded, contained in a closed and fastened case, gunbox, or securely tied package.

Subd. 10. **False representations.** A person who gives or causes to be given any false material information in applying for a permit to carry, knowing or having reason to know the information is false, is guilty of a gross misdemeanor.

Subd. 11. **No limit on number of pistols.** A person shall not be restricted as to the number of pistols the person may carry.

Subd. 11a. **Emergency issuance of permits.** A sheriff may immediately issue an emergency permit to a person if the sheriff determines that the person is in an emergency situation that may constitute an immediate risk to the safety of the person or someone residing in the person's household. A person seeking an emergency permit must complete an application form and must sign an affidavit describing the emergency situation. An emergency permit applicant does not need to provide evidence of training. An emergency permit is valid for 30 days, may not be renewed, and may be revoked without a hearing. No fee may be charged for an emergency permit. An emergency permit holder may seek a regular permit under subdivision 3 and is subject to the other applicable provisions of this section.

Subd. 12. **Hearing upon denial or revocation.**

(a) Any person aggrieved by denial or revocation of a permit to carry may appeal by petition to the district court having jurisdiction over the county or municipality where the application was submitted. The petition must list the sheriff as the respondent. The district court must hold a hearing at the earliest practicable date and in any event no later than 60 days following the filing of the petition for review. The court may not grant or deny any relief before the completion of the hearing. The record of the hearing must be sealed. The matter must be heard de novo without a jury.

(b) The court must issue written findings of fact and conclusions of law regarding the issues submitted by the parties. The court must issue its writ of mandamus directing that the permit be issued and order other appropriate relief unless the sheriff establishes by clear and convincing evidence:

   (1) that the applicant is disqualified under the criteria described in subdivision 2, paragraph (b); or

   (2) that there exists a substantial likelihood that the applicant is a danger to self or the public if authorized to carry a pistol under a permit. Incidents of alleged criminal misconduct that are not investigated and documented may not be considered.

(c) If an applicant is denied a permit on the grounds that the applicant is listed in the criminal gang investigative data system under section 299C.091, the person may challenge the denial, after disclosure under court supervision of the reason for that listing, based on grounds that the person:

(1) was erroneously identified as a person in the data system;

(2) was improperly included in the data system according to the criteria outlined in section 299C.091, subdivision 2, paragraph (b); or

(3) has demonstrably withdrawn from the activities and associations that led to inclusion in the data system.

(d) If the court grants a petition brought under paragraph (a), the court must award the applicant or permit holder reasonable costs and expenses including attorney fees.

Subd. 12a. **Suspension as condition of release.** The district court may order suspension of the application process for a permit or suspend the permit of a permit holder as a condition of release pursuant to the same criteria as the surrender of firearms under section 629.715. A permit suspension must be promptly reported to the issuing sheriff. If the permit holder has an out-of-state permit recognized under subdivision 16, the court must promptly report the suspension to the commissioner for inclusion solely in the database under subdivision 15, paragraph (a).

Subd. 13. **Exemptions; adult correctional facility officers.** A permit to carry a pistol is not required of any officer of a state adult correctional facility when on guard duty or otherwise engaged in an assigned duty. *Subd.* 14. **Records.**

(a) A sheriff must not maintain records or data collected, made, or held under this section concerning any applicant or permit holder that are not necessary under this section to support a permit that is outstanding or eligible for renewal under subdivision 7, paragraph (b). Notwithstanding section 138.163, sheriffs must completely purge all files and databases by March 1 of each year to delete all information collected under this section concerning all persons who are no longer current permit holders or currently eligible to renew their permit.

(b) Paragraph (a) does not apply to records or data concerning an applicant or permit holder who has had a permit denied or revoked under the criteria established in subdivision 2, paragraph (b), clause (1), or subdivision 6, paragraph (a), clause (3), for a period of six years from the date of the denial or revocation.

Subd. 15. **Commissioner; contracts; database.**

(a) The commissioner must maintain an automated database of persons authorized to carry pistols under this section that is available 24 hours a day, seven days a week, only to law enforcement agencies, including prosecutors carrying out their duties under subdivision 8a, to verify the validity of a permit.

(b) The commissioner may maintain a separate automated database of denied applications for permits to carry and of revoked permits that is available only to sheriffs performing their duties under this section containing the date of, the statutory basis for, and the initiating agency for any permit application denied or permit revoked for a period of six years from the date of the denial or revocation.

(c) The commissioner may contract with one or more vendors to implement the commissioner's duties under this section.

Subd. 16. **Recognition of permits from other states.**

(a) The commissioner must annually establish and publish a list of other states that have laws governing the issuance of permits to carry weapons that are not similar to this section. The list must be available on the Internet. A person holding a carry permit from a state not on the list may use the license or permit in this state subject to the rights, privileges, and requirements of this section.

(b) Notwithstanding paragraph (a), no license or permit from another state is valid in this state if the holder is or becomes prohibited by law from possessing a firearm.

(c) Any sheriff or police chief may file a petition under subdivision 12 seeking an order suspending or revoking an out-of-state permit holder's authority to carry a pistol in this state on the grounds set forth in subdivision 6, paragraph (a), clause (3). An order shall only be issued if the petitioner meets the burden of proof and criteria set forth in subdivision 12. If the court denies the petition, the court must award the permit holder reasonable costs and expenses including attorney fees. The petition may be filed in any county in the state where a person holding a license or permit from another state can be found.

(d) The commissioner must, when necessary, execute reciprocity agreements regarding carry permits with jurisdictions whose carry permits are recognized under paragraph (a).

Subd. 17. **Posting; trespass.**

(a) A person carrying a firearm on or about his or her person or clothes under a permit or otherwise who remains at a private establishment knowing that the operator of the establishment or its agent has made a reasonable request that firearms not be brought into the establishment may be ordered to leave the premises. A person who fails to leave when so requested is guilty of a petty misdemeanor. The fine for a first offense must not exceed $25. Notwithstanding section 609.531, a firearm carried in violation of this subdivision is not subject to forfeiture.

(b) As used in this subdivision, the terms in this paragraph have the meanings given.

   (1) "Reasonable request" means a request made under the following circumstances:

      (i) the requester has prominently posted a conspicuous sign at every entrance to the establishment containing the following language: "(INDICATE IDENTITY OF OPERATOR) BANS GUNS IN THESE PREMISES."; or

      (ii) the requester or the requester's agent personally informs the person that guns are prohibited in the premises and demands compliance.

   (2) "Prominently" means readily visible and within four feet laterally of the entrance with the bottom of the sign at a height of four to six feet above the floor.

   (3) "Conspicuous" means lettering in black arial typeface at least 1-1/2 inches in height against a bright contrasting background that is at least 187 square inches in area.

(4) "Private establishment" means a building, structure, or portion thereof that is owned, leased, controlled, or operated by a nongovernmental entity for a nongovernmental purpose.

(c) The owner or operator of a private establishment may not prohibit the lawful carry or possession of firearms in a parking facility or parking area.

(d) This subdivision does not apply to private residences. The lawful possessor of a private residence may prohibit firearms, and provide notice thereof, in any lawful manner.

(e) A landlord may not restrict the lawful carry or possession of firearms by tenants or their guests.

(f) Notwithstanding any inconsistent provisions in section 609.605, this subdivision sets forth the exclusive criteria to notify a permit holder when otherwise lawful firearm possession is not allowed in a private establishment and sets forth the exclusive penalty for such activity.

(g) This subdivision does not apply to:

(1) an active licensed peace officer; or

(2) a security guard acting in the course and scope of employment.

Subd. 18. **Employers; public colleges and universities.**

(a) An employer, whether public or private, may establish policies that restrict the carry or possession of firearms by its employees while acting in the course and scope of employment. Employment related civil sanctions may be invoked for a violation.

(b) A public postsecondary institution regulated under chapter 136F or 137 may establish policies that restrict the carry or possession of firearms by its students while on the institution's property. Academic sanctions may be invoked for a violation.

(c) Notwithstanding paragraphs (a) and (b), an employer or a postsecondary institution may not prohibit the lawful carry or possession of firearms in a parking facility or parking area.

Subd. 19. **Immunity.** Neither a sheriff, police chief, any employee of a sheriff or police chief involved in the permit issuing process, nor any certified instructor is liable for damages resulting or arising from acts with a firearm committed by a permit holder, unless the person had actual knowledge at the time the permit was issued or the instruction was given that the applicant was prohibited by law from possessing a firearm.

Subd. 20. **Monitoring.**

(a) By March 1, 2004, and each year thereafter, the commissioner must report to the legislature on:

    (1)   the number of permits applied for, issued, suspended, revoked, and denied, further categorized by the age, sex, and zip code of the applicant or permit holder, since the previous submission, and in total;

    (2)   the number of permits currently valid;

    (3)   the specific reasons for each suspension, revocation, and denial and the number of reversed, canceled, or corrected actions;

    (4)   without expressly identifying an applicant, the number of denials or revocations based on the grounds under subdivision 6, paragraph (a), clause (3), the factual basis for each denial or revocation, and the result of an appeal, if any, including the court's findings of fact, conclusions of law, and order;

    (5)   the number of convictions and types of crimes committed since the previous submission, and in total, by individuals with permits including data as to whether a firearm lawfully carried solely by virtue of a permit was actually used in furtherance of the crime;

    (6)   to the extent known or determinable, data on the lawful and justifiable use of firearms by permit holders; and

    (7)   the status of the segregated funds reported to the commissioner under subdivision 21.

(b) Sheriffs and police chiefs must supply the Department of Public Safety with the basic data the department requires to complete the report under paragraph (a). Sheriffs and police chiefs may submit data classified as private to the Department of Public Safety under this paragraph.

(c) Copies of the report under paragraph (a) must be made available to the public at the actual cost of duplication.

(d) Nothing contained in any provision of this section or any other law requires or authorizes the registration, documentation, collection, or providing of serial numbers or other data on firearms or on firearms' owners.

Subd. 21. **Use of fees.** Fees collected by sheriffs under this section and not forwarded to the commissioner must be used only to pay the direct costs of administering this section. Fee money may be used to pay the costs of appeals of prevailing applicants or permit holders under subdivision 8, paragraph (c); subdivision 12, paragraph (e); and subdivision 16, paragraph (c).

Fee money may also be used to pay the reasonable costs of the county attorney to represent the sheriff in proceedings under this section. The revenues must be maintained in a segregated fund. Fund balances must be carried over from year to year and do not revert to any other fund. As part of the information supplied under subdivision 20, paragraph (b), by January 31 of each year, a sheriff must report to the commissioner on the sheriff's segregated fund for the preceding calendar year, including information regarding:

(1) nature and amount of revenues;

(2) nature and amount of expenditures; and

(3) nature and amount of balances.

Subd. 22. **Short title; construction; severability.** This section may be cited as the Minnesota Citizens' Personal Protection Act of 2003. The legislature of the state of Minnesota recognizes and declares that the second amendment of the United States Constitution guarantees the fundamental, individual right to keep and bear arms. The provisions of this section are declared to be necessary to accomplish compelling state interests in regulation of those rights. The terms of this section must be construed according to the compelling state interest test. The invalidation of any provision of this section shall not invalidate any other provision.

Subd. 23. **Exclusivity.** This section sets forth the complete and exclusive criteria and procedures for the issuance of permits to carry and establishes their nature and scope. No sheriff, police chief, governmental unit, government official, government employee, or other person or body acting under color of law or governmental authority may change, modify, or supplement these criteria or procedures, or limit the exercise of a permit to carry.

Subd. 24. **Predatory offenders.** Except when acting under the authority of other law, it is a misdemeanor for a person required to register by section 243.166 to carry a pistol whether or not the carrier possesses a permit to carry issued under this section. If an action prohibited by this subdivision is also a violation of another law, the violation may be prosecuted under either law.

History: *1975 c 378 s 4; 1976 c 269 s 1; 1977 c 349 s 3; 1983 c 264 s 10; 1986 c 444; 1992 c 571 art 15 s 8,9; 1993 c 326 art 1 s 32; 1994 c 618 art 1 s 45,46; 1994 c 636 art 3 s 38-40; 1998 c 254 art 2 s 69; 2003 c 28 art 2 s 4-28,34; 2005 c 83 s 1,3-10*

Permit to Acquire

624.7131 TRANSFEREE PERMIT; PENALTY.

Subdivision 1. **Information.**

Any person may apply for a transferee permit by providing the following information in writing to the chief of police of an organized full time police department of the municipality in which the person resides or to the county sheriff if there is no such local chief of police:

(1) the name, residence, telephone number, and driver's license number or nonqualification certificate number, if any, of the proposed transferee;

(2) the sex, date of birth, height, weight, and color of eyes, and distinguishing physical characteristics, if any, of the proposed transferee;

(3) a statement that the proposed transferee authorizes the release to the local police authority of commitment information about the proposed transferee maintained by the commissioner of human services, to the extent that the information relates to the proposed transferee's eligibility to possess a pistol or semiautomatic military-style assault weapon under section 624.713, subdivision 1; and

(4) a statement by the proposed transferee that the proposed transferee is not prohibited by section 624.713 from possessing a pistol or semiautomatic military-style assault weapon.

The statements shall be signed and dated by the person applying for a permit. At the time of application, the local police authority shall provide the applicant with a dated receipt for the application. The statement under clause (3) must comply with any applicable requirements of Code of Federal Regulations, title 42, sections 2.31 to 2.35, with respect to consent to disclosure of alcohol or drug abuse patient records.

Subd. 2. **Investigation.**

The chief of police or sheriff shall check criminal histories, records and warrant information relating to the applicant through the Minnesota Crime Information System, the national criminal record repository, and the National Instant Criminal Background Check System. The chief of police or sheriff shall also make a reasonable effort to check other available state and local record-keeping systems. The chief of police or sheriff shall obtain commitment information from the commissioner of human services as provided in section 245.041.

Subd. 3. **Forms.**

Chiefs of police and sheriffs shall make transferee permit application forms available throughout the community. There shall be no charge for forms, reports, investigations, notifications, waivers or any other act performed or materials provided by a government employee or agency in connection with application for or issuance of a transferee permit.

Subd. 4. **Grounds for disqualification.**

A determination by the chief of police or sheriff that the applicant is prohibited by section 624.713 from possessing a pistol or semiautomatic military-style assault weapon shall be the only basis for refusal to grant a transferee permit.

Subd. 5. Granting of permits.

The chief of police or sheriff shall issue a transferee permit or deny the application within seven days of application for the permit. The chief of police or sheriff shall provide an applicant with written notification of a denial and the specific reason for the denial. The permits and their renewal shall be granted free of charge.

Subd. 6. Permits valid statewide.

Transferee permits issued pursuant to this section are valid statewide and shall expire after one year. A transferee permit may be renewed in the same manner and subject to the same provisions by which the original permit was obtained, except that all renewed permits must comply with the standards adopted by the commissioner under section 624.7151. Permits issued pursuant to this section are not transferable. A person who transfers a permit in violation of this subdivision is guilty of a misdemeanor.

Subd. 7. Permit voided.

The transferee permit shall be void at the time that the holder becomes prohibited from possessing a pistol under section 624.713, in which event the holder shall return the permit within five days to the issuing authority. Failure of the holder to return the permit within the five days is a misdemeanor unless the court finds that the circumstances or the physical or mental condition of the permit holder prevented the holder from complying with the return requirement.

Subd. 8. Hearing upon denial.

Any person aggrieved by denial of a transferee permit may appeal the denial to the district court having jurisdiction over the county or municipality in which the denial occurred.

Subd. 9. Permit to carry.

A valid permit to carry issued pursuant to section 624.714 constitutes a transferee permit for the purposes of this section and section 624.7132.

Subd. 10. Transfer report not required.

A person who transfers a pistol or semiautomatic military-style assault weapon to a person exhibiting a valid transferee permit issued pursuant to this section or a valid permit to carry issued pursuant to section 624.714 is not required to file a transfer report pursuant to section 624.7132, subdivision 1.

Subd. 11. Penalty.

A person who makes a false statement in order to obtain a transferee permit knowing or having reason to know the statement is false is guilty of a gross misdemeanor.

Subd. 12. Local regulation.

This section shall be construed to supersede municipal or county regulation of the issuance of transferee permits.

History:

1977 c 349 s 4; 1986 c 444; 1992 c 571 art 15 s 5,6; 1993 c 326 art 1 s 28-30; 1994 c 618 art 1 s 41,42; 1994 c 636 art 3 s 29-31; 1998 c 254 art 2 s 67; 2003 c 28 art 2 s 34; 2009 c 139 s 4

Carrying while intoxicated

624.7142 CARRYING WHILE UNDER THE INFLUENCE OF ALCOHOL OR A CONTROLLED SUBSTANCE.

Subdivision 1. Acts prohibited. A person may not carry a pistol on or about the person's clothes or person in a public place:

(1) when the person is under the influence of a controlled substance, as defined in section 152.01, subdivision 4;

(2) when the person is under the influence of a combination of any two or more of the elements named in clauses (1) and (4);

(3) when the person is knowingly under the influence of any chemical compound or combination of chemical compounds that is listed as a hazardous substance in rules adopted under section 182.655 and that affects the nervous system, brain, or muscles of the person so as to impair the person's clearness of intellect or physical control;

(4)   when the person is under the influence of alcohol;

(5)   when the person's alcohol concentration is 0.10 or more; or

(6)   when the person's alcohol concentration is less than 0.10, but more than 0.04.

Subd. 2. **Arrest.** A peace officer may arrest a person for a violation under subdivision 1 without a warrant upon probable cause, without regard to whether the violation was committed in the officer's presence.

Subd. 3. **Preliminary screening test.** When an officer authorized under subdivision 2 to make arrests has reason to believe that the person may be violating or has violated subdivision 1, the officer may require the person to provide a breath sample for a preliminary screening test using a device approved by the commissioner for this purpose. The results of the preliminary screening test must be used for the purpose of deciding whether an arrest should be made under this section and whether to require the chemical tests authorized in section 624.7143, but may not be used in any court action except: (1) to prove that the test was properly required of a person under section 624.7143, or (2) in a civil action arising out of the use of the pistol. Following the preliminary screening test, additional tests may be required of the person as provided under section 624.7143. A person who refuses a breath sample is subject to the provisions of section 624.7143 unless, in compliance with that section, the person submits to a blood, breath, or urine test to determine the presence of alcohol or a controlled substance.

Subd. 4. **Evidence.** In a prosecution for a violation of subdivision 1, the admission of evidence of the amount of alcohol or a controlled substance in the person's blood, breath, or urine is governed by section 169A.45.

Subd. 5. **Suspension.** A person who is charged with a violation under this section may have their authority to carry a pistol in a public place on or about the person's clothes or person under the provisions of a permit or otherwise suspended by the court as a condition of release.

Subd. 6. **Penalties.**

(a) A person who violates a prohibition under subdivision 1, clauses (1) to (5), is guilty of a misdemeanor. A second or subsequent violation is a gross misdemeanor.

(b) A person who violates subdivision 1, clause (6), is guilty of a misdemeanor.

(c) In addition to the penalty imposed under paragraph (a), if a person violates subdivision 1, clauses (1) to (5), the person's authority to carry a pistol in a public place on or about the person's clothes or person under the provisions of a permit or otherwise is revoked and the person may not reapply for a period of one year from the date of conviction.

(d) In addition to the penalty imposed under paragraph (b), if a person violates subdivision 1, clause (6), the person's authority to carry a pistol in a public place on or about the person's clothes or person under the provisions of a permit or otherwise is suspended for 180 days from the date of conviction.

(e) Notwithstanding section 609.531, a firearm carried in violation of subdivision 1, clause (6), is not subject to forfeiture.

Subd. 7. **Reporting.** Suspensions and revocations under this section must be reported in the same manner as in section 624.714, subdivision 12a.

History: 2003 c 28 art 2 s 29,34; 2005 c 83 s 1

Chemical testing

624.7143 CHEMICAL TESTING.

Subdivision 1. **Mandatory chemical testing.** A person who carries a pistol in a public place on or about the person's clothes or person is required, subject to the provisions of this section, to take or submit to a test of the person's blood, breath, or urine for the purpose of determining the presence and amount of alcohol or a controlled substance. The test shall be administered at the direction of an officer authorized to make arrests under section 624.7142. Taking or submitting to the test is mandatory when requested by an officer who has probable cause to believe the person was carrying a pistol in violation of section 624.7142, and one of the following conditions exists:

(1) the person has been lawfully placed under arrest for violating section 624.7142;

(2) the person has been involved while carrying a firearm in a firearms-related accident resulting in property damage, personal injury, or death;

(3) the person has refused to take the preliminary screening test provided for in section 624.7142; or

(4) the screening test was administered and indicated an alcohol concentration of 0.04 or more.

Subd. 2. **Penalties; refusal; revocation.**

(a) If a person refuses to take a test required under subdivision 1, none must be given but the officer shall report the refusal to the sheriff and to the authority having responsibility for prosecution of misdemeanor offenses for the jurisdiction in which the incident occurred that gave rise to the test demand and refusal. On certification by the officer that probable cause existed to believe the person had been carrying a pistol on or about the person's clothes or person in a public place while under the influence of alcohol or a controlled substance, and that the person refused to submit to testing, a court may impose a civil penalty of $500 and may revoke the person's authority to carry a pistol in a public place on or about the person's clothes or person under the provisions of a permit or otherwise for a period of one year from the date of the refusal. The person shall be accorded notice and an opportunity to be heard prior to imposition of the civil penalty or the revocation.

(b) Revocations under this subdivision must be reported in the same manner as in section 624.714, subdivision 12a. *Subd. 3.* **Rights and obligations.** At the time a test is requested, the person must be informed that:

(1) Minnesota law requires a person to take a test to determine if the person is under the influence of alcohol or a controlled substance;

(2) if the person refuses to take the test, the person is subject to a civil penalty of $500 and is prohibited for a period of one year from carrying a pistol in a public place on or about the person's clothes or person, as provided under subdivision 2; and

(3) that the person has the right to consult with an attorney, but that this right is limited to the extent it cannot unreasonably delay administration of the test or the person will be deemed to have refused the test.

Subd. 4. **Requirement of blood or urine test.** Notwithstanding subdivision 1, if there is probable cause to believe there is impairment by a controlled substance that is not subject to testing by a breath test, a blood or urine test may be required even after a breath test has been administered.

Subd. 5. **Chemical tests.** Chemical tests administered under this section are governed by section 169A.51 in all aspects that are not inconsistent with this section.

History: *2003 c 28 art 2 s 30; 2005 c 83 s 1*

2015 Minnesota Legislature Changes

The 2015 Minnesota legislature accomplished the passing of several changes to state statutes that affected gun owners generally in Minnesota.

Although still subject to all Federal laws, Public Safety Bill SF 878 amended Minnesota Statutes 2014, section 609.66, subdivision 1a to allow the ownership or possession of suppressors (also referred to as silencers).

Subd. 1a. Felony crimes; suppressors; reckless discharge. (a) Whoever does any of the following is guilty of a felony and may be sentenced as provided in paragraph (b):

   (1) sells or has in possession a suppressor that is not lawfully possessed under federal law;

   (2) intentionally discharges a firearm under circumstances that endanger the safety of another; or

   (3) recklessly discharges a firearm within a municipality.

   (b) A person convicted under paragraph (a) may be sentenced as follows:

   (1) if the act was a violation of paragraph (a), clause (2), or if the act was a violation of paragraph (a), clause (1) or (3), and was committed in a public housing zone, as defined in section 152.01, subdivision 19, a school zone, as defined in section 152.01, subdivision 14a, or a park zone, as defined in section 152.01, subdivision 12a, to imprisonment for not more than five years or to payment of a fine of not more than $10,000, or both; or

   (2) otherwise, to imprisonment for not more than two years or to payment of a fine of not more than $5,000, or both.

   (c) As used in this subdivision, "suppressor" means any device for silencing, muffling, or diminishing the report of a portable firearm, including any combination of parts, designed or redesigned, and intended for use in assembling or fabricating a firearm silencer or firearm muffler, and any part intended only for use in such assembly or fabrication.

To be sure suppressors are not used to illegally take game, the following penalties were added.

Sec. 3. Minnesota Statutes 2014, section 97A.421, is amended by adding a subdivision to read:

Subd. 3a. License revocation after conviction; firearm suppressor. (a) A person who is convicted of a violation under paragraph (b) and possessed a firearm with a suppressor may not obtain a hunting license or hunt wild animals for five years from the date of conviction.

(b) The revocation under this subdivision applies to convictions of:

(1) trespass as provided in section 97A.315, subdivision 1, paragraph (b);

(2) hunting game in closed season;

(3) hunting game more than one-half hour before legal shooting hours or more than one-half hour after legal shooting hours; or

(4) using artificial lights to spot, locate, or take wild animals while in possession of a firearm.

Minnesota residents may now purchase firearms from any dealer in any state. The restriction that the state must be contiguous to Minnesota has been removed.

624.71 GUN CONTROL; APPLICATION OF FEDERAL LAW.

Subdivision 1. Application. Notwithstanding any other law to the contrary, it shall be lawful for any federally licensed importer, manufacturer, dealer, or collector to sell and deliver firearms and ammunition to a resident of any state in any instance where such sale and delivery is lawful under the federal Gun Control Act of 1968 (Public Law 90-618).

Subd. 2. Contiguous state purchases. Notwithstanding any other law to the contrary, it shall be lawful for a resident of Minnesota to purchase firearms and ammunition in any state in any instance where such sale and delivery is lawful under the federal Gun Control Act of 1968 (Public Law 90-618). During the times of emergency declared by the governor relating to a public disorder or disaster, the Police or anyone acting within the authority of the color of law may not seize and confiscate firearms or arbitrarily suspend or revoke a valid permit to carry.

Sec. 34. [624.7192] AUTHORITY TO SEIZE AND CONFISCATE FIREARMS.

(a) This section applies only during the effective period of a state of emergency proclaimed by the governor relating to a public disorder or disaster.

(b) A peace officer who is acting in the lawful discharge of the officer's official duties without a warrant may disarm a lawfully detained individual only temporarily and only if the officer reasonably believes it is immediately necessary for the protection of the officer or another individual. Before releasing the individual, the peace officer must return to the individual any seized firearms and ammunition, and components thereof, any firearms accessories and ammunition reloading equipment and supplies, and any other personal weapons taken from the individual, unless the officer: (1) takes the individual into physical custody for engaging in criminal activity or for observation pursuant to section 253B.05, subdivision 2; or (2) seizes the items as evidence pursuant to an investigation for the commission of the crime for which the individual was arrested.

(c) Notwithstanding any other law to the contrary, no governmental unit, government official, government employee, peace officer, or other person or body acting under governmental authority or color of law may undertake any of the following actions with regard to any firearms and ammunition, and components thereof; any firearms accessories and ammunition reloading equipment and supplies; and any other personal weapons:

(1) prohibit, regulate, or curtail the otherwise lawful possession, carrying, transportation, transfer, defensive use, or other lawful use of any of these items;

(2) seize, commandeer, or confiscate any of these items in any manner, except as expressly authorized in paragraph (b);

(3) suspend or revoke a valid permit issued pursuant to section 624.7131 or 624.714, except as expressly authorized in those sections; or

(4) close or limit the operating hours of businesses that lawfully sell or service any of these items, unless such closing or limitation of hours applies equally to all forms of commerce.

(d) No provision of law relating to a public disorder or disaster emergency proclamation by the governor or any other governmental or quasi-governmental official, including but not limited to emergency management powers pursuant to chapters 9 and 12, shall be construed as authorizing the governor or any other governmental or quasi-governmental official of this state or any of its political subdivisions acting at the direction of the governor or another official to act in violation of this paragraph or paragraphs (b) and (c).

(e)(1) An individual aggrieved by a violation of this section may seek relief in an action at law or in equity or in any other proper proceeding for damages, injunctive relief, or other appropriate redress against a person who commits or causes the commission of this violation. Venue must be in the district court having jurisdiction over the county in which the aggrieved individual resides or in which the violation occurred.

(2) In addition to any other remedy available at law or in equity, an individual aggrieved by the seizure or confiscation of an item listed in paragraph (c) in violation of this section may make application for the immediate return of the items to the office of the clerk of court for the county in which the items were seized and, except as provided in paragraph (b), the court must order the immediate return of the items by the seizing or confiscating governmental office and that office's employed officials.

(3) In an action or proceeding to enforce this section, the court must award the prevailing plaintiff reasonable court costs and expenses, including attorney fees.

The Public Safety Bill also made changes to Minnesota Statutes that specifically affected holders of a Minnesota Permit to Carry.

Sec. 20. Minnesota Statutes 2014, section 609.66, subdivision 1g, is amended to read:

Subd. 1g. Felony; possession in courthouse or certain state buildings. (a) A person who commits either of the following acts is guilty of a felony and may be sentenced to imprisonment for not more than five years or to payment of a fine of not more than $10,000, or both:

(1) possesses a dangerous weapon, ammunition, or explosives within any courthouse complex; or

(2) possesses a dangerous weapon, ammunition, or explosives in any state building within the Capitol Area described in chapter 15B, other than the National Guard Armory.

(b) Unless a person is otherwise prohibited or restricted by other law to possess a dangerous weapon, this subdivision does not apply to:

(1) licensed peace officers or military personnel who are performing official duties;

(2) persons who carry pistols according to the terms of a permit issued under section 624.714 and who so notify the sheriff or the commissioner of public safety, as appropriate;

(3) persons who possess dangerous weapons for the purpose of display as demonstrative evidence during testimony at a trial or hearing or exhibition in compliance with advance notice and safety guidelines set by the sheriff or the commissioner of public safety; or

(4) persons who possess dangerous weapons in a courthouse complex with the express consent of the county sheriff or who possess dangerous weapons in a state building with the express consent of the commissioner of public safety.

(c) For purposes of this subdivision, the issuance of a permit to carry under section 624.714 constitutes notification of the commissioner of public safety as required under paragraph (b), clause (2).

Prior to August 1, 2015, if a permit holder intended to go armed at the Minnesota State Capitol complex, a written notice to the commissioner of public safety was required to secure the exemption provided for under Minnesota Statutes, section 609.66, subdivision 1(g)(b)(2). Now merely possessing the permit to carry constitutes the required notification to the commissioner of public safety for purposes of going armed at the State Capitol Complex.

However, should you wish to carry while conducting routine business at a courthouse, you are still required to notify the Sheriff of the county in which the courthouse is located. Permit holders may not go armed in a courtroom even if you have sent the sheriff the required notice.

Minnesota statutes language concerning the recognition of permits issued by other states was relaxed from "substantially similar" to just "similar". This change loosened the reading of other states laws so they did not have to be substantially similar to the Minnesota permit to carry law. Minnesota now recognizes more states permits due to this change. The current list can be found at www.handgunlaw.us.

Appendix B

Important Minnesota Case Law

Statutes rarely cover all the different ways that people and elected official "read" the law. It is incumbent upon the courts to knowledgeable interpret the law and provide resolution to criminal violations and civil disputes. Self defense law is no different. Over the years the MN Appellate and Supreme court has written several key decisions regarding the lawful use of violence to protect oneself. For our purposes there are four cases that direct when, where and how a Minnesota citizen can claim self defense.

Each of the following cases deal with the four elements or the requirements for raising the affirmative defense of Justification. the important section of each case have been highlighted, but for those interested in law, the entire opinions will provide a bit of insight into how the Appellate and Supreme Courts of Minnesota come to decisions. Whether you agree or disagree with their decision is less important than the insight gained by understanding the process and the reasoning of the courts.

Look through each. Review the highlighted point of each case and you will be better prepared to handle a DGU. Hopefully these cases will help you better articulate your DGU in a fashion that will keep your case from ever reaching the higher courts of Minnesota. For if it does it is because you are trailblazing new concepts of law or your attorney and yourself have failed to convince the country prosecutor responsible for charging and trying your case that you fulfilled each and every one of the four elements throughout your entire DGU.

Happy reading!

STATE OF MINNESOTA

IN SUPREME COURT

C5-96-493

Court of Appeals	Stringer, J.
State of Minnesota, Respondent, vs. Jack Allen Basting, Appellant.	Filed: December 18, 1997 Office of Appellate Courts

SYLLABUS

Defendant's experience and training as a professional boxer, while relevant to a dangerous weapon analysis, does not alone convert a fist into a dangerous weapon; as a matter of law, the defendant did not use his left fist in such a manner as to render it a dangerous weapon under Minn. Stat. § 609.222, subd. 2 (1996).

Reversed in part, affirmed in part, and remanded.

Heard, considered, and decided by the court en banc.

OPINION

STRINGER, Justice.

Defendant Jack Basting challenges his conviction for second-degree assault with a dangerous weapon. The circumstances of his conviction arose from a confrontation with his ex-wife's boyfriend. Jack Basting admits to punching the boyfriend twice in the face, but claims that his fist did not constitute a dangerous weapon. The trial court determined that Basting's left fist was a dangerous weapon because of Basting's status as a professional boxer. Likewise, the court of appeals affirmed, again relying on Basting's professional boxing experience. Under our case law and under Minnesota's statutory definitions however, the proper legal standard for determining whether a fist or a foot is a dangerous weapon includes a broader spectrum of considerations than simply an assailant's athletic career. This court uses a de novo standard of review in determining whether the court below erred in its application the law. *Art Gobel, Inc. v. North Suburban Agencies*, 567 N.W.2d 511, 515 (Minn. 1997). Because we conclude that the courts below misapplied the proper legal standard, we reverse in part, affirm in part, and remand.

On March 9, 1995, Jack Basting and his girlfriend, Julia Ervin, went out to dinner to celebrate Ervin's birthday and arrived home at approximately 1:00 a.m. While they were out, Jack Basting's ex-wife, Theresa Basting, left a message on his answering machine indicating that there might be a problem with their daughter, Shanna. Upon hearing the message, Jack Basting called his ex-wife but received no answer. Worried, he and Ervin drove to Theresa Basting's house where she lived with her boyfriend, Brian Bowling, and her three children from her marriage with Jack Basting.

When they arrived, Ervin waited in the Jeep while Jack Basting went to check on his children. The door to the house was standing open and neither Theresa Basting nor Bowling were home. Jack Basting went inside and found his children sleeping safely. Meanwhile, Bowling and Theresa Basting had returned home and Theresa

Basting approached the Jeep and began banging her fists on the window and shouting at Ervin, who was still inside the Jeep.

There was conflicting testimony as to what occurred next. According to Jack Basting and Ervin, as Jack Basting emerged from the house and approached his Jeep, Bowling walked over to him and, without warning, punched him on the side of the face. Jack Basting testified that he was stunned and just "reacted" by punching Bowling twice in the face. Theresa Basting, however, testified that while she saw Jack Basting hit Bowling, she never saw Bowling strike Jack Basting. Theresa Basting also testified that Jack Basting tried to kick Bowling, but she stopped him by jumping on his back, an account Ervin denied. Bowling, who is 6 feet tall and weighs 200 pounds, suffered a broken nose and a deep cut requiring 12 stitches.

At the time of the altercation, Jack Basting had almost 20 years of professional and amateur boxing experience. He was 39 years old, 5 feet, 10 inches tall, and weighed 195 pounds. Although he had fought only four bouts in the last five years, he continued to train regularly. Basting testified that he can hit harder than an average man and that he is trained to hit in order to disable his opponent.

Basting was subsequently charged with (1) one count of assault in the first degree in violation of Minn. Stat. § 609.221 (1996); [1] (2) two counts of assault in the second degree in violation of Minn. Stat. § 609.222, subds. 1 and 2 (1996); [2] (3) one count of assault in the third degree in violation of Minn. Stat. § 609.223, subd. 1 (1996); [3] and (4) one count of possession of a firearm by a felon in violation of Minn. Stat. § 624.713 (1996). [4]

After a court trial, Basting was found not guilty of first degree assault and guilty on all of the remaining charges. The court imposed a 36 month executed sentence for second-degree assault with a dangerous weapon [5] and felon in possession of a firearm. The two other assault charges were dismissed as lesser included offenses.

Basting appealed his conviction claiming insufficient evidence and the court of appeals affirmed. Basting now appeals to this court asserting that his fist was not a "dangerous weapon" as required for second degree assault. Basting also alleges that the state failed to disprove his self-defense claim and that his federal and state constitutional rights were violated.

I.

We begin by addressing Basting's claim that the courts below erred in concluding that his fist was a dangerous weapon. The elements of Basting's assault conviction are: (1) an assault; (2) use of a dangerous weapon; and (3) infliction of substantial

bodily harm. [6] 10 Minn. Dist. Judges Ass'n, *Minnesota Practice*, CRIMJIG
13.06 (3rd ed. Supp. 1997); Minn. Stat. § 609.222, subd. 2. A dangerous weapon
includes "any * * * device or instrumentality that, in the manner it is used or intended to be used, is calculated or likely to produce death or great bodily harm."
[7] Minn. Stat. § 609.02, subd. 6 (1996). The issue then, is whether Basting used or
intended to use his fist *in a manner* calculated or likely to cause great bodily harm.

It is well-settled in Minnesota that under some circumstances, a fist or a foot may
constitute a dangerous weapon. *State v. Born*, 280 Minn. 306, 159 N.W.2d 283
(1968). While there are no specifically enumerated factors essential to determining
whether a fist or a foot is a dangerous weapon, in prior cases appellate review has
focused on a variety of factors such as the strength and size of the aggressor and
the victim, the vulnerability of the victim, the severity and duration of the attack,
the presence or absence of victim provocation, and the nature and the extent of the
injuries. *See Born*, 159 N.W.2d 283; *State v. Mings*, 289 N.W.2d 497 (Minn. 1980)
reh'g denied, (Mar. 25, 1980); *State v. Davis*, 540 N.W.2d 88 (Minn. App. 1995),
pet. for rev. denied (Jan. 31, 1996).

The circumstances in which Minnesota courts have found that a defendant's hands
or feet constitute a dangerous weapon have involved particularly brutal and pro-
longed attacks against vulnerable and sometimes defenseless victims. For example, in *Born* the defendant, without provocation, began shaking and pushing the
victim. 280 Minn. at 307, 159 N.W.2d at 284. As the victim tried to escape, the
defendant chased him, knocked him down with his fist and kicked him as he was
lying on the floor. *Id.* The victim was hospitalized for five days and could not return to work for two weeks. *Id.* Similarly, in *State v. Mings*, a fight ensued between
the defendant and the victim. 289 N.W.2d at 498. The defendant, who was wearing
cowboy boots, continued to beat and kick the victim numerous times about his
head and chest after the victim was unconscious. *Id.* Still more malicious was the
assault in *State v. Davis*. 540 N.W.2d at 89. There, the victim was 7 months preg-
nant at the time defendant attacked her. When she tried to run from the defendant,
he grabbed her and she fell to the ground on her hands and knees. *Id.* at 89-90. He
then slapped her and repeatedly kicked her in the side as if he was "jump-starting
a Harley." *Id.* at 89. One witness saw the defendant punch the victim five to ten
times in her face, torso and chest. *Id.*

In stark contrast, here the assault was of only momentary duration, Basting struck
Bowling only twice and left the scene shortly thereafter, Basting and Bowling
were of approximately equal height and weight, the incident took place in early
morning hours in a moment of confusion, and prior to the brief altercation there
were no words of provocation exchanged between them. While Bowling did suffer

a broken nose and a cut on his face, unlike the victims in *Born, Davis,* and *Ming,* Bowling's injuries did not require extensive hospitalization nor was he rendered incapacitated. In addressing the definition of a dangerous weapon in *Born* we suggested that something more than "a mere injury by fist, such as is likely to occur in ordinary assault and battery" is needed. *Born,* 280 Minn. at 307, 159 N.W.2d at 284 (*quoting State v. Peters,* 274 Minn. 309, 317, 143 N.W.2d 832, 837 (1966)). Absent here are any facts indicating that the manner in which Basting used his fist rose to a level of severity beyond that involved in an ordinary assault.

We do not suggest however, that whether an object is a dangerous weapon turns on the nature or severity of the victim's injuries. Such a conclusion would lead to a backward analysis which would begin and end with assessing the ensuing injury, a result inconsistent with both the legislature's definition of a dangerous weapon and with the structure of the criminal second-degree assault statute, which establishes infliction of bodily harm and use of a dangerous weapon as two separate elements. [8]

The trial court's findings that Basting's left fist constituted a dangerous weapon rested upon Basting's formal training and experience as a professional boxer. Immediately after the trial court determined that Basting used his left fist to hit Bowling twice in the face, it found:

3. Defendant is a professional prize fighter, last licensed in Minnesota in 1992, but who fought professionally as recently as the Fall of 1994 outside of Minnesota. Further, Defendant continued to train as a fighter as recently as March 14, 1995.

4. The left fist of Defendant, under the facts of this case, constitutes a dangerous weapon.

No other circumstances regarding the assault were referred to in the court's factual findings.

Similarly, the court of appeals focused primarily on Basting's status as a professional boxer. It affirmed, stating, "[t]he facts here present a strong case that appellant's fists are dangerous weapons, given that he is a professional boxer." *State v. Basting,* C5-96-493, slip op. at 3 (Minn. App. Jan. 14, 1997). When determining whether an object, even an inherently dangerous object, is a dangerous weapon, the court must examine not only the nature of the object itself, but also the manner in which it was used. *See, e.g., State v. Patton,* 414 N.W.2d 572, 574 (Minn. App. 1987) (stating that the defendant "brandished [a] knife *in such a manner* that the jury could have found it was used as a dangerous weapon") (emphasis added). While a defendant's prior professional athletic training may be relevant to and properly considered in a dangerous weapon analysis, it alone is not determinative. Raising the level of a defendant's criminality based on his or her career, physique, or expertise in a particular field of athletics is not consistent with the legislature's clear differentiation between assault and assault with a dangerous weapon. We hold, as a matter of law, that the manner in which Basting used his fist did not constitute the use of a dangerous weapon for purposes of an analysis under Minn. Stat. § 609.222, subd. 2.

II.

We now turn briefly to Basting's assertion that the state failed to prove beyond a reasonable doubt that he did not act in self-defense when he struck Bowling. The elements of self-defense are (1) the absence of aggression or provocation on the part of the defendant; (2) the defendant's actual and honest belief that he or she was in imminent danger of death or great bodily harm; (3) the existence of reasonable grounds for that belief; and (4) the absence of a reasonable possibility of retreat to avoid the danger. State v. McKissic, 415 N.W.2d 341, 344 (Minn. App. 1987) (citing State v. Johnson, 277 Minn. 368, 373, 152 N.W.2d 529, 532 (1967)); Minn. Stat. § 609.06, subd. 1(3) (1996). [9] The degree of force used in self-defense must not exceed that which appears to be necessary to a reasonable person under similar circumstances. McKissic, 415 N.W.2d at 344 (citing State v. Bland, 337 N.W.2d 378, 381 (Minn. 1983)). A defendant has the burden of going forward with evidence to support a claim of self-defense. State v. Graham, 371 N.W.2d 204, 209 (Minn. 1985). Once it is raised, the state has the burden of disproving one or more of these elements beyond a reasonable doubt. State v. Spaulding, 296 N.W.2d 870, 875 (Minn. 1980).

The trial court specifically found that Basting did not act in self-defense and the court of appeals affirmed. There was conflicting testimony as to who initiated the attack, and the trial court was free to credit the testimony that was adverse to Basting's position. Furthermore, the trial court could have determined that Basting used more force than was necessary to protect himself. Viewing the evidence in a light most favorable to the verdict, the trial court's finding that Basting was not acting in self-defense when he committed the assault was not clearly erroneous.

III.

Basting's final contention is that the courts below violated his constitutional rights when they classified his fist as a dangerous weapon "solely on the basis of [his] vocation as a professional boxer." Basting alleges that such a classification was discriminatory and in violation of the United States and Minnesota Equal Protection Clauses. Basting did not claim constitutional violations in either court below.

While this court may choose to hear an issue raised for the first time to this court when the interests of justice require, in light of our ruling that Basting's fist did not constitute a dangerous weapon, the interests of justice do not require our review of Basting's equal protection issue. *Roby v. State*, 547 N.W.2d 354, 357 (Minn. 1996) (citing *State v. Sorenson*, 441 N.W.2d 455, 457 (Minn. 1989)).

We reverse Basting's conviction of second-degree assault with a dangerous weapon under Minn. Stat. § 609.222, subd. 2, but because the evidence is sufficient to establish that he committed an assault resulting in substantial bodily harm, his conviction is reduced to the lesser included offense of assault in the third degree in violation of Minn. Stat. § 609.223, subd. 1.

Reversed in part, affirmed in part, and remanded for resentencing for violation of Minn. Stat. § 609.223, subd. 1, assault in the third degree.

Footnotes

[1] Minnesota Statutes § 609.221 provides:

Assault in the first degree. Whoever assaults another and inflicts great bodily harm may be sentenced to imprisonment for not more than 20 years or to payment of a fine of not more than $30,000, or both.

[2] Minnesota Statutes § 609.222 provides:

Assault in the second degree Subdivision 1. Dangerous weapon. Whoever assaults another with a dangerous weapon may be sentenced to imprisonment for not more than seven years or to payment of a fine of not more than $14,000, or both.Subd. 2. Dangerous weapon; substantial bodily harm. Whoever assaults another with a dangerous weapon and inflicts substantial bodily harm may be sentenced to imprisonment for not more than ten years or to payment of a fine of not more than $20,000, or both.

[3] Minnesota Statutes § 609.223 provides:

Assault in the third degree Subdivision 1. Substantial bodily harm. Whoever assaults another and inflicts substantial bodily harm may be sentenced to imprisonment for not more than five years or to payment of a fine of not more than $10,000, or both.

[4] There was no gun involved in the assault. This charge resulted from Basting's

possession of a pistol at the time of his arrest four days after the assault. Minnesota Statutes § 624.713 provides that certain people are ineligible to have pistols or semiautomatic military-style assault weapons, including a person who has been convicted of a crime of violence unless 10 years have elapsed. Basting had been convicted of assault in the second degree within the past 10 years.

[5] Because this was Basting's second offense with a dangerous weapon, he was sentenced pursuant to Minn. Stat. § 609.11 (1996) which provides: Minimum sentences of imprisonment Subd. 4. Dangerous weapon. Any defendant convicted of an offense listed in subdivision 9 in which the defendant or an accomplice, at the time of the offense, used, whether by brandishing, displaying, threatening with, or otherwise employing, a dangerous weapon other than a firearm, shall be committed to the commissioner of corrections for not less than one year plus one day, nor more than the maximum sentence provided by law. Any defendant convicted of a second or subsequent offense in which the defendant or an accomplice, at the time of the offense, used a dangerous weapon other than a firearm, shall be committed to the commissioner of corrections for not less than three years nor more than the maximum sentence provided by law.

[6] The elements of assault and infliction of substantial bodily harm are not disputed in this appeal.

[7] "Great bodily harm" means "bodily injury which creates a high probability of death, or which causes serious permanent disfigurement, or which causes a permanent or protracted loss or impairment of the function of any bodily member or organ or other serious bodily harm." Minn. Stat. § 609.02, subd. 8 (1996).

[8] Minnesota's second-degree assault statute is divided into two parts, each carrying a different penalty. Minn. Stat. § 609.222. For a conviction of second-degree assault under Minn. Stat. § 609.222, subd. 1, the victim need not suffer *any* bodily harm, but the defendant must have used a dangerous weapon. Under subdivision 2, the defendant must have used a deadly weapon *and* caused substantial bodily harm.

[9] Minnesota Statutes § 609.06, subdivision 1(3) provides that "reasonable force may be used upon or toward the person of another without the other's consent when the following circumstances exist or the actor reasonably believes them to exist * * * * when used by any person in resisting or aiding another to resist an offense against the person * * *."

STATE v. SPAULDING No. 49618.

296 N.W.2d 870 (1980)

STATE of Minnesota, Respondent,
v.
James Montgomery SPAULDING, Appellant.

Supreme Court of Minnesota.

August 29, 1980.

C. Paul Jones, Public Defender, Michael F. Cromett and Robert Streitz, Asst. Public Defenders, Minneapolis, for appellant.Warren Spannaus, Atty. Gen., St. Paul, Thomas L. Johnson, County Atty., Vernon E. Bergstrom, Chief, App. Section, David W. Larson and Toni A. Beitz, Asst. County Attys., Minneapolis, for respondent.

Heard before KELLY, TODD, and WAHL, JJ., and considered and decided by the court en banc.

WAHL, Justice.

Defendant appeals from his conviction by a Hennepin County jury of aggravated assault and felon in possession of a pistol.[1] He was sentenced to three to five years on the aggravated assault conviction. Defendant raises the following issues on appeal: (1) whether he was denied his constitutional right to due process of law when the State reinstated two charges in the complaint on retrial after the defendant successfully set aside his conviction; (2) whether the State violated Minn.Stat. § 609.035 (1978) by reinstating two charges in the complaint on retrial after the defendant successfully set aside his conviction; (3) whether the evidence was sufficient to support defendant's conviction for aggravated assault and felon in possession of a pistol; (4) whether the prosecutor committed reversible error in his final argument; and (5) whether the trial court committed reversible error in its instructions to the jury. We reverse and remand for a new trial.

1. Defendant first argues that he was denied due process of law because the State was allowed to reinstate two charges in the complaint on retrial after he had successfully set aside his conviction on appeal. A resolution of this issue requires discussion of the procedural history of the case.

The incident from which defendant's convictions arose occurred on April 25, 1977. Defendant was charged initially with aggravated robbery, aggravated assault, and felon in possession of a pistol. On July 15, 1977, the attorney for the State and defendant's attorney negotiated an agreement which resulted in a dismissal of the counts of aggravated robbery and aggravated assault, with the defendant being tried to the court on stipulated facts on the charge of felon in possession of a pistol. He was found guilty by the Hennepin County District Court and sentenced to a term of 0 to 5 years. This conviction was set aside by the court in September 1977, on a petition for post-conviction relief, on the ground that defendant had not properly waived his right to a jury trial. The State subsequently moved to reinstate the previously dismissed counts of aggravated robbery and aggravated assault, which motion was granted. The County Attorney offered to again dismiss the counts of aggravated robbery and aggravated assault if the defendant would either plead guilty to the charge of felon in possession of a pistol or agree to have it tried to a court on stipulated facts. Defendant rejected the offer and was convicted by the jury on two of the three counts and sentenced on one of them.

Defendant argues that the reinstatement of the two charges after his successful appeal in effect penalized him for exercising his constitutional right to a jury trial. He relies on Blackledge v. Perry, 417 U.S. 21, 94 S.Ct. 2098, 40 L.Ed.2d 628 (1974), and North Carolina v. Pearce, 395 U.S. 711, 89 S.Ct. 2072, 23 L.Ed.2d 656 (1969), to support his position.

The United States Supreme Court in North Carolina v. Pearce held that whenever a judge imposes a more severe sentence on a defendant after a new trial conducted because his previous conviction was set aside, due process requires that reasons for the more severe sentence must affirmatively appear, based on objective information in the record. Otherwise, the defendant's fear of retaliatory motivation on the part of the sentencing judge might chill his right to appeal.

In Blackledge v. Perry, the defendant exercised his statutory right to a trial de novo after conviction of a misdemeanor in a lower court. After filing his notice of appeal, but before the trial de novo, the prosecutor obtained an indictment charging the defendant with a felony based on the same conduct which underlay the misdemeanor charge. The court held that due process requires that a person convicted of an offense is entitled to pursue his statutory right to a trial de novo without apprehension that the State will retaliate by substituting a more serious charge for the original one, thus subjecting him to a significantly increased potential period of incarceration. 417 U.S. at 28, 94 S.Ct. at 2102. The court noted, however, that due process is not violated wherever increased punishment is a possibility upon retrial after appeal, but only where there is a "realistic likelihood of 'vindictiveness,'"[2] such as in the case that was before the court. 417 U.S. at 27, 94 S.Ct. at 2102.

These cases make clear that a defendant may not be given a greater sentence after retrial on the same charges, where the possibility of vindictiveness is strong. In the instant case, however, there is little possibility of vindictiveness. The prosecutor did not file new, more serious charges after the appeal; he reinstated the charges from the original complaint. Moreover, he offered the defendant the same "deal" before the second trial as he had before the first trial, but the defendant refused the offer.

The State relies on several federal cases holding that no due process violation occurs when the state reinstates counts after defendant's guilty plea is set aside or withdrawn by the defendant, which counts were previously dismissed pursuant to the guilty plea. Those cases rely on the "possibility of vindictiveness" test and hold that there can be no appearance of vindictiveness under these circumstances because after the guilty plea is set aside and the original counts reinstated, the State and the defendant are placed in the same positions they were in before the plea bargain was accepted. See Chapman v. Estelle, 593 F.2d 687 (5th Cir. 1979); United States v. Osborne, 591 F.2d 413 (8th Cir. 1978), cert. denied, 440 U.S. 973, 99 S.Ct. 1539, 59 L.Ed.2d 791 (1979); United States v. Johnson, 537 F.2d 1170 (4th Cir. 1976); United States v. Anderson, 514 F.2d 583 (7th Cir. 1975); Arechiga v. Texas, 469 F.2d 646 (5th Cir. 1972), cert. denied, 414 U.S. 932, 94 S.Ct. 236, 38 L.Ed.2d 162 (1973); United States v. Rines, 453 F.2d 878 (3rd Cir. 1971); United States ex rel. Williams v. McMann, 436 F.2d 103 (2d Cir. 1970), cert. denied, 402 U.S. 914, 91 S.Ct. 1396, 28 L.Ed.2d 656 (1971); Sefcheck v. Brewer, 301 F.Supp. 793 (S.D.Iowa 1969). These decisions establish a distinction between defendants who were convicted and received a greater sentence for the same offense on retrial and those defendants who pled guilty, withdrew their plea, and received a greater sentence on conviction for the more serious charges originally brought.[3]

This distinction is also present in the few Minnesota cases dealing with the same issue. In State v. Holmes, 281 Minn. 294, 161 N.W.2d 650 (1968), this court held that the imposition of a longer sentence after a new trial and second conviction for the same offense was a violation of public policy.[4] In Beltowski v. State, 289 Minn. 215, 183 N.W.2d 563 (1971), the defendant was charged with burglary, permitted to plead guilty to a lesser included offense, and was sentenced. Later, after the defendant successfully moved to withdraw his guilty plea, the original charge was reinstated. On conviction, defendant received a greater sentence than for the lesser charge, which he claimed violated due process. This court disagreed, stating:

Here petitioner, permitted as he was to be relieved from the consequences of his plea agreement, now insists that the prosecution be held to the sentence for the lesser charge for which he successfully negotiated. To do so would permit a defendant to use his plea of guilty as a tactical device to limit the charge which could be brought against him. This is not a case where a greater charge was reinstated or increased punishment imposed after a reversal of a conviction on appeal. State v. Holmes, 281 Minn. 294, 161 N.W.2d 650. Nor is there any evidence that the 10-year sentence resulted from any vindictiveness on the part of the sentencing court because petitioner was afforded his election to stand trial. It is simply a case where petitioner refused to be bound by his plea agreement, thereby justifying the court in reinstating the original charge so as to place the parties in the positions which existed prior to the plea agreement.

289 Minn. at 220, 183 N.W.2d at 566. See also State v. Ackerley, 296 Minn. 495, 207 N.W.2d 272 (1973), where we held that the Holmes rule did not apply to limit defendant's final sentence where the State offered a limited sentence in exchange for a plea of guilty but the defendant declined the offer, went to trial, and was convicted.

The defendant here did not receive a greater sentence after retrial on the same offense, nor did the prosecutor substitute, after reversal on appeal, more serious charges than were originally brought. The State merely reinstated the charges from the original complaint and offered the defendant the same deal he had been offered before the first trial. Defendant, in effect, accepted a plea bargain which was set aside by his appeal, thereby returning the parties to their original positions. We can find no indication of judicial or prosecutorial vindictiveness on the record before us, and therefore we find no due process violation.

2. Defendant further contends that the reinstatement of the two charges on retrial after his successful appeal violates Minn.Stat. § 609.035 (1978). That statute provides:

Except as provided in section 609.585 [burglary], if a person's conduct constitutes more than one offense under the laws of this state he may be punished for only one of such offenses and a conviction or acquittal of any one of them is a bar to prosecution for any other of them. All such offenses may be included in one prosecution which shall be stated in separate counts.

Defendant's conviction of both aggravated assault and pistol possession was permissible under the statute, and his sentence for only one of these convictions was proper. Defendant contends, however, that the State waived its right to prosecute him on the dismissed charges by proceeding to trial initially on the pistol possession charge.

Only a prior conviction or acquittal bars prosecution for other offenses arising out of a single behavioral incident. State v. Simon, 275 N.W.2d 51 (Minn.1979); State v. Gaulke, 281 Minn. 327, 161 N.W.2d 662 (1968). Defendant's first conviction, which was set aside on appeal, was never a final conviction under the statute so as to bar the State's prosecution of the other offenses arising out of the same conduct. Therefore, defendant's arguments under Minn.Stat. § 609.035 must fail.

3. Defendant maintains that the evidence was insufficient to support

his conviction for felon in possession of a pistol because the State failed to prove that the pistol was operable and/or that its possession was not justified. He also argues that the conviction for aggravated assault must be vacated because the State failed to prove that defendant did not act in self-defense.

We need not decide whether, in order to convict the defendant of the pistol possession charge, the State was required to prove that the pistol was operable, because there were sufficient facts presented at trial which tended to show that it was, in fact, operable. The gun was loaded. The defendant claimed he was afraid he would be killed when he first saw the gun. The defendant also testified he was afraid to drop it on the sidewalk once the police arrived, because if it fired, the police would shoot him. The gun was received into evidence so the jury could inspect it. Finally, defendant introduced no evidence tending to show inoperability.

The more difficult questions are whether there was sufficient evidence to prove that the defendant did not act in self-defense and whether the evidence was sufficient to prove that defendant's possession of the gun was not justified. The State must prove beyond a reasonable doubt that the defendant did not act in self-defense, once the defense is raised. State v. White, 295 Minn. 217, 225, 203 N.W.2d 852, 858 (1973). To do so, the State must disprove at least one of the following elements of self-defense: (1) the absence of aggression or provocation on the part of the defendant; (2) the actual and honest belief of the defendant that he was in imminent danger of death or great bodily harm and that it was necessary to take the action he did; and (3) the existence of reasonable grounds for such belief. State v. Johnson, 277 Minn. 368, 373, 152 N.W.2d 529, 532 (1967).

The record indicates that in the early evening of April 25, 1977, Sandra Anderson backed into the car defendant had borrowed from a friend when she was attempting to pull out of a parking space. Defendant, who is a felon, and who did not have a gun in his possession, crossed the street with two friends to question Anderson about the accident. Anderson's companion, Leon Kirby, a drug dealer whom defendant had known in Stillwater Prison as a dangerous man who always carried a gun, got out of Anderson's car and drew a gun from under his jacket. In the ensuing fight for possession of the weapon, defendant prevailed. The fight continued briefly until Kirby fled the scene with minor injuries, throwing some live cartridges into a flower box as he ran. Although we have little doubt that the defendant's initial reaction in taking the gun from Kirby was in self-defense, the closer questions are whether the defendant, even if justified in wresting the gun away from Kirby, continued his aggression beyond the limits of self-defense or his possession of the pistol beyond justifiable possession. Defendant admits that twice during the incident the gun was pointed at Kirby but claims this was a reasonable action of self-defense. The evidence was conflicting as to how long defendant continued beating Kirby once he wrested the gun away from him. Furthermore, defendant did not rid himself of the gun once he had gotten possession of it and Kirby had left the field of battle. There was testimony that at one point one of defendant's friends had possession of the gun but when the police arrived on the scene minutes later and ordered defendant from his car, he was holding the gun in his hand, holding it, according to his testimony, by the barrel. Considering that the entire incident lasted no more than 15 minutes, defendant's conduct and possession of the gun does not seem unreasonable. The jury, however, the finder of fact, evidently found that the defendant's actions after obtaining the gun from Kirby were not justified either as to self-defense or possession.

When the sufficiency of the evidence is raised on appeal, this court's scope of review is limited to determining whether, viewing the evidence in the light most favorable to the jury verdict, the jury could reasonably have found the defendant guilty of the crime charged. State v. Swain, 269 N.W.2d 707, 712 (Minn.1978). Given this limited scope of review on fact questions, we must affirm defendant's conviction unless we determine that substantial trial errors occurred which require reversal.

4. Defendant maintains that the prosecutor made several improper and prejudicial remarks to the jury in his final argument. None of these comments was objected to below by counsel; and, therefore, in the usual case the objection is waived. State v. Flom, 285 N.W.2d 476 (Minn.1979). However, because this case is a close one, it is appropriate to determine whether the prosecutor erred and, if so, whether his misconduct likely played a substantial part in influencing the jury to convict. State v. Caron, 300 Minn. 123, 218 N.W.2d 197 (1974).

Defendant argues that the prosecutor misled the jury regarding its duties and the State's burden of proof, improperly commented on the defendant's credibility, and improperly interjected broader issues than defendant's guilt or innocence into his argument. It is improper for the prosecutor to inject into closing argument his personal opinion about the veracity of a witness or the guilt or innocence of the defendant. State v. Williams, 297 Minn. 76, 210 N.W.2d 21 (1973); State v. Jones, 277 Minn. 174, 152 N.W.2d 67 (1967). Nor may counsel introduce issues broader than the guilt or innocence of the accused into his argument. State v. Clark, 291 Minn. 79, 189 N.W.2d 167 (1971); State v. Gaulke, 281 Minn. 327, 161 N.W.2d 662 (1968). Although the prosecutor's comments in the instant case were in some measure improper, our review of the record persuades us that those comments were unlikely to have played a substantial part in influencing the jury's verdict.

5. Defendant urges error in the trial court's instructions to the jury. Defendant requested that the court instruct the jury that self-defense is a defense to aggravated assault and felon in possession of a pistol. The court instructed the jury on self-defense with respect to the aggravated robbery and aggravated assault charges. No instruction on self-defense was given with respect to the pistol possession charge, but the court instructed the jury on justification or necessity as follows:

If you find that the defendant obtained a pistol in defense of himself or another, that is justified and the defendant has not violated this law. However, once the necessity for his possession is reasonably over he no longer may possess the pistol. It is for you to determine if continued possession is reasonably justified.

At the end of its instructions to the jury, the court asked counsel whether they had any objections or corrections to make, and defendant made none.

Defendant argues first that the court's instruction on necessity was confusing because it failed to give the jury any guidance in defining necessity and failed to inform them that the State had the burden to establish beyond a reasonable doubt that defendant's possession was not justified. He also argues that the court's failure to instruct the jury on self-defense for the pistol possession charge was reversible error.

Instructions to the jury should be considered as a whole. State v. Columbus,258 N.W.2d 122 (Minn.1977). Taking all of the court's instructions together, the charge was sufficient to convey to the jury that the State must prove defendant's guilt beyond a reasonable doubt on every element of the offense, including proof beyond a reasonable doubt that defendant's possession of the gun was not justified. The court instructed the jury as to the presumption of innocence, that the defendant need not prove his innocence, and that the State must prove defendant's guilt beyond a reasonable doubt. The court also told the jury that whatever evidence was offered, the State retained the burden of proof beyond a reasonable doubt. The State's burden was mentioned again with respect to each of the offenses and with respect to the defense of self-defense. Finally, the court instructed the jury that it was proper for them to find the defendant not guilty unless they were convinced he was guilty beyond a reasonable doubt. Although the court did not elaborate on the meaning of "necessity," defendant offered no specific suggestions as to how the court's instruction could have been improved, and the instruction was not complex or confusing. Moreover, we find no error in the court's failure to instruct on self-defense on the pistol possession charge where an instruction on justification mentioning self-defense was given and the defendant did not object to that instruction at the time of trial.

Lastly, defendant argues that the court abused its discretion by instructing the jury that no testimony would be reread and by refusing to consider the jury's request to read defendant's testimony. Before the jury began its deliberations, the court told the jury that they must rely on their memory of the evidence because no testimony would be read to them. After more than nine hours of deliberation, the jury sent the court a note saying, "We are deadlocked in disagreement in what the law is and in the testimony of the defendant. We ask you to clarify these matters for us if you can." The court's response was, "I think I've explained to you that we weren't going to reread any testimony, but if you would like me to reread some law?" After the jury had deliberated for a total of about 15 hours, they returned to court, stating that they were deadlocked. After rereading an instruction on the jury's duty to attempt to reach a decision, the jury was allowed to continue its deliberations. Less than an hour later, they reached a verdict.

Rule 26.03, subd. 19(2) of the Minnesota Rules of Criminal Procedure provides as follows:

1. If the jury, after retiring for deliberation, requests a review of certain testimony or other evidence, the jurors shall be conducted to the courtroom. The court, after notice to the prosecutor and defense counsel, may have the requested parts of the testimony read to the jury and permit the jury to re-examine the requested materials admitted into evidence.2. The court need not submit evidence to the jury for review beyond that specifically requested by the jury, but in its discretion the court may also have the jury review other evidence relating to the same factual issue so as not to give undue prominence to the evidence requested.

Whether or not to grant a jury's request for a reading of trial testimony is within the discretion of the trial court. In State v. Scott, 277

N.W.2d 659 (Minn.1979), this court upheld the trial court's conclusion that the jury's request for rereading of nearly half of the total trial testimony was unreasonable. Similarly, in State v. Schluter,281 N.W.2d 174 (Minn.1979), we held that it was not error for the trial court to refuse to give the jury a transcript which amounted to over one-third of the entire trial testimony.

Defendant's testimony covered 35 pages out of approximately 393 pages of testimony. The trial court did not attempt to narrow the jury's request to specific parts of the testimony. He categorically refused to honor any requests for rereading evidence. In fact, the court refused to exercise its discretion at all by determining at the outset of deliberations, and before any requests from the jury, that no testimony would be reread. Under the circumstances of this case, the trial court abused its discretion to the defendant's prejudice. The effect of the court's inaction was to force the jury to decide the case on the basis of sketchy memory of the evidence. The error was especially prejudicial since the requested testimony was the testimony of the defendant, the witness who most clearly presented evidence supporting the claim of self-defense. Defendant's testimony went to the core of the case, and it is clear from the record that the jury needed assistance. Under these circumstances, even though the defendant failed to object at trial, the trial court committed prejudicial error by refusing the jury's request in such a close case. Justice requires a new trial. See People v. Butler,47 Cal.App.3d 273, 120 Cal.Rptr. 647 (1975); LaMonte v. State,145 So.2d 889 (Fla.App.1962).

Reversed and remanded for a new trial.

KELLY, J., took no part in the consideration or decision of this case.

AMDAHL, J., not having been a member of this court at the time of argument and submission, took no part in the consideration or decision of this case.

FootNotes

1. Minn.Stat. § 609.225, subd. 2 (1978) provides as follows: "Whoever assaults another with a dangerous weapon but without inflicting great bodily harm may be sentenced to imprisonment for not more than five years or to payment of a fine of not more than $5,000, or both." [This statute has been recodified at Minn.Stat. § 609.222 (Supp.1979).]Minn.Stat. § 624.713, subd. 1 (1978) provides: "The following persons shall not be entitled to possess a pistol: * * *"(b) A person who has been convicted in this state or elsewhere of a crime of violence * *."Subd. 2 provides: "A person named in subdivision 1, clause (b) who possesses a pistol is guilty of a felony. * * *"

2. The court relied on two other cases adopting the "possible vindictiveness" test, Chaffin v. Stynchcombe,412 U.S. 17, 93 S.Ct. 1977, 36 L.Ed.2d 714 (1973), and Colten v. Kentucky,407 U.S. 104, 92 S.Ct. 1953, 32 L.Ed.2d 584 (1972). The court held in Chaffin that due process does not bar a jury from rendering a higher sentence on retrial following a reversal of a prior conviction, because there is so little potential for vindictiveness in jury sentencing. The court held in Colten that Kentucky's two-tiered system for prosecuting misdemeanors, which allowed for a possible greater penalty after an appeal and a trial de novo, was constitutional because there was no possibility of vindictiveness inherent in it.

3. In Corbitt v. New Jersey,439 U.S. 212, 223-24, 99 S.Ct. 492, 500, 58 L.Ed.2d 466 (1978), the United States Supreme Court reaffirmed that "withholding the possibility of leniency" from those defendants who go to trial rather than plead "cannot be equated with impermissible punishment as long as our cases sustaining plea bargaining remain undisturbed."

4. Subsequently, in State v. Johnson, 299 Minn. 143, 216 N.W.2d 904 (1974), we held that after a trial de novo in the district court on appeal from a conviction in lower court, the district court may impose a sentence greater than that imposed by the lower court, absent an actual showing of vindictiveness. In State v. Alexander,290 N.W.2d 745 (Minn.1980), we held that where there is no possibility

of vindictiveness, the amendment of a complaint after mistrial, adding new counts to an original charge, does not constitute a denial of due process. 290 N.W.2d at 748-49.

STATE v. GRAHAM No. C4-84-1905.

366 N.W.2d 335 (1985)

STATE of Minnesota, Appellant,
v.
Thomas Elmer GRAHAM, Respondent.

Court of Appeals of Minnesota.

April 16, 1985.

Hubert H. Humphrey, III, Atty. Gen., Thomas Johnson, Hennepin County Atty., Paul R. Jennings, Asst. County Atty., Minneapolis, for appellant.

Rick E. Mattox, Asst. Public Defender, Minneapolis, for respondent.

Heard, considered, and decided by HUSPENI, P.J., and FOLEY and WOZNIAK, JJ.

OPINION

HUSPENI, Judge.

The State appeals dismissal of a charge of assault in the second degree, assault with a dangerous weapon. The trial court ruled that the definition of dangerous weapon in Minn.Stat. § 609.02, subd. 6 (1982), was unconstitutional because it was vague and diluted the State's burden of proof. We reverse and remand for trial.

FACTS

On March 7, 1984 respondent Thomas Elmer Graham allegedly struck Suzanne Olson on the face, legs, and arms with a four-foot metal floor lamp with a large metal base. They had shared living quarters intermittently for approximately two years. The complaint indicates that, during the alleged assault, Olson curled up into a defensive position attempting to shield herself from repeated blows aimed at her head. The complaint states that Olson suffered a cut around one eye and severe bruising during the assault, and suffered headaches and substantial pain as a result, but did not incur great bodily harm.

On September 26, 1984 Graham moved the trial court to declare, under the facts of this case, Minn.Stat. § 609.02, subd. 6 (1983), unconstitutional. Written arguments were submitted to the trial court, as were photographs of Olson's injuries. The trial court had also formerly viewed the lamp.

The trial court found that Olson suffered no substantial harm, held that Minn.Stat. § 609.02, subd. 6, was unconstitutionally vague and diluted the State's burden of proof, and granted Graham's motion to dismiss the complaint.

The State of Minnesota now brings this appeal to reinstate the complaint and moves this court to declare that Minn.Stat. § 609.02, subd. 6, is not vague, and does not dilute the State's burden of proof.

ISSUES

1. Is the definition of dangerous weapon found in Minn.Stat. § 609.02, subd. 6, impermissibly vague?

2. Does the definition of dangerous weapon found in Minn.Stat. § 609.02, subd. 6, unconstitutionally dilute the State's burden of proof?

ANALYSIS

The Minnesota statutes relevant to this appeal read as follows:

609.222 (1982) Assault in the Second Degree Whoever assaults another with a dangerous weapon but without inflicting great bodily harm may be sentenced to imprisonment for not more than five years or to payment of a fine of not more than $5000 or both.609.02, subd. 6 (1982) Dangerous weapon"Dangerous weapon" means any * * * device or instrumentality which, in the manner it is used or intended to be used, is calculated or likely to produce death or great bodily harm.1. The void for vagueness doctrine: * * * requires that a penal statute define the criminal offense with sufficient definiteness that ordinary people can understand what conduct is prohibited and in a manner that does not encourage arbitrary and discriminatory enforcement.

Kolender v. Lawson,461 U.S. 352 at 357, 103 S.Ct. 1855, 1858, 75 L.Ed.2d 903 (1983), citations omitted.

Graham asserts that, since conceivably any object is "likely to produce death or great bodily harm" under the right circumstances, the phrase encourages arbitrary and discriminatory enforcement by law enforcement officials.

In recent years, the requirement that legislatures establish minimal guidelines to govern law enforcement has become the more important element of the two-pronged void-for-vagueness doctrine. Id. at 358, 103 S.Ct. at 1858, citing Smith v. Goguen,415 U.S. 566 at 574, 94 S.Ct. 1242, 1247-48, 39 L.Ed. 605 (1974). Such guidelines are important to ensure that police, prosecutors, judges and juries follow a legal standard rather than their personal predilections. Kolender, 461 U.S. at 358, 103 S.Ct. at 1859. Due process, however, does not require "impossible standards of clarity." Id. at 361, 103 S.Ct. at 1860; United States v. Petrillo,332 U.S. 1, 7-8, 67 S.Ct. 1538, 1542, 91 L.Ed. 1877 (1947).

It would be impossible to specify any and all objects capable of producing death or great bodily harm when used to inflict injury on another. Thus, by necessity, the definition of dangerous weapon in subdivision 6 must be expressed in flexible terms and be broad and inclusive. See State v. Reynolds,243 Minn. 196, 204, 66 N.W.2d 886, 891 (1954).

A statute proscribing a class of behavior in flexible terms is not unconstitutional for vagueness if it can be determined with reasonable certainty or definiteness the conduct that is disapproved. Id. Graham is charged with using a four-foot long metal lamp as a bludgeon in an assault upon another. The victim incurred injuries, but great bodily harm was not inflicted. Unquestionably, it can be determined that the alleged conduct is reasonably within the boundaries of the proscribed class of conduct. Whether the lamp as allegedly used in this case does constitute a dangerous weapon is for the jury to determine after a full trial on the merits.

The trial court's finding that Olson suffered no substantial bodily harm appears to be an acceptance of Graham's argument that the lamp cannot be a dangerous weapon unless it caused great or substantial bodily harm. Such argument is contrary to the valid legislative intent supporting the specific statutory definitions of a dangerous weapon and second degree assault. The assaultive conduct while using an object capable of inflicting great bodily harm is proscribed regardless of whether bodily harm is actually incurred.

2. Graham argues that the term "likely" in the definition of dangerous weapon in subdivision 6 allows for a lower standard of proof than the constitutionally required standard of beyond a reasonable doubt.

The issue presented here is analagous to that addressed by the supreme court in State v. Tibbets,281 N.W.2d 499 (Minn. 1979), and State v. Bicknese,285 N.W.2d 684 (Minn.1979).

At issue in Tibbets and Bicknese was the following portion of the definition of sexual contact:

"Sexual contact" includes any of the following acts committed without the complainant's consent, if the acts can reasonably be construed as being for the purpose of satisfying the actor's sexual or aggressive impulses * * *.

Minn.Stat. § 609.341, subd. 11 (1978).

It was argued in Tibbets, and the supreme court agreed, that the phrase "can reasonably be construed" impermissibly diluted the requirement of proof from acts which must be proved beyond a reasonable doubt to that which is possible from several reasonable alternatives. Tibbets, 281 N.W.2d at 500.

Similarly, we find that the portion of the definition of dangerous weapon containing the challenged term, "likely," could be construed by a jury so as to dilute the state's burden of proof. See Id. at 500, State v. Bicknese, 285 N.W.2d at 686. However, the remedy is not to declare the statute void as Graham asserts, but to give the jury an instruction which informs it of the substance of the statute without using the offending or confusing language.[1]Id.

DECISION

1. The definition of dangerous weapon set forth in Minn.Stat. § 609.02, subd. 6 (1982), is not unconstitutionally vague.

2. The definition of dangerous weapon set forth in Minn.Stat. § 609.02, subd. 6 (1982), does not dilute the State's burden of proof when appropriate jury instructions are given.

Reversed and remanded for trial.

FootNotes

1. We recognize that the Minnesota Jury Instruction Guide in Crim. JIG 13.06 contains the statutory language to which Graham objects. Unlike the situation in Bicknese, the Crim. JIG drafting committee apparently did not foresee a constitutional attack. We note with approval the following definition of "deadly weapon" set forth by the National Conference of Commissioners on Uniform State Laws: * * * any firearm, or other weapon, device, instrument, material or substance, whether animate or inanimate, which in the manner it is used or is intended to be used is known to be capable of producing death or serious bodily injury.Model Penal Code § 210.0 (1974).

STATE v. BLAND No. CX-82-771.

STATE of Minnesota, Respondent,
v.
Gary L. BLAND, Appellant.

Supreme Court of Minnesota.

August 12, 1983.

Rehearing Denied September 27, 1983.

C. Paul Jones, State Public Defender, Robert D. Goodell, Asst. State Public Defender, Minneapolis, for appellant.

Hubert H. Humphrey, III, Atty. Gen., St. Paul, Thomas L. Johnson, County Atty., William A. Neiman, Asst. County Atty., Minneapolis, for respondent.

Considered and decided by the court en banc without oral argument.

AMDAHL, Chief Justice.

Defendant was found guilty by a district court jury of a charge of assault in the second degree, Minn.Stat. § 609.222 (1982) (assault with a dangerous weapon). Pursuant to Minn.Stat. § 609.11 (1982) and Minnesota Sentencing Guidelines and Commentary, II.E., the trial court sentenced defendant to 54 months in prison. Defendant appeals from judgment of conviction and from the order denying his motion for a new trial. Defendant seeks an outright reversal on the ground that the state failed to prove that he did not act in self-defense. Alternatively, he seeks a new trial on the grounds that (a) he was prejudiced because the prosecutor failed to call a witness referred to in the prosecutor's opening statement, (b) the trial court improperly restricted defense counsel's cross-examination of the victim about his prior acts of violence, (c) the prosecutor committed plain error in eliciting evidence that defendant's possession of the weapon he used, a sawed-off shotgun, was a separate crime, and (d) the trial court erred in its instructions on self-defense. We affirm.

This prosecution arose from an episode that occurred on the evening of Friday, October 9, and the morning of Saturday, October 10, 1981, in Minneapolis. Defendant and the victim, Jeffrey Larson, who were friends, became involved in an argument at their usual hangout, Moore on University. Police, who were called when the two became disruptive and disorderly, asked Larson and his brother to leave. Larson returned later and a fight ensued, with defendant throwing the first punch but with Larson getting the better of the fight before it was stopped by police. After the fight, defendant walked home. Some time later Larson went to defendant's residence and asked defendant why he had "sucker punched" him. Defendant then began to get up from where he was sitting and said, "I suppose you want to go outside." Larson replied, "That sounds about right." Larson testified that as defendant got up, defendant pulled out his sawed-off shotgun and, from a distance of 9 feet, fired it once.

Defendant, who was the only other witness to the actual shooting, testified that Larson woke him up and kicked him in the head notwithstanding his statement that he did not want to fight. He testified that after Larson banged his head on a chandelier and ripped the chandelier down, Larson stood about 8 or 9 feet away from him and said, "Come on, Gary." He testified that he then reached down, got the gun, aimed it at Larson's legs, and, without warning, fired it. He testified that he did not shoot to kill, just to stop Larson, that he did this because he feared that Larson was going to beat him up so severely that he would have to go to the hospital.

1. Defendant contends first that the state did not meet its burden of proving that the shooting was not in self-defense. Minn.Stat. § 609.06(3) (1982) allows the use of reasonable force by a person to resist or to aid another to resist an offense against the person. The person may use force to defend himself against an assault if he believes it to be reasonably necessary and if it would appear to a reasonable person under similar circumstances to be reasonably necessary, with the amount of force used to defend himself being limited to that which a reasonable person in the same circumstances would believe to be necessary. The state concedes on appeal that defendant reasonably believed that Larson was going to assault him but it argues that defendant's own testimony established that his response was unnecessary, unreasonable, and excessive. We agree. In fact, defendant admitted in his testimony that Larson was about 8 feet from him at the time of the shooting (which was consistent with Larson's testimony and the expert testimony), that Larson was standing still, and that he shot Larson without warning. Under the circumstances, the jury clearly was justified in concluding that the state had met its burden of proving that defendant did not act in self-defense.

2. Defendant's next contention is that he was prejudiced because a witness did not testify after the prosecutor told the jury in his opening statement that the witness would testify.

In Frazier v. Cupp,394 U.S. 731, 89 S.Ct. 1420, 22 L.Ed.2d 684 (1969), the prosecutor had been told by defense counsel that an accomplice, Rawls, might invoke the privilege against self-incrimination but had received apparently reliable information from another source that Rawls would testify against the defendant. Therefore, in his opening statement the prosecutor alluded to Rawls' expected testimony. The witness claimed the privilege and refused to testify. The defendant moved for a mistrial, which was denied. The trial court gave general limiting instructions to the effect that the statements of counsel were not evidence. Affirming defendant's conviction, the Court, while noting that a more specific limiting instruction might have been desirable but that it was not required, stated in relevant part as follows:

We believe that in these circumstances the limiting instructions given were sufficient to protect petitioner's constitutional rights. As the Court said in Bruton, 391 U.S. [123] at 135 [88 S.Ct. 1620, 1627, 20 L.Ed.2d 476], "Not every admission of inadmissible hearsay or other evidence can be considered to be reversible error unavoidable through limiting instructions; instances occur in almost every trial where inadmissible evidence creeps in, usually inadvertently." See Hopt v. Utah,120 U.S. 430, 438 [7 S.Ct. 614, 618, 30 L.Ed. 708] (1887). It may be that some remarks included in an opening or closing statement could be so prejudicial that a finding of error, or even constitutional error, would be unavoidable. But here we have no more than an objective summary of evidence which the prosecutor reasonably expected to produce. Many things might happen during the course of the trial which would prevent the presentation of all the evidence described in advance. Certainly not every variance between the advance description and the actual presentation constitutes reversible error, when a proper limiting instruction has been given. Even if it is unreasonable to assume that a jury can disregard a coconspirator's statement when introduced against one of two joint defendants, it does not seem at all remarkable to assume that the jury will ordinarily be able to limit its consideration to the evidence introduced during the trial. At least where the anticipated, and unproduced, evidence is not touted to the jury as a crucial part of the prosecution's case, "it is hard for us to imagine that the minds of the jurors would be so influenced by such incidental statements during this long trial that they would not appraise the evidence objectively and dispassionately." United States v. Socony-Vacuum Oil Co.,310 U.S. 150, 239 [60 S.Ct. 811, 852, 84 L.Ed. 1129] (1940). 394 U.S. at 735-36, 89 S.Ct. at 1423 (footnote omitted).

In this case the jury knew that the state wanted to call one Weme, who aided Larson after Larson was shot, and the jury knew that he not only took the fifth amendment but that he did not appear later when he was supposed to appear and testify. However, contrary to defendant's argument, there is nothing in the record to suggest that Weme knew anything about the actual shooting itself or that the jury was led to believe that his testimony would shed any light on the actual shooting. Under the circumstances, we hold that defendant was not prejudiced by Weme's failure to testify.

3. Defendant's next contention is that the trial court improperly restricted defense counsel's cross-examination of the victim about his prior acts of violence.

In State v. Keaton,258 Minn. 359, 104 N.W.2d 650 (1960), we noted that evidence of the victim's reputation for violence and quarrelsomeness may be admitted in self-defense cases for the purpose of determining (1) whether the defendant was reasonably put in apprehension of serious bodily harm or (2) who was the aggressor. Where the former purpose is involved, it is necessary that the defendant knew the victim's reputation, but where the latter purpose is involved, it is not necessary that the defendant knew the victim's reputation. We held in Keaton that evidence of a specific act of violence is not admissible to prove who was the aggressor. Later, in State v. Matthews, 301 Minn. 133, 221 N.W.2d 563 (1974), we held that evidence of a specific act of violence is admissible to prove that the defendant was reasonably put in apprehension of serious bodily harm, provided that the defendant knew about the prior act of violence. Then, in State v. Taylor,258 N.W.2d 615 (Minn.1977), we dealt with the issue of the admissibility of evidence of the victim's past criminal record where the defendant claiming self-defense did not know of it. Our opinion made no attempt to write the final word on the subject but held that the convictions of simple assault and disorderly conduct did not, by themselves, indicate a violent or quarrelsome disposition.

Minn.R.Evid. 404(a) provides generally that "Evidence of a person's character or a trait of his character is not admissible for the purpose of proving that he acted in conformity therewith on a particular occasion, except:

(1) Character of accused. Evidence of a pertinent trait of his character offered by an accused, or by the prosecution to rebut the same;(2) Character of victim. Evidence of a pertinent trait of character of the victim of the crime offered by an accused, or by the prosecution to rebut the same, or evidence of a character trait of peacefulness of the victim offered by the prosecution in a homicide case to rebut evidence that the victim was the first aggressor.(3) Character of witness. Evidence of the character of a witness, as provided in rules 607, 608, and 609."

The general rule of exclusion of Rule 404(a) applies only when character evidence is used to show that a person acted in conformity with his character. Thus, when character evidence is used for some purpose other than to show that a person acted in conformity with his character, it does not apply. Rule 404(b) deals with some of the most usual instances in which character evidence may be admitted for some other purpose. It provides:

Evidence of other crimes, wrongs, or acts is not admissible to prove the character of a person in order to show that he acted in conformity therewith. It may, however, be admissible for other purposes, such as proof of motive, opportunity, intent, preparation, plan, knowledge, identity, or absence of mistake or accident. Rule 404(c) is a specific rule dealing with past conduct of the victim of sex offenses.

Rules 608 and 609 deal with the use of character evidence to show the character of a witness for truth or veracity.

Rule 405 deals with methods of proving character. It provides:

(a) Reputation or opinion. In all cases in which evidence of character or a trait of character of a person is admissible, proof may be made by testimony as to reputation or by testimony in the form of an opinion. On cross-examination, inquiry is allowable into relevant specific instances of conduct.(b) Specific instances of conduct. In cases in which character or a trait of character of a person is an essential element of a charge, claim, or defense, proof may also be made of specific instances of his conduct.

As stated in 2 D. Louisell and C. Mueller, Federal Evidence § 150 (1978) (footnotes omitted):

It is of course true that specific instances of conduct may be shown in a wide variety of circumstances which are not specified in Rule 405(b). These include: (i) Prior acts, including crimes and convictions, to show intent, knowledge, plan, and so forth pursuant to Rule 404(b); (ii) prior acts by a party (or events in his life), including crimes and even arrests, brought out pursuant to Rule 405(a) upon cross-examination of the party's character witness who has given character evidence to show the party's conduct under Rule 404; (iii) prior acts of a witness (or events in his life), whether or not a party, and again including crimes and even arrests, brought out pursuant to Rule 608 upon cross-examination of another witness who has testified to the character of the first for truth and veracity; and (iv) prior convictions of a witness, whether or not a party, elicited by way of cross-examination of the witness or established by public record during cross-examination, pursuant to Rule 609.

Rule 405(b) cannot be relied upon as justifying admission of specific evidence of prior acts of violence by the victim in a criminal case in which the defendant claims self-defense. Professors Louisell and Mueller state:

[It cannot be said] that specific instances of past violence by the victim may be proved where these are relevant solely as tending to show his probable actions at the time of the alleged crime. Rule 405(b) allows evidence of specific instances only where these amount to an "element of a charge, claim, or defense": It is clear that specific instances of the victim's past conduct do not amount to such an element in cases of homicide or criminal assault â□" they amount at most to circumstantial evidence that the victim was the first aggressor, and it is this latter fact which amounts to an element of the defense of self defense.

2 D. Louisell and C. Mueller, Federal Evidence § 139 (1978) (footnote omitted). However, they add that "If it can be established that the accused knew at the time of the alleged crime of prior violent acts by the victim, such evidence is relevant as tending to show a reasonable apprehension on the part of the accused. Since this is not the circumstantial use of character evidence to prove conduct, such use is not barred either by Rule 404 or by Rule 405." 2 D. Louisell and C. Mueller, Federal Evidence § 139 (1978). See also 11 P. Thompson, Minnesota Practice, Evidence § 404.04 (1979). Rule 404(b) provides another exception to the limit of Rule 405 on the use of evidence of specific acts in cases of this sort. Thus, if defendant offers the evidence not to show that the victim acted in conformity with his bad character but to show his intent, knowledge, plan, and so forth, the evidence is admissible under Rule 404(b).

In this case the trial court admitted a wealth of reputation evidence and evidence concerning specific past acts of violence by the victim, but defendant nonetheless claims that he was prejudiced by the trial court's limiting rulings with respect to two prior acts by the victim. One of these incidents was a 1977 act of damage to property and possession of an uncased rifle and the other involved a fight in the house of a friend, also in 1977. Defendant had no knowledge of the first incident and, in any event, the acts committed by the victim at that time bear little, if any, relation to a predisposition for violence or quarrelsomeness. State v. Taylor,258 N.W.2d 615 (Minn.1977). Detailed evidence was admitted concerning the second incident. With respect to the trial court's rulings on both items of evidence, it may also be said that, given the wealth of evidence that was admitted relating to the victim's violent past, it would be hard to find any prejudice even if there was error. Stated differently, the evidence excluded was cumulative evidence.

4. Defendant also argues that the prosecutor committed plain error in eliciting evidence that defendant's possession of the weapon he used, a sawed-off shotgun, was a separate crime. In State v. Underwood,281 N.W.2d 337 (Minn.1979), we reversed an aggravated assault conviction because the prosecutor improperly and over defense objection cross-examined the defendant about the fact that the gun he used was unregistered and the fact that it was a gross misdemeanor to possess it without a permit. In State v. Swanson, 307 Minn. 412, 240 N.W.2d 822 (1976), on the other hand, we held that a similar error was nonprejudicial, particularly in view of the trial court's cautionary instructions. In the instant case defense counsel did not object or move for a cautionary instruction. Further, the fact that the weapon used was a sawed-off shotgun was properly admitted and the jury probably knew,

without being told, that it is illegal for citizens to possess one of these. Finally, defendant used the fact that his possession of the gun was illegal as an explanation for his incriminating post-act conduct, which included throwing the gun into the river. Clearly, therefore, defendant was not prejudiced by the admission of the evidence.

5. Defendant's final contention is that the trial court's instructions were inadequate with respect to "retreat." The original version of CRIMJIG 7.08, which the defendant contends the trial court should have given, reads:

A person who has been attacked and who is exercising his right of self-defense is not required to retreat and he not only may stand his ground and defend himself against the attack but may also pursue his assailant until he has secured himself from danger if that course appears to him, and would appear to a reasonable person in the same situation, to be reasonably necessary, and this is his right even though he might more easily have gained safety by withdrawing from the scene.

The original version was based on a misinterpretation by the drafters of the instruction of language which we used in State v. Love, 285 Minn. 444, 173 N.W.2d 423 (1970). See State v. Jones, 271 N.W.2d 534 (Minn. 1978). The amended version, which the trial court gave in this case, provides:

The legal excuse of self-defense is available only to those who act honestly and in good faith. This includes the duty to retreat or to avoid the danger if reasonably possible.

We hold that the trial court's instructions were correct and fairly informed the jury of the parameters of the law of self-defense in Minnesota. State v. Duke, 335 N.W.2d 511 (Minn., 1983).

Affirmed.

Appendix C

Minnesota Criminal Penalties

What follows are charts showing various levels of crimes and the associated penalties. The MPPA does not have any felony crimes for permit holders, but it does not provide any immunity against being charges or prosecuted for other crimes either. It does contain a number of petty misdemeanor, misdemeanor and gross misdemeanor crimes. So forewarned is forearmed.

Levels of Offenses

In Minnesota, as in all states, criminal offenses are grouped by category as a way to roughly distinguish offense severity. The four categories in Minnesota are:

Category	Maximum Sanction	Examples
Petty Misdemeanor	Fine of up to $300. Not a crime because incarceration is not an allowable sanction	Most traffic violations
Misdemeanor	90 days in jail and/or up to $1,000 fine	Driving without a license; Simple assault (such as punching someone); First-time DWI; Theft of property worth less than $500*
Gross Misdemeanor	One year in jail and/or up to $3,000 fine	Second DWI in ten years; Second assault in ten years against same victim; Theft of property worth between $500 and $1,000*
Felony	Over one year imprisonment and/or up to maximum fine specified in law. Maximum imprisonment penalties range from 366 days to life imprisonment.	Murder and manslaughter; Most criminal sexual conduct crimes; Theft of property worth more than $1,000*
*Theft thresholds are effective August 1, 2007.		

The chart on the next page provides sentencing guidelines for felonies. Presumptive sentence lengths are in months. Italicized numbers within the grid denote the discretionary range within which a court may sentence without the sentence being deemed a departure. Offenders with stayed felony sentences may be subject to local confinement.

4.A. Sentencing Guidelines Grid

Presumptive sentence lengths are in months. Italicized numbers within the grid denote the discretionary range within which a court may sentence without the sentence being deemed a departure. Offenders with stayed felony sentences may be subject to local confinement.

SEVERITY LEVEL OF CONVICTION OFFENSE (Example offenses listed in italics)		CRIMINAL HISTORY SCORE						
		0	1	2	3	4	5	6 or more
Murder, 2nd Degree (intentional murder; drive-by-shootings)	11	306 *261-367*	326 *278-391*	346 *295-415*	366 *312-439*	386 *329-463*	406 *346-480*[2]	426 *363-480*[2]
Murder, 3rd Degree Murder, 2nd Degree (unintentional murder)	10	150 *128-180*	165 *141-198*	180 *153-216*	195 *166-234*	210 *179-252*	225 *192-270*	240 *204-288*
Assault, 1st Degree Controlled Substance Crime, 1st Degree	9	86 *74-103*	98 *84-117*	110 *94-132*	122 *104-146*	134 *114-160*	146 *125-175*	158 *135-189*
Aggravated Robbery, 1st Degree Controlled Substance Crime, 2nd Degree	8	48 *41-57*	58 *50-69*	68 *58-81*	78 *67-93*	88 *75-105*	98 *84-117*	108 *92-129*
Felony DWI	7	36	42	48	54 *46-64*	60 *51-72*	66 *57-79*	72 *62-84*[2]
Controlled Substance Crime, 3rd Degree	6	21	27	33	39 *34-46*	45 *39-54*	51 *44-61*	57 *49-68*
Residential Burglary Simple Robbery	5	18	23	28	33 *29-39*	38 *33-45*	43 *37-51*	48 *41-57*
Nonresidential Burglary	4	12[1]	15	18	21	24 *21-28*	27 *23-32*	30 *26-36*
Theft Crimes (Over $5,000)	3	12[1]	13	15	17	19 *17-22*	21 *18-25*	23 *20-27*
Theft Crimes ($5,000 or less) Check Forgery ($251-$2,500)	2	12[1]	12[1]	13	15	17	19	21 *18-25*
Sale of Simulated Controlled Substance	1	12[1]	12[1]	12[1]	13	15	17	19 *17-22*

☐ Presumptive commitment to state imprisonment. First-degree murder has a mandatory life sentence and is excluded from the Guidelines under Minn. Stat. § 609.185. See Guidelines section 2.E. Mandatory Sentences, for policies regarding those sentences controlled by law.

▨ Presumptive stayed sentence; at the discretion of the court, up to one year of confinement and other non-jail sanctions can be imposed as conditions of probation. However, certain offenses in the shaded area of the Grid always carry a presumptive commitment to state prison. Guidelines sections 2.C. Presumptive Sentence and 2.E. Mandatory Sentences.

[1] 12[1]=One year and one day

[2] Minn. Stat. § 244.09 requires that the Guidelines provide a range for sentences that are presumptive commitment to state imprisonment of 15% lower and 20% higher than the fixed duration displayed, provided that the minimum sentence is not less than one year and one day and the maximum sentence is not more than the statutory maximum. Guidelines section 2.C.1-2. Presumptive Sentence.

Appendix D

Eligibility to Qualify for LEOSA

LEOSA Trainers, Inc. (LTI) is authorized under Federal and State law to administer the Annual Firearms Test to eligible Retired and Separated Law Enforcement Officers. LTI provides firearms qualifications for those separated law enforcement officers who are:

(1) Retired or Separated Minnesota resident law enforcement or police officers who reside in Minnesota;
(2) Retired or Separated federal law enforcement officers and agents, and certain DOD individuals who reside in Minnesota or;
(3) Retired or Separated out-of-state law enforcement officers who reside in Minnesota.

All applicants must have their permanent residence in the State of Minnesota to begin the application process. Verification of a permanent residence in the State of Minnesota must be provided by all applicants with 1) a Minnesota driver's license, 2) US Passport or 3) other valid government issued identification card. The LTI firearms qualification card is valid only while you maintain your primary residence in the State of Minnesota.

LTI reserves the right to deny the issuance of the LEOSA firearms certification card if your status as an eligible separated law enforcement officer cannot be established. LTI will not conduct research on your behalf to prove your eligibility.

The Law Enforcement Officers Safety Act (LEOSA) first enacted July 22, 2004 as Pub. L. 108-277, 118 Stat. 865 (204) and subsequently modified and signed into law on October 12, 2010, codified as 18 U.S. Code §926B and §926C, permits the nationwide carrying of concealed handguns by qualified current, and certain retired and separated law enforcement officers. The Act amends the Gun Control Act of 1968 (Pub. L. 90-618, 82 Stat, 1213) and exempts qualified current, and certain retired and separated law enforcement officers from state and local laws prohibiting the carry of concealed firearms.

Federal statute mandates certain conditions and provisions for a separated individual to be eligible for the issuance of a LEOSA certification. Federal law defines a qualified separated or retired law enforcement officer as an individual who:

(1) Separated or retired in good standing from service with a public agency as a law enforcement officer;

(2) Before such separation or retirement, was authorized by law to engage in or supervise the prevention, detection, investigation, or prosecution of, or the incarceration of any person for, any violation of law, and had statutory powers of arrest;

a. Before such separation or retirement, served as a law enforcement officer for an aggregate of 10 years or more; or
b. Separated from service with such agency, after completing any applicable probationary period of such service, due to a service-connected disability, as determined by such agency;

(3) During the most recent 12-month period, has met, at the expense of the individual, the standards for qualification in firearms training for active law enforcement officers, as approved by any agency within the State of Minnesota, and

(4) Has not been officially found by a qualified medical professional to be medically unqualified for reasons relating to mental health and

as a result of this finding will not be issued a photographic identification from your former agency as described; or

(5) Has not entered into an agreement with the agency from which you have separated or retired from service in which you acknowledged that you are not qualified for reasons relating to mental health and for those reasons you will not receive or accept the photographic identification as described.

(6) Is not under the influence of alcohol or another intoxicating or hallucinatory drug or substance; and

(7) Is not prohibited by State or Federal laws from possessing a firearm.

In addition to these qualifications, 18 U.S. Code §926B and §926C requires the applicant to possess a photographic identification issued by the governmental agency from which the individual separated or retired from service as a law enforcement officer.

The LTI Process

All new LTI applicants are required to initially pass a written exam.

Once you have:

1) Submitted all required paperwork and fee to LTI;
2) Passed the written exam; and
3) Passed the firearm qualification requirements;

You will be issued a firearms qualification card.

LTI charges a non-returnable fee for each application submitted for consideration. Our fee reduces for up to the next four years or until the renewal of your Minnesota permit as shown in the table below. Your written knowledge test replaces the need for LEOSA classroom training.

You will be required to annually meet the established firearms qualification and training standards by the expiration date of the previous firearm qualification in order to maintain your LEOSA authority.

LTI reserves the right to deny the issuance of the LEOSA firearms qualification card if you cannot establish and/or verified your status as a qualified retired or separated law enforcement officer, you fail to pass the knowledge test or if you fail the shooting qualification.

Documents you need to submit to LTI along with your completed application.

- A Minnesota driver's license, US Passport or other valid government issued identification card.
- A copy of your current LEOSA qualification card and Minnesota permit to carry, if you have one.
- A photocopy of your photo identification card issued by your former agency.

A caution about school zones:

Title 18 U.S.C §922(q) known as the Federal Gun Free School Zones Act of 1995

Although Congress intended to allow nationwide carry the act does not provide a qualified individual any exemptions from Federal Law, LEOSA qualified individuals are subject to the restrictions of Title 18 U.S.C §922(q) known as the Federal Gun Free School Zones Act of 1995. It is therefore a Federal Crime for a LEOSA qualified individual to travel armed on any public sidewalk, road, or highway which passes within one-thousand (1000) feet of the property line of any 1-12 public or private school in the nation. Violation of the Federal GFSZA by an individual is punishable by five (5) years in Federal Prison, a $5,000 fine and the permanent loss of gun-rights.

18 USC 922(q)(2)

(A) It shall be unlawful for any individual knowingly to possess a firearm that has moved in or that otherwise affects interstate or foreign commerce at a place that the individual knows, or has reasonable cause to believe, is a school zone.

(B) Subparagraph (A) does not apply to the possession of a firearm—

(i) on private property not part of school grounds;
(ii) if the individual possessing the firearm is **licensed to do so by the State in which the school zone is located** or a political subdivision of the State, and the law of the State or political subdivision requires that, before an individual obtains such a license, the law enforcement authorities of the State or political subdivision verify that the individual is qualified under law to receive the license;

(iii) that is—
(I) not loaded; and
(II) in a locked container, or a locked firearms rack that is on a motor vehicle;
(iv) by an individual for use in a program approved by a school in the school zone;
(v) by an individual in accordance with a contract entered into between a school in the school zone and the individual or an employer of the individual;
(vi) by a law enforcement officer acting in his or her official capacity; or
(vii) that is unloaded and is possessed by an individual while traversing school premises for the purpose of gaining access to public or private lands open to hunting, if the entry on school premises is authorized by school authorities.

To safely enter a school zone while armed, the individual must have a Minnesota permit to carry or a permit recognized by Minnesota. Minnesota law does specifically extend all rights and privileges to out-of-state permit holders including to enter school zones. Some other states have taken a similar approach which reduces the risk of schools if an individual possesses a permit recognized by the visiting or destination state, when traveling around the country. Minnesota's permit is currently recognized by twenty three other states and our permit to carry training is recognized by Florida which is the premier non-resident permit.

If you do not currently have a Minnesota permit to carry, LTI offers a one day carry class which is combined it with your initial LEOSA shooting qualification. Our class is very comprehensive and includes information how you can be properly insured should you have a defensive gun use.

We strongly recommend that you have a Minnesota permit in addition to your LEOSA authority.

Be A **Victim**

or

Be A **Survivor**

LEOSA Trainers, Inc.